The Deeper Meaning Behind the Pillars of Islam

Shaykh Muhammad al-Jamal ar-Rifa`i as-Shadhili
translated by
Dr. Rosina Fawzia al-Rawi

Bismi'llah ir-Rahman ir-Rahim
In the Name of Allah, the Merciful, the Compassionate

Sidi Muhammad Press is committed to publishing the spiritually significant teachings of Shaykh Muhammad al-Jamal ar-Rifa`i as-Shadhili. We will be happy to give you information on the availability of these books: SMP, 2656 First Street #413, Napa CA, 94558.

Other titles by Sidi Shaykh Muhammad:
Music of the Soul
Fruits from the Tree of Life
Stories of the Prophets

Sidi Muhammad Press

The Deeper Meaning Behind the Pillars of Islam

cover: a Ladik prayer rug with a mosque lamp in its niche.
inside cover: The Shahada in rectangular Kufic script.
"La ilaha illa'llah Muhammadun Rasullah"

بسم الله الرحمن الرحيم

At-Tawhid
The Religion of the Unity

Praise be to Allah, the one who appears in His Hiddenness, and who is unrevealed in His Manifestness, until He disappears from the sight of His worshippers through the brilliance of His manifestation, and by the magnitude of His light. And He disclosed all things in the state of His manifesting when He revealed Himself in the mountain of the heart; and He was made known in this revelation.

Thus He has been known to them, and they have recognized Him and have drawn nearer to the place of manifestation. And they have seen Him, and they have described Him. Yet in accordance with His complete and brilliant wisdom, He has been unrevealed to others than them; although He is closer to them than their jugular vein, and yet they cannot see Him.

For He has revealed Himself in different stages, in order that His Omnipotence might become manifest; and He has appeared in all times, in accordance with the capacity and capability of the minds, and their willingness and acceptance to carry and to endure. And these are His Family, and through them His Mercy is extended. And in this way the whole world is in His hand and the whole earth is in His grip, and no one can accord Him the true place.

I praise Him and I thank Him for the opening of the heart to His subtlety, and for being able to see His Light of Oneness. He has unveiled for us what was hidden and has given us, through Him, greatness.

I witness *la ilaha illa 'llah*, there is no god but Allah. He has no partner: this witnessing is that of a slave needy of His grace; one who has been taken by Him on the righteous path of Divine guidance and love, to His knowing.

Thus he spoke out, and he confessed before Him to the absoluteness of His Oneness in the Essence, the Attributes and the Actions; and I bear witness that our Lord and Master Muhammad, the Prophet, is the *soul of the world*, and the *owner of the revealed appearance*, and the *origin of existence*, and that he is the Lord of all those who give birth and of all those who are born, and that he is the secret of beings, may the peace and blessings of Allah be upon him, and upon his family, and the followers of his true Path, may peace and blessings be upon us, protecting us with a true and great protection, and a strong refuge from sorrow, grief, pains, and all misfortunes.

Know, that this knowledge is that of the People of Allah. It is the knowledge of the Sufi, and it is the best of knowledge and the purest of understanding; and no one knows it except the ones who are in His Compassion, not knowing anything else but Him. True are the words of the poem of the Shaykh 'ibn `Arabi, who said:

"Complete your Truth which you have not yet completed,
And leave the body in its lower parts.
The body is for the precious nafs an instrument.
If the nafs is clear and beautiful so will the body be.
For without them the body cannot reach the Truth.
For the body disappears, and the nafs remains
In happiness or unhappiness, praising what it has reached.
If you have been a slave to your body,
You have forgotten your Promise in the First World."

And true are the words:

"Whoever has tasted the drink of the Folk knows it
And whoever knows it with his soul, buys it."

And know, that this knowledge is the most noble of all, the nobility of which is joined to the nobility of the known, its degree being in accordance with the rank of he who is connected to it, since it is related to the Essence of the Everlasting One. And by Allah! he has gained the honor, above which there is no more honor; and all the other sciences compared with it, are of lesser importance and rank, for they are as slaves to it, as is said:

"O you hurried Man, if you ask for knowledge
All knowledge is a slave to the knowledge of words.
You ask for fiqh so that you can straighten your way according to the rules,
And at the same time, you close the doors of the One,
Who has brought down these rules.
There is a difference between the one who stands by the outer rules,
And the one who reaches to the One."

For in every knowledge or science there are controversies and arguments amongst its followers, and conflicts, differences, and conjectures between them, but the noble knowledge is far removed from quarrels and arguments. Thus `Umar 'ibn Farid said, "How much conflict exists amongst the clever and the skillful, but none exists between the lovers and the Beloved."

The reason lies in that, in the knowledge of the Folk there is no *interpretation* or *application*, and this is contrary to the other knowledges which are based upon evidence and proofs; and some of which are founded upon the copying of every tradition and custom. But the knowledge of the People of Allah comes from revelation and inspiration, and nothing else, and therefore neither conflict nor divisions are found in it, because it is the hidden Qur`an and the revealed Qur`an, which does not change, either in its hidden or its revealed meaning. Allah, Exalted is He, said, "We have sent down the Qur`an and you should preserve It." So He appointed for its revealed form, scholars who follow the outer rules, and He appointed for its hidden meanings, scholars of the perception of the heart. So the people of the heart come to it for drowning in its inner meanings, and the people of the outer come to it caring for it, like the people of the material world (*ad-dunya*) care about the Garden of Eden. As our Master, the Prophet of Allah, may peace and blessings be upon him, said, "The Qur`an is a Garden and a Paradise for those who know."

So, my brother, do not be influenced by the words of those who are deceived, because their words try to belittle the friends of Allah, over whom they seek to gain an influence, by insisting upon evidences and proofs, thinking that, through them, they can gain power over His people. But they are like small boys compared with the Folk of Allah, for they do not know the ocean into which they have plunged, nor do they know in which direction they are traveling.

As the Shaykh Muhyi-id-din 'ibn `Arabi, may Allah be pleased with him, said, "We have left the overflowing seas behind us, for how should the people know where we have drifted to?" Through that they have become the most noble of all people, and their knowledge is the most noble of all agreed knowledges.

So hurry, my brother, to seek for it and to believe in its followers; and if you do not want to follow it, at least do not try to fight against It.

Al-Ghazzali, one of the knowers, may Allah be pleased with him, said, as follows, in his book *Ihya al-`Ulum-id-din*, "The one who is not grateful for having this knowledge (of revelation), the lowest rank of which is the surrendering to the Folk of Allah, I worry that his end will not be good."

Abu-l-Hasan ash-Shadhili, may Allah be pleased with him, said, "He who does not have this knowledge of ours dies insisting on the great sins, and the greatest sin, for the Folk of Allah, is polytheism (*ash-shirk*)." The only one who can flee from this misfortune is the one who is humble, and who follows the People of Allah to their doors, even if he be one of the distinguished scholars. So go to them, my brother, and may you walk in their footsteps, and believe in their knowledge.

And my Master al-Junayd said, "To believe in our knowledge is to become a Saint." And as-Siqiti said, in his book *Al-Kitab Nur al-Qulub Fi-`Ilm al-Mawhub,* "The one who believes in this knowledge belongs to the *special ones*, and the one who witnesses it and speaks about it, and who acts according to it, is like a star which cannot be revealed, and like a sea which cannot be abandoned."

And the Doctor Razi, the author of *Marginal Notes to the Qur`an,* says, "It is not right for a scholar to absorb all the knowledge, and to believe in it, so as to become the leader of his time; but rather it is his duty to meet the People of the Path and that they may show him the righteous way, so that he then becomes of the People to whom Allah reveals His

Secrets, because their inner world has become very pure, thus permitting them to absorb the light from the Prophet." And I have asked, "How is a scholar able to transmit the knowledge if his understanding is not yet complete?"

And we know from the 'Imam al-Ghazzali, may Allah be pleased with him, who said, when he was working on the purification of his inner *self* through walking on the Path of the People of Allah, "We lost our life in inactivity, and how lost was my existence in all those days!" Someone answered him, "Have you not become, in this time, the authority of the Religion?" He said, "Leave me in peace with the past things, for have you not heard the words of the Prophet, may peace and blessings be upon him, "Allah places this religion even in a hypocritical Muslim."

So look, my brother, at the humility of this great scholar, and his confession to his shortcomings regarding right actions before he met with the Folk. And do not think that he said, what he said, out of lack of respect for the law (*ash-shari`a);* far from that, but rather he said what he said because through it he came to know, whereas before that he had been ignorant. And although he was outwardly leading the life of a Muslim, yet he was ignorant of the inner Reality of Islam; and although he had amassed all the knowledges, yet he was ignorant of the true Knowledge of the Reality of Allah. But when Allah opened the doors for him, through the Sufi Path, he obtained knowledge of Him, whereas before he had knowledge only of the outside of the Law of God.

Al-`Iz `Abd as-Salam, may Allah have mercy upon him, said, "The Sufi Way is founded on the rules of the law (*ash-shari`a*) which cannot change either now or in the Hereafter, whereas other people rest upon the outside knowledges and pictures. And what establishes the Sufis (*al-mutasawwifa*) is that their knowledge and wisdom, and the power which they create through their words, reaches to people and honors all beings, with the result that those who sit with them gain more from them than they can from any others.

An-Nawawi, in his book *Al-Muhaddab*, mentions the words of as-Shaf`i, may Allah be pleased with him, who said, "I have gained two sayings while sitting with the Sufis; one of them is, 'Time is like a sword, and if you do not break it, it will break you!' And the second saying is, 'If you do not keep your *nafs* busy doing good things, it will keep you busy with bad ones.'"

To sum this up, it is said, generally, that this knowledge is that of those who are sincere, and that the one who partakes of it belongs to those who are *near* to Allah, for they are closer to Him than those who belong to the outside Islam. How immensely fortunate is the one who has even the smallest part of it! How poor is the one who, with his arguments and ideas without understanding, is in conflict with it; for he is a poor man who fights against those who are stronger than he is. Some scholars say, "Any man who fights something stronger and greater than himself brings down misfortune upon himself."

My brother, trust in Allah and His righteous followers, and especially the People of Allah, the Sufis who know Allah and His Prophet, for to be in conflict with them is like a deadly poison. May Allah protect us, and all the Muslims, from that.

The Determination of the Path.

The Path, and the Way are similar words for the journey by which the reaching to what is intended is made easier, and through which the safeguarding of the follower himself, his possessions and his safe *return*, are ensured against all hazards. The follower on the Path of Allah, Exalted is He, must leave behind him many realities which are relative for him, but if he does not leave them behind, his reaching to the Reality of the Truth is made more difficult, because each of these relative realities is like a mountain which blocks his Path to Allah, Exalted is He.

The foundations of the religion rest on four principles: belief, prayer, behavior, and manners. Success comes from the first of these, which is belief, and the likelihood of a person *reaching* is according to the strength of his belief. The Companions of the Prophet, may peace and blessings be upon him, were the first in the strength of their belief, and we were before the ones who came after them, in our striving for knowledge; and we came and we reached, through arduous work. But all this is as nothing compared with the power of belief; and even if we know nothing except that which is absolutely necessary for us to know, and if we abandon all effort except that which is a duty entrusted upon us from

Allah, any striving for knowledge, and any effort towards gaining it, if combined with a weak faith, is of no help at all. From true belief comes true worship, devotion, pure manners, good behavior and the following of the Orders of Allah, all of which enable a Muslim to live in Allah, and to strengthen the existence of Allah in him. As the Prophet, may peace and blessings be upon him, said, "If you do not see Him, yet surely He sees you."

Those who observe the Law of Allah, Praised and Exalted is He, and the knowledge of His orders and His rules, and the observance of the special days of the Muslim year, these are the Inheritors of the Prophet, may the peace and blessings of Allah be upon him. And this is the great happiness for whoever surrenders to Allah, who follows His Prophet, and who embraces his safe berthing-places. Allah, Praised and Exalted is He, said to the Prophet, "The person who harms a friend of Mine, I am at war with him." Meaning that the true follower is the complete image of the Prophet of Allah, who is the representative of Allah, and he is the *owner of the proof*, and he is the *manifest way,* therefore Allah protects him. And from this follows the meaning of Allah's Words, "The ones who fear Allah the most are His knowers." Then come the ones who praise Allah; then comes the man who follows His love for he is an ascetic slave, and Allah has given him godliness in his religion and humbleness in his devotion. And next comes the man whom Allah has cleansed of his *self* (*nafs*) and purified his manners until his *nafs* has become completely humble in his own eyes, and whose manners manifest pure desires. The gifts of Allah, and the qualities which a person has, can most clearly be seen in his manners, for he carries in his hands as much as Allah has given him of His Attributes. Each Muslim who does not grow by the hand of a Master does not taste the sweetness of faith, nor does he taste the sweetness of the fear of Allah, so that he is in danger of falling down and being influenced by evil. And how many followers have slipped on their Path, and have fallen on their faces, so that there is no way for them to be rescued from the wiles of Allah. But the follower who is taken by a Master is safe from the evils and deceptions of the *nafs*, and so he moves forward with sure steps in repentance, fear, hope, love, trust, eye-witnessing, contentment, yearning, and other praise-worthy qualities, until he reaches the station (*maqam*) of the *people brought near to Allah*, and he becomes of the Folk, the righteous ones, upon whom Allah has bestowed comfort, such as the Prophets, the holy people and the martyrs; and these are the best companions. Each

Muslim should reach to the knowledge of the secrets so that he may follow the Master in his actions, and that the people, through him, may have an example of the manners of the Prophet, may peace and blessings be upon him. But any Muslim who has not followed a complete Master may arouse doubts, both in his actions and in his honor, of concealed polytheism and hidden self-deception. We ask Allah to relieve us of these shortcomings, and to strengthen our yearning for Him; and He is the one who hears our prayers, and who answers them.

Some Explanations of the Rules of Conduct for the Shaykh, Master and Guide

It is important for the Guide to know in what it is necessary for a seeker to be knowledgeable concerning the orders and the decrees of the Unity (*at-tawhid*), and he should know about the *ripeness*, maturity and grace of the hearts; and about the weakness of the *self* and its ailments, and to uphold and safeguard its health and equilibrium. The Master must be gentle and compassionate towards the Muslims, and especially towards the seekers, and he must be ready with advice for them, and be able, at all times, to see the *state* of those who want to follow, and he must be able to show them how to do so. And he should make it easy for the seeker on the Path to leave behind him all reasoning, and everything that hinders him in his walking on the Path, and which prevents him from giving all that he is able, and wanting, to give.

One of the attributes of an honest Guide is to keep to himself his knowledge of the weaknesses of his followers, and to take a middle course in all his actions, whether it be concerning physical hunger and the satisfying of this hunger, or whether it be in sleep or in wakefulness, in anger or in joy. The middle way lies between excess and indulgence on one hand and total abstinence and inadequacy on the other; and it is only the *complete man*, the Perfect One, who can find the right balance between these states. Therefore he who possesses this balance is ready to be a Guide.

Another attribute for the Guide, and one which is a rule of conduct for him, is that both food and clothing have become of no importance for him. Also, his *self* must be balanced and well-mannered, so that he shows no anger except for the sake of Allah. So that if someone comes to him for guidance and help, he does not frown at him, but he is always well-disposed to all comers. In other words, his majesty (*jalal*) should be combined with his beauty (*jamal*), his anger with his good-pleasure, his compulsion with his kindness and generosity. May Allah give us His grace and His generosity in these Attributes.

The 'Imam al-Junayd said, in giving a description of the Guide, "He who has not listened to the *hadith* of the Prophet, and who has not sat with the *fuqara* and taken his manners from those who are well-mannered, deludes those who follow him, although he claims that his knowledge stems from the Book *(al-Qur'an)* and the *sunna* of the Prophet." The Shaykh 'ibn `Arabi said, "Through working with them, the two honest witnesses (meaning the Qur'an and the sunna), you arrive."

Our Master Abu al-Hasan ash-Shadhili said, "If your revelation is in contradiction with the Book and the *sunna*, then hold to the Book and the *sunna*, and leave the revelation, and say to yourself, "Allah has given me the protection (*i`sma*) in the Book and the *sunna*. One must only be certain of one's revelations, illuminations, and visions after referring them to the Book and the *sunna*.

Some of the knowers say, "Our sources are seven in number, namely: the holding to the Book, being inspired by the *hadith*, the eating of only *halal* food, the abandoning of evil deeds, repentance, and the avoiding and washing away of sins. The basis of the Sufi Path is to hold to the Book and the *sunna,* and to leave any inclinations towards heresy and innovation in the glorifying of the holiness of the knowers of Allah, and in the making of excuses for not praying, and for such dilatory practices as the substitution of two *ruku* for prayers that may be combined when a person is traveling on a journey. Also this applies to the establishing of certain supererogatory devotions, and of *interpretation*, all of which should be avoided, together with the indulging in committing *ruhas*, or *the taking of the easy way out*. Anyone who follows such practices loses his way and falls down from the rank of *men*.

Thus, it is the responsibility of the Shaykh towards the seeker to care about him, and from the beginning to make the Way clear for him, and in the end to transform him. And it is the duty of the seeker towards the

Shaykh to surrender to his orders, to keep his secrets, and to honor his power.

My Master al-Hawas said, "We only consider a man to be of the Folk of the Path if he knows the pure *shari`a* in its generality and in its particularities; in the aspect in which it abrogates and in the aspect in which it is abrogated, both in its parts and in its entirety. He who is ignorant of even one of these, falls down from the rank of *men*.

The 'Imam al-Junayd said, "A man is not worthy to be called a Shaykh except if he has knowledge of all the *shari`a*, and if he is cautious about all that is forbidden, if he is ascetic in the world (*ad-dunya*), and if he does not set out to heal others before he has healed himself." Then he, may Allah be pleased with him, said, "The person who does not have these qualities belongs to the people of the Devil." So weigh the words, the actions, and the *states* of a man by the measure in which he follows the *shar`ia* and the Path (*at-tariqa*), and if you see anything which is contrary to them, turn away from him. But if the man is really true, and of true caring and inspiration, you should not turn away from him, but you should take him as a spiritual Guide, in accordance with the *shari`a*. True are the words of the poet:

"If a Shaykh does not have the following five qualities, he can with ease guide to ignorance:
He walks according to its rules,
That he seeks in the knowledge of the Essence of the Reality (al-Haqiqa),
That he is generous to the people,
That he is humble in his words,
And actions towards those who are poor."

This is the praiseworthy Shaykh who, having all these qualities, is able to distinguish between that which is *halal* and permitted, and that which is *haram* and forbidden.

A Further Determination of the Sufi Path

There are many definitions of the knowledge of the Sufi Path, of the *songs which it sings*, and its blessing; may the seeker be helped by it. We can see that it is a way through which the inner world is cleansed from weaknesses coming from the *self* (*nafs*), and the low qualities of the *nafs*, such as hatred, jealousy, pride, the love of praise, of being generous in front of others, of anger and of showing off, or greed, of meanness, of admiration of the rich and the disdaining of the poor, and so on.

The Sufi Path is to shun everything that is debased, and to cling to every kind of virtue. It is the protection of the senses and the guarding of the private parts. It is said, also, that its way is the devotion to work, and the shunning of shortcomings.

It is said also, that the Path of the Sufi is to use the time for the most valuable things, and it is for this that he is referred to as *the son of the moment*. How sweet, then, are the words of 'Ibn al-Farid, "Be sharp like time, because time is like a sword. Do not say *later*, or *I have time*, because procrastination is more dangerous than any sickness."

Al-Junayd said, "The Sufi Path is the knowledge that the Reality is that by which one is killed, and it is the Reality by which one is brought back to life." He, may Allah be pleased with him, means by this that Allah kills you in the eyes of your *nafs,* and He brings you back to life through the remembrance of Him; and this is the highest *state* of the Sufi. And it is true that the Sufi Path is known through *tasting.*

And the 'Imam ash-Sha`rami said in his book *Tabaqat*, "Sufism is a knowledge which is ignited in the hearts of the *awliya* (the friends of Allah), the heart which is illumined through working with the Book and the *sunna* of the Prophet, and whosoever works with them is illumined, through them, with knowledge, good manners, secrets, and realities of which the tongue is unable to give expression. For this reason it is said, "The knowledge of the Sufi Path is only for those to realize who, in the beginning were created to understand it. And how can a man *know*, without being able to see that which is to be known; and how can a blind man see the light of the sun?"

The Sufi Path is concerned with actions of the heart and the senses, regarding the awareness of them, followed by their purification. Its matter is concerned with the benefits and blessings coming from this, and the changing of a human being for the *good*, both in his outer and his inner manifestation; for the Sufi is he who is purified from distress and suffering, and who is filled with Divine Wisdom and realities, and who through his bondsmanship to Allah, has abandoned all his human shortcomings, and for whom both *gold* and *mud* are alike. He is the one about whom it is said, "The Sufi Path does not mean the wearing of patched wool (*suf*) nor is it to weep and cry out when music or words move him to wish to weep or to cry out. A Sufi does not give vent either to crying out, dancing, music or confusion, as if he were behaving like a madman."

"But Sufism is to purify the heart from all sickness,
And to follow the Truth (al-Haqq) and the Qur'an.
To exist in this material world.
And to see Allah in humility,
Sorrowing about the sins one has committed throughout one's lifetime,
And to regret the bondage of one's former days."

The Sufis in the material world are ascetics, and the love in their bondsmanship to Allah is said to be of the quality of the *people of the bench* (*'ahli 's-saffah*) who were the followers of the Prophet Muhammad, may peace and blessings be upon him. They abandoned everything to come to be near to the presence of the Prophet, who had a porch of molded stones covered with a roof, built uniquely for them, as a shelter beside his mosque in al-Madina.

It is said that the word *Sufi* comes from the word *safiy* (meaning pure). And it is also said that the Sufis were associated with wool (*as-suf*) because they wore woolen garments in the *dunya*.

Know that the Path of the Sufi is that of righteousness, and it contains both the humblest of people and the most elevated of the believers, and those who follow them (*at-tabi`un*). They are those who follow the Path of the Truth (*al-Haqq*) and of true Guidance, the basis of which is the love of bondsmanship and the abandoning of everything that is other than Allah, the avoidance of the trifling things of the *dunya*, and of all ornamentation.

In the second century after the death of the Prophet Muhammad, may peace be upon him, the people, although they called themselves Muslims and claimed that they loved the Prophet and followed his Way, started to become absorbed by the material life (*ad-dunya*) around them. But some of the people remained steadfast in their devotion to serving

Allah, and these were the people who called themselves Sufis (*al-mutasawwifa*). All the books and commentaries on the Religion, and on the subject of the Unity, which are concerned with the rules of piety and of the examination of the *self* (*nafs*) in relation to the giving and taking, were written by the learned ones of this Community. Some of them wrote about the right behavior (*as-suluk*) of the People of the Path, and others wrote about good manners, and about the knowledge of those who are the inheritors, and how anyone who follows this knowledge will be granted, from Allah, knowledge that he did not have before.

What is Needed from the seeker

Before committing himself to the remembrance (*ad-dhikr*) and to the spiritual practices, the seeker should obtain knowledge about the *Oneness of God* (the Unity) and of what will familiarize him in the school of the orthodox Muslims, *the people of the sunna* (*'ahi 's-sunna*) and the Community so that he can become aware of all practices which are not a part of it, because without the true Religion, the heart that is accustomed to drink from heresy and illusions cannot become enlightened. The *sunna* of the Prophet is the doctrine of the great *sunni* Masters, and it is that which every Muslim should follow. He must believe, without any doubts, that Allah, Exalted is He, is One, and that He has no partner, no wife nor child, and that He exists through existence, without there being any beginning for it, nor any end. He is free from all *being* except for His Being, yet all that is not He has need of Him. He stands by Himself alone and without any space in His Indivisible Essence. He cannot be touched because He has no body to be touched, and He is Self-Sufficient without specific direction, and free from *sides* or places. He is seen in this world through the hearts of His believers, and in the Hereafter with *the eyes of witnessing*, seated on the Throne, controlling all things from it, with the meaning that He desires, wishes and wills, both in this material world (*ad-dunya*) and in the world of the Hereafter. And this is not hard for Him, to be the Guardian of all living beings, for He is everywhere, in all places and all directions, and He is Holy beyond words and space. These are the qualities of time which He has established, for He, Praised and Exalted is He, is not limited by either time or space; for He *was* before either time or space, and He *is* now as He has always been, without time or space. The heavens and the earths are held in His grip, and He it is who created the Tablet and the Pen with which, through His knowledge, He wrote what He had destined for His Creation - what was to be, and what will be, from the beginning without any beginning until the end without any ending.

No atom moves except from Him. He created all things without the need for anything, and nothing obliged Him to create. But the knowledge of Allah came before all things, and therefore He created what He created. His capability is but the measure of what He wishes, for He desires only that which He desires. He has knowledge of everything that He creates, before He creates it, and He knows its manifest numbers. He knows the Secret, and what is behind it, as it is said, "My Lord sees the black ant on the dark stone on the moonless night, and He knows its resting-place; and He gives it what it does not expect." He has knowledge of all things before they come into existence, and He creates all beings on the seven earths and in the seven heavens, as He wishes, and no one knows of how He creates, for He is the All-Subtle (*al-latif*) the All-Knowing (*al-khabir*). Nothing exists either of obedience or disobedience, nor of increase nor of diminution, no life nor death, no *reaching* nor nourishing, no movement nor standing still, no outer nor inner that is other than He, as He wishes and wills; great is His glory. Nothing can halt Him, and nothing can refuse His Order. He gives power to whomsoever He chooses, and He removes it from whomsoever He chooses. He brought the world into existence with two *faces*, and He gave them two states of being. He said, "These are for the Garden, and I am heedless of them, and these are for the Fire, and I am heedless of them." Allah does not distribute injustice and cruelty, nor is He questioned with *why*? and *how*? as to what He does, for He, Praised and Exalted is He, is not asked about His actions, but we are asked about ours. So if you see someone who does not follow this belief, do not think that he is one who is lost, and do not turn your eyes away from him, but say, "Allah alone has the complete power, and if He willed He would show all people the right Path." He moves out of the stillness, He speaks out of the silence with ancient words devoid of letters, all means of expression, and all language. Likewise His hearing is without ears or auditory organs, and His seeing is without eyes or eyelids, and His knowldege is without theories or proofs, and His life is without beginning and without end, and far from material considerations. And He, Praised and Exalted is He, is attributed with perfection far removed from all shortcomings, because He is the Greatest One, the most Sublime; and He is not like anything that takes place, nor anything that comes to the mind, for He is the other than all that exists.

It is also the *sunna* to believe that Allah, Exalted is He, has Prophets and Messengers who warn and proclaim from Him, and that our Master Muhammad, the Messenger of Allah, who was sent to all creatures, was the last of all the Prophets and Messengers. Allah addressed him with the Words, "O Prophet! We have sent you as a witness and a bearer of good tidings and a warner calling to Allah by His permission, and a lamp bearing light." He bore witness to all that was sent down to him from Allah; and he bore witness to belief, and performed the prayer,and he counseled all creatures.

And it is to be believed that everything to which the Prophet, may peace be upon him, bore witness is the Truth, and that *the questioning in the grave* is the Truth, and that the *hour* will come of which there is no doubt. And also to believe that Allah returns to life all those who are in the graves, and that *the standing in lines before Allah on the Day of Judgment* is the Truth, and that the Path is the Truth, and that *the recording of actions* is the Truth, and that the Garden is the Truth, and that one group will be in heaven and another in the fire. "A party in paradise and a party in the blaze." (42:7) And it is to believe that the intercession of the prophets, the angels, the knowers, the martyrs, and the righteous believers is the Truth, and that everything that has come through the prophets is the Truth.

This is the belief of the people of the *sunna* and of the Community, and it is our belief, praised is Allah, until *the time of the hour*. I ask Him that He may grant us to strive in this life with clear and unambiguous words, and that in the Hereafter He will grant us to look upon His Omnipotent Face.

It is also important that the seeker should take from the knowledge of those who are learned in the outside law, so that his deeds may become in accordance with the pure *shari`a*, otherwise he, as well as his fortunes, will be mindless.

An Understanding of the Path According to its People

Know, that the People of Allah understand every word that is spoken to them as coming from Allah. This is because of their *state*, and this is what Allah wishes for them; and they do not use this knowledge for themselves, but for Him, and through Him. So, do not be surprised my brother, if their understanding of a word in a specific case is absolutely different from how others understand it, because this is the most noble *state* for them, and it is of the highest rank, since in this they understand the matters of Allah. And the Folk believe that understanding is from Allah according to a person's *state*, so that they do not of necessity agree that a word carries only one meaning, but that it may be understood with many uncountable meanings and striking wonders, which the mind could not penetrate. All of this indicates that the seeker should not hear anything except the word of Allah, or His Messenger, and whatever brings him closer to them. It may also be that the outer form of a word has an ugly sound, but the knower is enabled to gain something of good from it because he does not stop with the outside sense of the word, nor with its speaker, but he is able to put the word in its right place, without any picture.

Briefly, therefore, the family of Allah may agree with others as to the outer meaning of a word, yet for them it has a different inner meaning; just as they may agree upon things seen, yet differing as to what lies behind them, and likewise agreeing as to what is heard yet differing about the meaning of what they hear. He, Who is the one to be praised, said, "All drink the same water, but for food We prefer some to others."

Thus the Sufi may hear all, but he neglects what is not important, taking only the best of what is said. These are they about whom Allah said, "They hear the saying but they follow only the best of it." They are those to whom Allah has given righteousness, and they are *the first ones*, and *the people of the core of Essence*. Praise be to the one who has shown them the Righteous Path and who has brought them in proximity to Him, and has chosen them so that they come to take their orders and actions from Allah, their Lord. Thus they come to hear what other beings could not hear, and they come to see what others could not see, as some have said, "Their bodies are with us but their souls are with the

Truth (*al-Haqq*)." Also, as has been said, "My heart is with my Beloved talking to Him, but my tongue is with you." Therefore they come to hear things which are not heard by others, and they come to take their knowledge from things which, in the eyes of the people, are of little consequence. But for the Folk of Allah nothing is lowly because, for them, everything in existence reveals the Oneness of He Who is worshiped; until even evil words become, to their hearing, praiseworthy.

We heard it said about the Master of the Masters, the Shaykh al-`Arabi ad- Daqawi, may Allah be pleased with him, that he was walking one day with a group of his followers when they came upon a singer singing a banal song. The Shaykh, to the astonishment of the followers, bowed his head as he listened to the song. When the singer had finished, the Shaykh gave him what money he had and appeared content with what he had heard. Some of his *fuqara* said to him, "Master, how are you able to listen to things which should not be listened to?" The Shaykh, may Allah be pleased with him, answered them, "Why should I not listen to the *nafs* which through his singing left him, and in so doing freed him from what had been confusing him, so that he found peace?"

And know, that the Sufis (*al-mutasawwifa*) do not stop with the outside pictures of words, but they look for the meanings that are needed, and they do not care about the rhythms or the grammar of language, but they take the meaning of it as they find it, as it comes to them, because they look at what the soul wishes to indicate, and they are not concerned with the pronunciation of the tongue. You see that they are always with Allah in all their *states* for, "He is every day on a different matter." But in order to reach this victory they have absented themselves from the world, and have plunged into the *seas of realization* in which their only concern is for their heart, which is the house of God. And this is because their hearts have been chosen to see their Lord, and therefore He takes their hearts and purifies them, and in so doing the *nafs* are purified. Allah, Praised and Exalted is He, says, "The kings when they enter a town destroy it and make its lords the lowest of people." And He, Praised and Exalted is He, also says, "Allah never takes an ignorant person for a friend; and if He took such a person He would make him knowledgeable."

But as for the other arts of, for example, grammar, syntax, inflections, illustrations and linguistics, it is not necessary for the saint to have a mastery in them, for they only serve as a complimentary addition to true meanings, about which most Sufis know little, because their goal is Allah, and they are therefore raised up above others, because of the richness of what they realize about which the Prophet, may the peace and blessings of Allah be upon him, said, "He who is not enriched with the realization of Allah is he who is mischievous." Therefore it is not considered to be a shortcoming in their obligations if they are ignorant of sophisticated arts, which are other than bondsmanship to their Lord, but rather it is a sign of *ripeness* and a state of completion (*kamal*), although lacking in complete perfection. My Master Ahmad 'ibn Ujayba al-Mughrabi, may Allah be pleased with him, said, "The pious tongue without a pious heart is sinfulness and a straying from the Truth. The pious heart without the pious tongue is an imperfect completion, but the pious heart and the pious tongue is a completion above all completions."

I said, "What benefit is there in a pious tongue without a pious heart? Have you ever seen anybody who is satisfied with the words, but without the station (*maqam*); with speech, but without actions? Does the tongue have no need of faith, or has hearing no need of seeing Allah?"

The Imam of the grammarians, Sibawayh, answered, saying:

"Talking with a pure Arabic tongue
Will not save a man on the Day of Judgment.
Is grammar of any benefit if the heart is lacking in Allah?
Compare this with one who does not speak Arabic
But whose heart is devoted to Allah."

It is said, "The worst of all disgraces is when a person learns through the tongue, and then teaches by it; and does not learn through the heart nor does he teach by it." If his tongue together with his heart is towards his Lord their possessor is safe and he does not need to worry about loss or disappointment on the day that he stands before the All-Merciful; for Allah, the All-Blessed, the All-High, does not judge His slaves according to their knowledge of grammar, but He judges them according to their hearts. As it is said in the *hadit,* "Allah does not look at your pictures, nor at your actions, but He looks into your hearts."

Know that all beings except the Sufis, are taught according to the outside *shari`a*, but the Sufis are taught according to both the outside and the inside *shari`a*. When they listen to the language which is customary amongst the people they understand it in a different way from how the people do, and this is for them a means of assessing their standing on the Path; so they measure with it, and they make use of it. In this way they keep themselves busy, and not only with the task of acquiring knowledges. However, if they hear anything from other knowledges they raise it up to have a nobler meaning than that which the outside people give it. It is enough for the Folk that they are united to Allah, and that they are called *the People of Allah.*

Thus they are joined to Him, and in this universe they do not see anything else but Him. All that pertains to words or that is written in their books is taken from *the Divine Flood*, and this is not because of their reading nor is it from their planning. But they stand facing their Lord, obedient to His authority both in their senses and their feelings. They take the wisdom from everywhere, wherever they find it; and they feel deeply towards all beings on this earth, depending only upon their Lord, and not on any other being. May Allah make us one of them even if only of those who stand at their doors; and O Merciful One, O Compassionate One, do not cut off our bond with them.

"I have Masters of their knowledge
Whose feet are above those of the people.
Even if I am not one of them,
My heart, in love for them, becomes strong and dignified."

And know that *completion* does not mean a separation between the Reality (*al-Haqiqa*) and the Law *(ash-shari`a)*, nor a separation of the law from the Reality. There is a saying of the Folk, "The Reality (*al-Haqiqa*) is the eye and the Law (*ash-shari`a*) is what surrounds it." And their saying, "Whoever reaches the Reality without the Law becomes an unbeliever, and whoever follows the Law without reaching the Reality becomes misguided, but he who combines both together finds the Truth."

The Shaykh Muhammad al-Buzaydi, may Allah be pleased with him, said, "The Reality is the body and the Law is its members, for there is no body without its members." It is also said that the Reality is a tree of which the Law forms the branches, and it is sufficient for us that the Prophet, may the peace and blessings of Allah be upon him, said, "The *shari`a* is my speech, the Path is my actions, and the Reality is what I am."

The meaning of *O Allah! send Your prayers and Your blessings upon Muhammad, his Family, his Companions and his followers* is that, for the People of Allah, prayer means the Divine Glory and the revelation of Allah upon His slave. This draws the slave to Him and brings him to His presence, and thus, from time to time, He reveals Himself to him, and also, from time to time He hides Himself, so that the slave longs for the revelation, because every time that He shows Himself to him his awe and yearning are quieted, his heart finds ease and is filled with peace. This happens, however, only to His prophets and the *special ones* of His followers, the saints (*awliya*). But it is not right to ask Allah to bless (*yusalli `ala*) anyone except the saints and the prophets; and praise on the Prophet Muhammad must come first, this being a noble station (*maqam*) to which only the *special ones* of the people of knowledge can reach. In this case the prayer, if it comes from Allah, means revelation, or it means the asking and requesting (*du`a*) of God, if it comes from His slave. So if it is said, "O Allah! bless our Master Muhammad and his Family," it is as if it is said, "O Allah! reveal Thyself to Muhammad and to his Family," and if the asking does not carry the meaning of asking for revelation, the Prophet does not desire it.

And we are asked to send our prayers upon the Prophet all the time, and in every *state*. Thus, what is meant by this is the revelation of the *self* of the Divine Qualities which contains all the Names and Qualities, until through revelation he comes to see only the Creator, and not what is created. This then becomes his *state* most of the time in which nothing but Allah can satisfy him and bring him contentment. The Prophet, may Allah bless him and grant him peace, said, "I have a time when no one suffices me except my Lord;" and this is the time of *O Allah! send Your prayers upon him*; meaning Your revelation.

And still he asks for this revelation, and the Community of the Muslims (*al-'umma*) will ask for it until the *day of the religion* (*yawm id-din*) for if it is meant here by the prayer, the Mercy, it would have been enough for Him, Exalted is He, to say, "And We have not sent you save as a Mercy for all the worlds." This would be enough. But the yearner does not stop with the Qualities, for ultimately the prayer of Allah upon His slaves is His most complete affection for them, and the utmost proximity to Him, because through those who have reached the prayer all can reach to it; and through it Allah brings out His special followers (*al-awliya*) from the bonds of their *nafs* to the seeing of their Lord. Therefore His Words, Exalted is He, "He it is who sends His prayers upon you, and His angels, to bring you out from the darkness into the light." Meaning, that He takes you out from the darkness of the Creation to the light of the Creator; or it can be said from the bondage of the human being to the world of the secrets. Therefore, no one is satisfied with the prayer alone, but all ask for what accompanies it. It is said that the Prophet, may the peace and blessings of Allah be upon him, benefits from the prayers upon him - yes, he benefits from them, and he is not lured by the gardens and suchlike dwellings and ornaments without the prayers upon him. "Some faces that day shall shine observing Allah." Meaning, in observing the prayer; and Allah is the one who is the All-Knowing.

Concerning the peace from Allah on His slaves: this means security and certainty for them in the revelation of the Reality. Therefore a person should not request the prayer alone, but request the prayer and peace together. Also, peace should not be mentioned before the prayer for it is a sign and a confirmation of the existence of revelation, and of the prayer. But if Allah, Praised and Exalted is He, is sought in the prayer upon a group of His slaves, and the peace upon them is omitted in the asking then the revelation comes to them in the form of imprudence, fearfulness, instability and uneasiness. As a result of this their apprehension grows, and their crying increases so that they give utterance to secret words of the Folk. Then the ordinary people call them untruthful, and judge them unjustly. And the reason for all that is because Allah only was invoked in the prayer which did not include the request for peace. If Allah, Praised and Exalted is He, is to save them and others with them, then the prayer upon the Prophet must be followed by the requesting of peace upon him, whereupon the fearfulness of the slaves calms down and their *state* becomes balanced so that their outward *state* is with the creation, and their inner *state* is with the Truth (*al-Haqq*). The uniting of these two worlds comes through the wisdom of the two stations (*maqamat*) of the Qur'an and the sunna.

This is the case of those who are the inheritors of the Prophet in his noble station (*maqam*), witnessing it with both intoxication and with sobriety (*al-fana' wa al-baqa'*), and suchlike expressions; and here intoxication is the sign of the prayer of Allah upon them, and sobriety is the sign of the peace of Allah upon them after they have dwelt in the sight of their Lord.

Know, that the Prophets, may the prayer and the peace of Allah be upon them, were exceptional in being able to bring together the prayer, and at the same time, the peace. But, as for the saints (*al-awliya*), may Allah be pleased with them, some of them favored the prayer without the peace in which case the station (*maqam*) is referred to as *intoxication*, as we have explained. Some of them died in that *state*, and those are the *martyrs of love*, and their death is paid for by Allah. Some of them came back to their senses and paid for their intoxication with the strengthening of their inner *state*. Both of these are gifts from Allah; and His Giving is never withheld from His slaves.

Finally, the prayer from Allah on His beloveds is a sign of *reaching* and union, just as the curse upon His enemies is a sign for being distant and cut off. May Allah protect us and all the Muslims from that. Amin.

Know that the Sufi should carry three ranks, and these ranks, which should be built into him, are as follows: That through the knowledge and understanding of the Qur'an, he in his actions and in his bondsmanship should copy one of the *'imams* and *special ones* of Allah. In his inwardness he should be prepared to bear witness to the Path of the 'Imam of the Sufis, al-Junayd, may Allah be pleased with him, one of the *'imams* of Sufism. And by this it is meant that he should not see anything other than the Creator in his existence. This he can realize through the Path of witnessing, manifestation, and knowledge. And if he, in himself is grounded in this station he should only speak of beliefs that are in accordance with the understandings of created minds such as the beliefs of *al-'Ash`ari* and the *'Ijma*, otherwise his words would be a trial and temptation (*fitna*) for them.

True are the words of the 'Imam as-Safi`i, may Allah be pleased with him, when he said, "Speak to the people about things which are familiar to them for in the ignorant there exists a great treachery, and if they were to be shown the Reality they would not recognize It."

If you ask, "Do the Folk have a belief which is different from that of al-'Ash`ari?" I say, "Yes, because al-'Ash`ari has a belief which is special for *men*, and which cannot be given to children." For it is said that the food of *men* is not suitable for small boys. The Prophet, may peace and blessings be upon him, said, "Hidden inside knowledge there is a knowledge which is only known by the knowers of Allah. If this hidden knowledge is shown to ignorant people they will reject it." So where do you halt with this knowledge? If you do not have any part in it you are as though non-existent after which anything of it that is said to you does not touch you; for the People of Allah do not speak to us solely about what concerns our minds. For this reason the Prophet, may peace be upon him, said, "Speak to the people in accordance with their minds."

Know that the first thing that the seeker on the Path of Allah meets with, and by means of which he arrives to the Reality of the knowledges, understands the meanings of the *Great Book*, and becomes qualified in being able to distinguish between what is right and what is wrong, is belief, and in his total dedication to the beginning of the Path so that he becomes of absolute certainty in its ending. And this will come to him because of the perfect freedom with which he faces his Lord on the Path, without hesitation or illusions; for these attributes will lead him to what he desires in his Way. But if these attributes are not present he will be cut off and forbidden from the *watering-places* of the Folk, for only sincerity is acceptable with them, and if he lacks this sincerity he will be cast out from the Path even if he is willing to follow it.

For this reason some say, "Our Way is founded on the *intention*; and honesty of intention does not come through searching and meticulousness. So it is important for the reasoning person to observe himself with the eye of true judgment, not measuring what he possesses of the Truth by what he has which is not of the Truth; for what a difference exists between the soil and the stars! The minds of ordinary people are not like those of the Folk; therefore how can a person who sees only the outside face of things compare what he has of knowledge with what the Folk who do not stop with what is ordinary have; for their knowledge contains all other knowledges.

Know that the wisdom of the minds of the Folk is a wonderful thing which cannot be measured by habit nor by anything pertaining to man, and this cannot be deposited except in the most *beloved being.* He who has such a mind is freed from all defects, for Allah created him for Himself, and He would not permit him to turn aside to anything else; and in the Truth any mind which contains anything that is other than Allah is not, in the eyes of the Folk, a mind.

Know that the above-mentioned mind can be divided into three parts, namely: the *obligatory*, the *impossible* and the *possible,* to which nothing can be added and nothing taken away. This is in regard to the minds of the great knowers who are *subsistent* in the world; but as for the beginners, those who are *attracted* to Allah (*al-majadhib*) in a state of intoxication, their mind has only two of these parts. Some of these only know what is obligatory, and they say that Allah is the Essence of the Creation and all that exists without Him is lost. The others do not say anything because they are absent from everything. But for those who are complete and live in the perfect subsistence *(baqa')*, giving to each one his *due* and whatever he needs, their inner part belongs to intoxication and their outer to *the people of sobriety.* Because of that their integrity is on the straight Path, and they are respected and honored amongst the people, since their *price* is Allah.

Know that the *image* of obligation which is required from the saint is to accept the annihilation in any face which manifests the Truth to him; and that revelation exists in every *state*. The 'Imam ash-Shadhili, may Allah be pleased with him, said, "Vision of the Truth came upon me and would not leave me, and it was stronger than I could bear so I asked Allah to set a veil between me and it. Then a voice called out to me saying, "If thou besoughtest Him as only His prophets and saints and Muhammad, His beloved, know how to beseech Him, yet He would not veil you from it. But ask Him to strengthen you for it." So I asked for strength, and He strengthened me, praise be to Allah."

And some say, "If I was commanded to see other than Allah I could not do so for the eye cannot see what is *lost*, or *other than He*."

This then, for them, is the image of obligation which accepts annihilation (*fana'*) in any state; but what is not permitted is the acceptance of subsistence in a state which is not from the Reality, and the existence of which cannot be proved. Some say:

"I have seen Allah and none other than He have I seen,
And every other thing for us is forbidden.
I feared to make a separation in the Unity,
And I have today arrived and reached to Union."

The knowers have finished with existence and they never see anything but the All-Mighty, the All-Supreme, for if a person sees anything other than Allah he can never arrive at dying *now*, both to the past and what lay before, and to the future and what lies ahead.

In brief: belief in the existence of anything other than Allah is forbidden, and it is destructive, for it cannot be described as either existent or non-existent; and this is the example of what is *impossible*. But what is permitted for the knowers, and what is a practice amongst them, is the affirmation that the Creation exists, and the denial that it is non-existent, thus uniting and thereby confirming both its existent and its non-existent state. This station (*maqam)* has two aspects, so that if a person wishes he believes in the existence of the creation, and at the same time he believes in its non-existence. For this reason our Master Abd al-Qadir al-Jilani, may Allah be pleased with him, said, "If I so wished you would be annihilated in a moment." Meaning briefly, that either to affirm the existence of the creation or to deny it is, in the eyes of the Folk, all the same thing, because in seeing the creation this does not mean that they do not, at the same time, see the Creator. No, but rather it is that they are not concerned about *this* or *that*, for if they affirm the existence of the Creation they do so in Allah, and if they deny its existence they deny it in Allah. This is the meaning of what, for them, is *permitted*; and Allah knows best.

Then the permitted (*ja'iz*), the obligatory (*wajib*) and the impossible (*mustahil*) are also divided into both what is obligatory and what is *visual.* What is obligatory can be recognized by the knower without being in a *state* of absence, whereas the *visual* is what he recognizes because of its exactitude and clarity through absence and eye-witnessing. Then the obligatory duty is the affirmation of the Unity (*al-wahdaniyah*) in Allah, which the knower recognizes without being absent from the world, nor through eye-witnessing, because it appears to the Folk as the sun appears to the world. But the obligation of *eye-witnessing* is like the witnessing of the Omnipotence through the witnessing of the existence of the Omnipotent, and this is not realized by everyone of them in his *state* of being drowned in the might of the Essence, but only after his absence, and when he returns to his senses in subsistence (*baqa`*) for it is in the manifestation of the Essence that the Names and the Attributes are made apparent. But he who has witnessed the might of the Essence is not able to bear witness to anything other than it because of its Indivisibility and the strength of its manifestation - a *state* which cannot be understood by anyone who has not *tasted* it, nor dwelt in it. As for there being impossibility in what is obligatory, this would be, for example, if the Essence were both elevated and also divisible, but Allah is high above all that, and moreover this Truth is made known to them without their being absent from the world.

What is the *visually impossible* is the forbidding of seeing the Truth through anything but its images. Meaning, that it is not possible for the knower to see Allah other than through witnessing Him in the world, for before the contemplation it is not certain what is forbidden and *impossible,* and it is only after he comes to be more experienced and is steadfast in his witnessing that he is able to recognize all things, and to put them in their right place; and that he will come to understand. For before that he will not be able to recognize the Reality even if he were to tear himself apart from the strength of his desire to do so. Moreover, whatever is partial and incomplete has no existence in the Truth. As the Shaykh Ibn `Arabi, may Allah be pleased with him, said, "The Essence cannot be reached without the manifestation even if a man were to tear himself apart from the strength of his yearning for it."

Therefore, when Moses (*Musa*), may the peace and blessings of Allah be upon him, asked to see Allah without His manifestation he was told, "You will not see Me, for I am not outside the world, and not inside it, not a part of it and also not separated from it, for I am every one of you, but why are you not aware of Me? If My nearness to you were made proof to you, you would become distracted. So, look inside yourself and return to your senses, and look at the place where you are standing, which is the mountain. If it stays in its place you will see Me." Then, when Allah revealed Himself to the mountain and He removed the veil of his existence from Moses, the mountain and every other place became as rubble before his eyes. Moses fell down unconscious, and this was because of the removing of the *between* (*bayna*) and the *where* (*`ayna*), so that he saw with his eyes. Moreover, the real meaning of these words cannot be understood by anyone who is not in the same *state* as was Moses, may peace and blessings be upon him. And this is an example of what is known by the Folk as the *seeing which is impossible*, or *visually impossible*.

An example of the obligation which is *permitted* is for the People of Allah, the attraction of one of the creation for the presence of the Reality as a result of which he becomes one of the *people of witnessing* (*ahl al-mushahada*) without having to go through the *great battle* (*al-jihad*); and this is what is known as the *permitted obligation*. The *permitted seeing* is when Allah, Praised and Exalted is He, picks out one of the beloved people of witnessing (*mushadah*) and brings him near to Him, and then cuts him off, and veils him. But no one knows about this *state* except the people who are given, or permitted to contemplate this proximity. May Allah protect us and all the Muslims!

Know, my brother, that the first necessity for those under obligation is a sound reason, and that for the Folk the meaning of maturity is the state in which his witnessing of the Truth is firm and established. This means that he has reached to the seeing of the Truth (eye-witnessing), and that the veil has been removed from him. This must take place in order for Allah to be known in every manifestation. But, for he who has not yet seen the Truth, and for whom the veil has not yet been removed he is not expected to *see* Him and to know Him in all His Attributes and revelations. The meaning of the word *obligated* refers to he who is the owner of the claim to the knowledge of Allah, and who has reached to the *state of men*, and who has emerged from the prison of limitation and illusion to the Unity without limitation or space. He is the one who is *obliged*, and it is for him to *reach* and to know Allah in all the Qualities as well as in the Essence; and to deny and refuse all that is contrary to these revelations for he who is ignorant of every Quality is ignorant of He who is the source of every Quality.

So my brother, if you have known Him in the witnessing (*ash-shuhud*) do not deny Him in existence (*al-wujud*), because whatever is manifested is nothing but Him. Beware of knowing Him in the Unity and denying Him in separation, or of being of those who, if Allah sends them something of His Majesty and Severity, say, "This is from you, O

Muhammad, but not from Allah." He wants you to know Him, and to love Him in every face of His faces, and to know Him in the way that He wants, and not in the way that you want.

So be with Him, as one guided, and not as one who thinks that he has free will, or as one who thinks that he has a choice. If you would know His Essence it is necessary not to deny Him in His revelations. He wants you to know Him in the state (*hal)* as well as in words (*maqal*). For this reason, O knower, He puts you to the test, and He fulfills all your demands so that you may subsist in the place to which you have arrived. Because if you are ignorant then your place of arrival is your ignorance, but if you are a knower your dwelling-place is the Truth; and that is your Lord. So free yourself to be able to see His Beauty in everything upon which your eye falls, for nothing exists, but He. And say, as the Master `Abd al-Karim al-Jili, the author of *Al-Insan al-Kamil* (*The Perfect Man*), may Allah be pleased with him, said:

"The Beloved was revealed in the appearances of His Beauty,
And in all appearances of the beloved is He revealed."

So it is important for you, my brother, to be the one who understands completely if Allah comes to you in any color or form, for whatever is revealed from Allah is only veiled by the world from the power of its true manifestation. But always be present with Him, and do not be veiled from Him by things which with Him are non-existent nor stop with the pictures of manifestation; and do not look at their outer appearances, but go through them to find the inner meaning in everything that manifests. Do not be veiled from Him through any of His pictures, for behind the veil of the eye there is a shining light. Open all the doors of the Truth in everything that you see, for these are the revelations of the *Doer*. This is the Straight Path, so do not go astray from it. Take hold of it and do not be attracted away from it.

Allah, Exalted is He, says, "This is My Straight Path therefore follow it, and do not follow the ways that lead you away from this Path." Therefore my brother, follow the Path of the Truth, and do not leave it once you have found it, or you will become forgetful of Allah which comes from not cherishing His manifestation, and from being neglectful of His appearances when He reveals Himself to you. For this reason you know Him in His Beauty (*jamal*) and you deny Him when He appears to you in His Severity and Majesty (*jalal).* But it is necessary to be strong with all His states and manifestations, and to know Him in all His contraries. Do not love Him only when He expands you, and turn away from Him when He contracts you. Or do not love Him only when He gives to You, and deny Him when He withholds from you. Or do not see Him only in knowledge, and deny Him in ignorance; or know Him in everything that is pleasing and easy, and deny Him in trials and difficulties, for all that is the knowledge of the pictures, and it is not the knowledge of realization. Allah in all His *states* is always the true Beloved, for His Beloved.

In relation to this there is a story told about Shibli, may Allah be pleased with him, and a group of his friends who visited him when he was confined to a mental hospital. He asked them, "Who are you?" They said, "We are your beloveds." But Shibli took up a stone and threw it at them, whereupon they all fled from him. Then he said, "They were lying in what they said, for if they had been my beloveds they would not have run away from my distress and misfortune;" and this is not the way of the true lover with his beloved.

So my brother, do not acknowledge your Lord only when He is generous to you, and deny Him when He repels you. No; because He is your Lord in all states and situations. Do not be with Him only in a limited place or for a limited time, but be with Him everywhere and at all times. And do not say, "He came to me joyfully," but you see Him through trouble, and do not say, "He forbade me," when He was generous to you and ennobled you. Rather be a slave for Him in every state, for no one knows what Allah knows. And this is a mighty obligation and a significant decree. And therefore it is necessary for he who is under obligation, and who has the power to see, to know the meaning of every word that Allah sends, and not to ignore it. The meaning of being able to *see*, is to see the Truth of the eye-witnessing when it comes to him, and to know Allah through the Qualities as well as through all other revelations. And it means to be able to take the knowledge from revelations of the Essence without losing the station of being the slave. For that, he says, "Allah and His prophets are known through the Qualities, and he who contains the prophets and gathers them together is Mustafa, may Allah bless him and grant him peace, because through him all the prophets can be known, and whoever is polite with him will be polite with them all. Through him the knower will seek, and will find what he is searching for if he knows Allah in the Essence and in the Qualities, and if he goes deeply into the witnessing (*ash-shuhud*). For in that case, he will not have taken the knowledge from the fringes, or borders, and therefore he remains firm in relating all outer matters with the outer (the Revealed), and all inner matters with the witnessing (*ash-shuhud*). Thus he is not veiled by multiplicity from seeing the Unity, nor is he veiled by the Unity from multiplicity, but he sees the Reality (*al-Haqiqa*) in inner existence and the Law (*ash-shari`a*) in all that is manifest. This is a noble *state* and an elevated rank in which the people of true knowledge (*at-ta`rif*) are found. Such a person is dearer than the *red sulphur* (*kibrit al-ahmar*), the highest, the most perfect medicine and healing, because none but he who holds the deepest station and mind can be the mediator between these two states of the Reality (*al-Haqiqa*) and the Law (*ash-shari`a).*

And know that the station of obligation is a matter of the mind and of maturity; the basis of which is the realization that all individual entities, in themselves, are non-existent, and this is without any exception. But if any one of the necessary conditions of this station is lacking then he who is under obligation is no longer in that station, because this noble *state* cannot be carried by a weakened obligation resulting from an incomplete mind and state of maturity. The meaning of maturity being that the person under obligation and who follows what is obligatory has reached to a knowing of Allah through eye-witnessing and extinction (*fana*') and has come to the deepest knowledge (*al-ma`rifa*) which is bereft of all illusion. He is now totally immersed in the Essence, and not in the presence of the Qualities, so that he is not aware of how the Essence brings to an end, and completes the disappearance of creations other than Itself. At the same time, it is not possible for he who follows what is obligatory, but who is not in the state of sound maturity and reason, to know Allah in other revelations, because he cannot know what the Essence contains of them. For if he is not both in obligation and mind, mature to this extent, he would lose his reason, because the mind is a created entity, and in such a station he would have left the created world, which is the case of the person who is attracted beyond his reason (*al-majdhub*). Therefore a person who is under obligation, but who does not possess a proper mind, could not be the mediator between the Reality and the Law, because he would not be able to be drowned in the witnessing whilst standing on the fringes of the knowledge (*al-ma`rifa*). It is only the prophets and the special friends of Allah who are able to do this because their minds, which recognize and understand what is witnessed, and which provide them with the details of the ranks which have passed away, have been destroyed in their annihilation in the Exalted One (*at-ta`ziym*).

Therefore, what of he who remains on the fringes of the knowledge and at the same time has left everything of existence (*al-wujud*)? How could he take care of those who have dissolved in the Oneness of the Truth, or how could he bear witness to the universe if he has not found the place for its existence? It is Allah, and no *place*, for He is what He is. Meaning that the Essence exists through Itself alone, and It does not need anything else in order for It to exist. Nor does it need any *place* or *space* in which to manifest, or on which to come to rest. How could He, Praised and Exalted is He, need a place when the place before it could have its existence is in need of Him? Is a place set apart, or isolated until there is a space found for it? No, but the *place* only exists in the eyes of youths- those who have not yet reached maturity. If a place were to have any existence in itself then that would come between it and Allah, as an existence together with Him. And for he who is in this *state*, how can his fears be removed from him if he is absent, but nevertheless still with his feelings in all his states? He cannot be blamed for his state if he is not of those who are complete, for he has arrived there by the hand of Allah. My Master Abu Madyan al-Ghawth, may Allah be pleased with him, said, "Do not blame the intoxicated one in his state of drunkenness, for Allah in our intoxication has taken away all obligation from us." Briefly, it is necessary that the balance between the Reality (*al-Haqiqa*) and the Law (*ash-shari`a)* be one of reason and maturity as I have already mentioned.

For this maturity there are five signs, and if any one of them is present in the seeker after the Sufi Path then the obligation falls upon him so that he will be led to preserve and to protect all the other revelations, and to uphold their ways and characteristics. One of these signs is that he should speak with wisdom, and that he should understand the Reality of the Names. Another is that, in the beginning of what is decreed for him, he should be absent from his senses whilst witnessing his Lord, and that he should speak with the tongue of his Lord, or his Shaykh. Also, that his brother should witness these states in him. If any one of these signs manifests in the *faqir* he will be entrusted with good manners in all his other behavior. These are the signs which outwardly should manifest from him. Concerning his inner signs of maturity he knows them for himself, and he should be trustworthy in his manners and behavior towards his Lord so that, because of his maturity he should not have to be excused for anything nor for any state. These are the signs of maturity.

As for he who is absent through attraction (*al-majdhub*), and who utters sayings, and who proclaims in front of people, he is not under obligation to combine and unite his states of intoxication with sobriety because of the strength of the revelations for him. In this case if it can be seen that his state is a question of his mind being in separation, and if this is confirmed in him, then he should be compelled to obligation. Such would be the case of a person making a separation between sense and meaning, but who, at the same time, is able to take care of his affairs, or a person who knows his rights from the rights of others, or a person who is answerable for himself being able to say, "No," and such-like cases. Meaning that when he returns to good sense and perception, he also comes closer to being under obligation, for obligation is never completely removed from any person whose state is that of separation.

The Mother of Books

Know, that the *Mother of Books* is the goal to which the knowers aspire, and it is that which is yearned for by all those who seek. It is the Essence which unites all the Names and Attributes. Therefore it is said, about what it contains, that: "All beliefs come about from this Book which is born from the Essence, and has its origin in It." It carries all the secrets of the decrees of Allah, and contains, in their entirety, from the highest to the lowest, the signs of Allah for His world. It is the Book of the Folk, the People of Allah, and it is the unifier of all knowledges to which they are returned, according to the words of the One, Praised and Exalted is He, who said, "Behold what is in the heavens and the earth!" And when they looked they found it true so they said, "O Lord, Thou didst not create all this in vanity, praise be to Thee." And when the veil was removed for them they understood the meanings of the Book, and they obtained the understanding of its lines. O what a Book!. He who has received it has gained abundant merit. The Exalted One has said, "And with Him is the Essence of Books." This means, to be the possessor of the Essence of the decrees of the Book, from which every reader draws his life, just as the milk of a mother gives life to her child. And there is no doubt but that the entire existence draws its support and strength from this Book, without which everything would perish. As it is said:

"He who is non-existent receives his Essence
From His Essence.
His true existence without Him is impossible.
So know, that you and all the worlds, without His existence,
Melt away and become non-existent."

Briefly, any person who desires to know Allah through the Essence sees that he has no existence of himself but only through the existence of his Creator. Therefore, it is necessary for the human being to know that his attributes are from the Attributes of his Lord, as it is said, " Know your attributes and He will then give you His Attributes." So, O seeker, if your eyes are opened, and you see what is from Allah and what is from yourself, you will find that you have completely no existence, as if you were a thing without mention. Therefore, purify your heart and your soul and walk, and be aware of your qualities.

Know, O seeker, what is from yourself, for if you describe yourself by qualities which are reserved for Allah alone you are contending with Him and making partners with Him. The Creation of Allah, Praised and Exalted is He, exists through Him, and it is the eye of the Creator. What is meant by this is the Creator in all His perfection, because His Universal Existence has no numbers, nor can it be determined; and there is no Creator together with this Creator because He is Indivisible, without numbers, and He is the All-mighty One, the All-Merciful, the All-Compassionate.

Know then, that in the eyes of the knowers this creation does not know of disappearance or dissolution, just as the senses in the eyes of those who are veiled by the senses (*al-mahjubin*) do not allow for extinction; for the manifestation of meanings to meaning is stronger than the manifestation of the senses to sensibility. For this reason the most complete manifestation appears in a Sufi, and therefore he lives in praising and thanking. Therefore, for that reason if he wanders in the fields of Eternity he will find no intention there, and he will return from this intoxicated strolling to subsistence (*al-baqa'*) to which he will find no limits and no ending. Then he will be immersed in the Hidden (*al-batin*) from which he cannot escape. Then he will say, "O my confusion! where shall I go for shelter, you who wanted to describe Him with *sides*? You are the center and the core of existence, the hidden of the Names and the Attributes." Then, what will be the case of he who has been created? He will surrender himself to this existence, and then he will know that there is no other existence, either existent or non-existent than this existence.

Briefly, the Self of the Essence is existence and Eternity is its Attribute, there being no specificity for the beginning of existence because subsistence in Allah (*al-baqa'*) excludes the existence of anything for which there is an ending. Allah, the Exalted, is timeless and there is no beginning for His timelessness, and there is no end to His everlastingness. This unlimited existence is all-rich, universal, and without any duration. The meaning is that the Essence exists through itself alone, and it does not need anything else but itself in order to have its existence.

Modern Innovations Contrary to What is Allah

This quality of innovation has no part in the pillars of the belief of the knowers. Any desires to innovate examples, likenesses or copies of what Allah has ordered come from the world of fantasies and shadows of the *how,* and these things, which are likenesses, or copies, do not enter into the minds of the knowers. Therefore, because they do not pay attention to these things, the barriers, for them, are broken down and the *sides*, shores and edges of witnessing disappear, so that the seer is rolled up in the existence of what is seen. For how can they see anything other than the existence of the King whom they worship? Yes, this quality of imagining, inventing, and the like is useful for those who are veiled, and it is even their *ship of safety*, for it does not hinder their hearts from being dependent upon the existence of simulation (*takhlif*), and of the *how?,* of sides, systems, inventions, partiality and distinctions. But the Reality, exalted is He, is free from all attributes of changeableness. He takes the veil, and in so doing removes all concept of diversity from His Divinity, so that the knowers are filled with wonder when they see the Truth freed from the things which manifest with the people; and if they desire to give expression to the marvelous secrets they are prevented from doing so lest words should escape from them which might resemble the attribution of human qualities to Allah; and that these could become a temptation (*fitna*) in the ears of the *people of the veil.* In truth, all this would come only from the paramount desire not to associate any human quality with the image of the Divinity.

Therefore, the only ones who can free themselves from the *why?* and from the possibility of making false attribution are the knowers who have followed the Path of the Unity. But how can he, who is far removed from the Truth, be saved from ascribing attributes and qualities, or how can he be saved from limitation when for him, the universe still has an existence in its own right?

So, my brother, if you do not die to your existence in the seeing of the one who is the worshiped, and if you do not search about to find the friend, the Perfect One, the door to the Way, you will fall down, and thereafter there will be no hope of rescue for you, except if you are found, and saved, by the caring of Allah. And may Allah care for us with His kindness, and may He protect us with His protection to save us from all innovations and suchlike things, and the making of comparisons, metaphors and likenesses (*al-amthal*).

And you, my brother, are not helped by merely professing with your tongue how remote the Divinity is from all influences, qualities and characteristics of the human being, nor is it helpful for you to make, from your heart, pictures of Him, because when you are veiled from Him then you describe Him from your ignorance of His Reality with likenesses and pictures coming from your heart. But if you knew Him, because your existence had disappeared in His existence, you would then know that He is far removed from any such pictures or likeness.

Briefly then, when the Folk make comparisons and ascribe likenesses, this is preferable to the false ascribing of qualities of holiness and piety to themselves or others in which the ordinary people indulge; and also their punctilious standing on ceremony, because they look at everything with the eye which belongs to the material world (*ad-dunya*) and therefore they are only capable of ascribing material qualities from the *dunya*, to what they see.

Therefore it is necessary for those who are veiled to avoid ascribing attributes to Allah which are not suitable for Him, and to not talk about things of which they have no knowledge; and to search for the help which will take them from their existence in the self (*nafs*) to the true knowledge of themselves in the witnessing of their Lord. For when the seeker knows how to *be* with his Lord all these things disappear, because Allah, in His Essence, His Qualities and His Actions, is One, and He is not composed of either similar or diverse parts. Therefore it is said, "The Unity in the Essence and the Qualities is what he who lives in illusion fears, when he hears of the Qualities and draws near to them, so that he comes to think of them as numerous, in the same way as the unbelievers of old thought of them." But Allah is above all that, for in His Unity the Truth has no numbers, nor does it permit of either increase or decrease, nor of superfluity nor of lack, because there is only Allah alone, and nothing else is with Him, and His *being* is through Himself alone. The Qualities have no existence in themselves, for they are not independent entities, nor are they capable of being detached from the one whom they describe; and that is the Essence. This is the meaning of the Oneness of the Essence and the Qualities; and as for the Actions, there cannot exit any action which is other than the action of Allah, Praised and Exalted is He.

Briefly then, the Folk are divided into three categories, the first of which sees that there is no *doer* except Allah, so that through unveiling *(kashf)*, they know the meaning of *oneness of actions*, and not by means of usual belief. They see that the *doer* is one even though the actions are many. These are the Folk of Allah, the children of the Path, in accordance with the Truth.

The second category are those who are certain of the Oneness of the Reality of the Qualities, so that when they *reach* to the recognition of this oneness they find no hearer, no seer, no living one, no speaker, no seeker, no knower, but Allah. These are they who, through witnessing, and not by means of reasoned proofs, perceive the Qualities in all creatures, because when any person comes to realize that there is no *doer* except Allah, it is not possible for him to ascribe the Qualities to anyone but He.

The third category of the Folk are those who have realized the oneness of the Reality of the Essence which is veiled from all creatures, for when they find the mightiness of the Essence they see that there is no place for the creation, in itself, to manifest. These are the *people of the*

Essence, and the knowers of the Unity; and all others, but they are veiled and therefore in ignorance, because they have not *tasted* the Oneness, nor have they smelt the fragrance of Uniqueness (*tafrid*), although word of the Unity has reached their ears. But because they have heard of it they consider themselves to be *people of the Unity*. No, for on the contrary they are far from the Truth, and are cut off from it because the Unity *(at-tawhid)* does not exist only on paper, in written texts, or as expressed by movements of the jaws of the mouth. For there is no *place* for it nor *space* for it, either on the earth or on the horizons; and it cannot be contained by the heavens, nor can it be found by any analogy, nor by the bringing together of opposites (*tibaq*); but only by the secrets in the hearts of the beloveds, who know Allah. The Prophet, may Allah bless him and grant him peace, said, in what he mentioned from his Lord, "Neither My heavens nor My earth contain Me, but only the heart of my trusting believer." O what a heart! O what a Lord! And O what a resting-place! O Lord, send peace to our hearts and do not leave us in emptiness!

Power, will, knowledge, life, hearing, speech, and sight are all obligatory Qualities which are veils for the Essence which, because of the strength of its manifestation is veiled by these Qualities, so that omnipotence is the veil of the Omnipotent, and will is the veil of the Willer, and hearing the veil of the Hearer, and sight the veil of the Seer, and words are the veil of the Speaker. And also it can be said briefly, that meanings are the veil for the intended. He who stops with actions is veiled from witnessing (*shuhud*) of the Qualities, and he who stops with the witnessing of the Qualities is veiled from the witnessing of the Essence. As for the Essence, he who knows it does not see anything of any other essence, for it, itself, is its veil just as, in the same way, the Qualities are themselves their own veil. Thus, omnipotence is veiled by power and will is veiled by desires, and thought and speech by meaning, sense, letters and sounds. Hearing and sight are veiled by the intensity of their manifestation in the creation, as knowledge is veiled by the strength of its revelations (*tajalli*) and the need for the gathering together of information on its behalf.

And know, that these Qualities are divided into three kinds, for each of which there exists a world which knows its own *kind*. Concerning the first kind, that of hearing, sight and speech, their world is that of the physical body. For the second kind, that of capability, will and knowledge, their world is that of the Dominion (*al-malakut*) and the world of life is that of Omnipotence *(al-jabarut*). These worlds are not separated from the Essence either in revelation or in the removal of *sides* for according to the witnessing of the People of Allah, the Qualities are one with the Creation, and their manifestation is expressed through it, because the Qualities encompass existence, but existence does not encompass the Qualities.

For that reason, even though a person may search throughout the entire Creation he will find there only the Divine Unity in the Essence, the Qualities, and the Actions. Action resides in the doer, just as with every other thing before it becomes manifest, and when it manifests it does not do so by itself alone, but only if Allah causes it to appear, and in the measure that He is manifest in it; for all things are in their essence non-existent until they are witnessed.

And know that everything, which in the eyes of Allah is permitted, is also obligatory for the eyes of the believer who, for the Folk of Allah, is the knower from the beginning which is without beginning until the end which has no ending. Meaning that everything breathes from the word *kun* (Be); and that is enough.

Therefore my brother, it is important that you make sure of your qualities and that you look with the eye of your heart to the beginning of your existence, to the point when you were brought out into existence from non-existence; for if you look into your qualities, and make a reckoning of them, He will expand you with His Qualities. Some of your qualities are those of non-existence which is your description, and that of the world as a whole. If you acknowledge your non-existence, He will expand you with His existence, but if you ascribe what is His existence to yourself, then you are in conflict with Him, and with His grace. And how can you ascribe existence to yourself when the proof of your non-existence lies in how you first appeared in this world, for you are a created being, and from your own self (*nafs)* you can know that yesterday you were non-existent? This fact has been passed down from Eternity to all human beings, from before any word was pronounced.

Therefore, from where do you have existence, and who was the one who made you to be manifest in what is seen? Who made you appear to the one who witnessed you? You continue to be non-existent until the existence, in which He is revealed, becomes your existence alone. For, if it were not for Allah's appearance in all appearances, what is seen could not be seen. For this reason some say, "He is the Creator of all things and He is the eye of their existence, and if it were not for His existence they could not be seen in their existence."

One of your qualities is that you are extinguished (*fana*), for you, my brother, are *dead* until you are annihilated, and you are faded away until you are made to fade away, and you have disappeared until you are made to disappear, because you are an illusion in all illusion and you are a non-existence in all non-existence. You are nothing but an illusion like a mirage in the desert which he, who is very thirsty, thinks is water. But when he approaches it he finds no water, he only finds Allah. In the same manner if you search for yourself you will not find anything other than Allah. Meaning that you will find Him in place of yourself, and only your name will remain without any pictures, because all existence is not yours, but it is Allah's.

Therefore, if you begin searching for what lies inside you, and you remove what is not for Allah, you will find that the self *(nafs)* is like the skins of an onion, because when you want to peel the onion you must take away the first skin, then the second, then the third, until nothing remains of the onion; and this is the case of the slave of Allah in the existence of the Truth.

Another of your qualities is that you have no essence for we have imagined you to have existence as though you existed, but this existence, of itself, is completely lacking in the Essence, and it is only affirmed, and made true, through its Creator; otherwise it would vanish and disappear from sight.

And with all that, meaning the recognition of the non-existence of the slave (*`abd*), and of his poverty in Allah until he comes to resemble the Truth (Praised and Exalted is He) in the world of the Unity, we can see that if a person tries to prove for himself an existence other than that of the Reality, or of annihilation (*fana'*) in the existence of the Unity which cannot disappear, then he tries to give proof of two existences: that of the Reality and that of the self. Then, where is the Unity *(at-tawhid)*, and where is the Oneness; and in the eyes of the Folk what he lives by is polytheism; and this is a sin not to be compared with any other thing, and Allah does not forgive the one who makes himself equal with Him.

It is said that Rabi`a al-Adawiyya, may Allah be pleased with her, once met one of the knowers whom she asked about his state *(hal)*. He answered, "I have followed the Path of obedience, for I have not committed any sin since Allah created me." She answered him, saying: "Be careful, my son, for your very existence is a sin not to be compared with any other."

So, my brother, follow the Path of the People of the Unity, and do not ascribe existence to anyone but Allah, for if anyone of the Folk ascribes existence to himself he has made a partner (*shirik*) with Allah, and may Allah preserve us from that. As for the ordinary people, they cannot escape from ascribing existence to other things than Allah, even if it were to that of *a faithful king* or *a Prophet ordained*, or to anything which cannot harm, or which is not useful, nor is it *able to create a fly* although they brought everything that they possess in order to do so - all of which is other than Allah. Therefore, know your incapacity and powerlessness, then He will give you of His power.

And one of the qualities of the slave, which is a Quality of the Truth (Mighty and Powerful is He), is a dislike of all that the "self" wills. So if you claim to have a will of your own, then, O slave, you ascribe to something which is not your Lord and in this case you will not succeed, for it is not possible for you, if you wish to be a knower, to desire anything to exist which is not your Lord. Therefore, know your capability, and what is permitted for you, or else you will fall down in the eyes of your Lord. But he who surrenders his will to Allah lives in peace, while he who fights against Him is a prisoner of struggle and distress. The Reality, (Mighty and Powerful is He) said, "O My slave, you desire and I desire, and if you surrender to Me in what I desire, I will give you what you desire; but if you battle with Me in what I desire I will make fire for you in what you desire; and nothing but what I desire will be."

So surrender your will to Allah, and do not choose any action except what Allah wishes, because for the knowers of Allah to nourish the will, and to fight against Destiny is the quality of he who is ignorant and foolish. In the beginning it is necessary for the seeker to direct his will towards what Allah, Mighty and Powerful is He, wishes, so that in the end he is deprived of any will of his *self*, and his will becomes the Will of Allah, and this is what was written for him from the beginning; and it is the goal of every knower, because whoever in the end still possesses a will has strayed away from the Path of Allah.

So know your quality my brother, which in the very beginning it is necessary for you to destroy, and *be* in accordance with the Quality of the Will of Allah, as some have said:

"Surrender to Salma, and walk in the Way that she walked,
And follow the wind of destiny, and turn in the direction that it turns."

And another of the qualities of the slave is that he is ignorant; for you, O slave, who are ignorant of yourself and of your origin, how can you ask to know your Lord? It is your duty and your right, to seek to know yourself and to know about your origin, but you have turned away to other things. Because of that you do not know who you are, nor from where you have come. But you have found yourself in this manifestation and so you began to stop with that, and you turned away so that most of what you know of yourself says, "I have no existence." Then you turned away from non-existence and in so doing, you gave it a special world. You have approached it, and then turned back from it. If this is so, you have given existence to what is, in the Truth, non-existent. For the Prophet, may peace and blessings be upon him, said, "Allah was, and there was nothing with Him." In the true existence there is nothing that is non-existent, so if you make claim to a thing, and believe in it, and it is something which passes away, you have no knowledge, and you are in a state of ignorance before the true knowing. Therefore, ask to be taken by the hand and to be guided to the presence of your Lord, then your illusions will be destroyed in the true understanding; and your ignorance will become true knowledge.

Another of the qualities of the slave is that he is *dead* because life does not come to him, even though he appears to be alive, until Allah breathes it into him. You are like the mad person (*al-majnun*) in whom a *jinn* lives. He says, "I am this and that," but he is not. But if you were, in the eyes of Allah, to know yourself, you would see your body to be like the body of your father Adam, may the peace and blessings of Allah be upon him, into which Allah breathed His Spirit; and He would restore you, by His Grace, and make you His Vice-Regent (*halifa*) upon this earth. Then you could say, "I am alive." And it is of His blessing to you that you should know that, without Him, you are dead and have no true life. You have already been made aware of this, and of the insignificance of your existence, because you have become *special* for Allah, the Mighty. He, the Mighty, the Supreme, the Exalted, says, "Has not man seen that We have created him from a sperm-drop, and behold he is a manifest adversary." So return, my brother, to your quality of being dead, and remain in your rightful place, and do not lay claim to what is not yours, until Allah, Exalted is He, raises you up with a Spirit from Him.

And another quality of the slave is to be *deaf,* for now, O slave, you are deaf, because hearing is not your own attribute since it is Allah who is the hearer, and if you attribute hearing to yourself you will become deaf, even though you still hear. But although you hear sounds and words you do not hear truly, because if you did so you would hear Allah speaking at all times, and in all your states, for He is always speaking since silence does not exist in His Reality. But where is your hearing of His voice and where your understanding of His words? You are deaf, and you are still in the arms of non-existence, because if you witnessed true existence you would also hear the words of your Lord. How can he, who is deaf to His calling, hear his Lord speaking to him; yet if he truly heard he would answer the Call. But how can a person who is also dumb answer the Call. If he is dumb than how can he speak, for speech is one of the Qualities of Allah? If he is a being endowed with speech he would have value as a teacher, but no one keeps company with anyone who is dumb. Therefore he is excluded from the station (*maqam*) of those who speak. But if he acknowledges his dumbness Allah will give him His words, and he will begin to speak with the Voice of Allah, and to talk by His permission, and to hear by His permission until his hearing becomes His, and he does not hear anything except what is from Allah.

Another of your qualities, O slave, is that of being *blind.* Now you are blind because if you were able to *see* you would witness His Name. But you only see the outside appearance of things, so where is your seeing of the Truth, when outside appearances are clearer to your eyes than He is? May Allah forbid that He should be veiled from sight, but if this is so, then it is because you are possessed by your quality of blindness, so that you have become blind. This is the case of the person who claims that the Quality of sight belongs to himself; but he who knows himself and attributes every Quality to Allah, draws near to Him and through what He desires from him, Allah becomes his hearing and his seeing, so that whatever he sees, he sees through Allah, and whatever he hears he hears with Allah. Then, because of his existence in Him, Allah becomes both his seeing and his hearing; and this is the highest proximity of the slave to his Lord.

So give thought, my brother, to your quality of blindness, and ponder the wisdom that lies beneath it, then you will be illumined with true vision, and you will hear what you have never heard before; and you will see what you have never seen before. But you cannot reach that except through the knowledge of yourself, and through the realization of the fact that, in the Truth, you are, in yourself, non-existent.

And know, that in His Reality it is possible for all the possibilities to be created at the same time that they are also non-existent in the Truth; for in this case, they will pass away with all things that pass away. Yet it is from the Order of Allah to create them, and at the same time, to leave them as non-existent, for so long as they remain possibilities their existence is relative, and therefore not part of true existence, because there cannot be any other existence together with His existence, O Allah! except if it is a manifestation of His, for nothing has true existence unless it is He; and nothing can be affirmed unless through His affirming it. It is not possible for anything to be made manifest by itself, and through itself, just as it is impossible for anything to come into being, or to remain and subsist, by itself, or through itself alone. For it is Allah himself, Praised and Exalted is He, who has caused them to be made manifest, through His appearance in them. As one of the knowers has said:

"You manifested Yourself in things when You created them,
And lo! in them the veils are lifted from Your very self.
And You have taken away Your veils through them.
You have carved out mankind as a slice from Your Essence,
And they have remained joined to You, and at the same time
He is neither joined to You, nor is he separate from You."

The world is proof of the existence of the Reality which is the means for arriving to the knowledge of the existence of Allah. All who stop with the things of the world are veiled from their Lord by their desire to know Him through what is not He. Some have said, "There is no proof for Allah except through Himself, and there is no reaching to Him through anyone but Himself." But the proof is a veil for the prover, and in the measure that you are veiled with the proof, so you are veiled from He who proves.

So take advice, my brother, and ask for His help, and be needy of seeking for Him, for Allah answers the call of the needy when he calls to him. The lover always longs for his Beloved, and he is not satisfied with anyone but Him; and how is it possible for that which is a created thing, and which is a *happening*, to be in need, or to be dependent upon itself alone? Therefore, it is not for you to be in need of that which is created and transitory, but to be in need only of He who is the Creator of all *being*.

And know that everything that takes place has no existence of itself until it manifests in existence; and it has no *state* in front of the presence of He who is timeless (*qadim*) and eternal. And it has no name nor picture, no mentioning, no message, no existence, no influence and no remains. How can that which is non-existent and transitory stand side by side with that which is timeless? As Ibn `Ata'illah, may Allah be pleased with him, said, "How can existence manifest in non-existence, or how can that which occurs, be made true by He who has the Quality of timelessness?" For nothing manifests by itself and through its own nature or its contingency, but it manifests through the appearance in it of He who allows it to manifest, because He only manifests Himself in it for the purpose of revealing the lights of the heavens and the earth; and not for any other pretext.

And know that the Creation of world and its occurrence and its coming into existence is a proof of Divine existence, and this proof is both the means and the stages by which Allah may be reached. In saying this I fear that the reader of my words will imagine that the world has no beginning. Therefore I begin by giving proofs of the Creation, and I say, "The coming into existence and the occurrence of the world, from its depths to its heights, in its elements and in its contingent parts is an unprecedented thing." Everything that is not Allah is a creation now, and which is new in the moment, by which I mean that it is an occurrence having a *color* which is not the color of its origin. But that which is timeless and eternal, and which is not subject to either occurrence, appearance, reappearance or disappearance is free from what is of the world. This truth the knowers come to understand through unveiling (*kashf*) and they do not need any proof of it because Allah has shown them the nature of timelessness and eternity, and they have witnessed the world of purity (*safa*) and at the same time, they have not found therein anything that would invalidate the existence of manifestations. Everything that occurs is subject to change, but the origin (the source) is pure, and there is no inclarity, no muddiness nor overclouding in it. As 'Ibn al-Farid, may Allah be pleased with him, said:

"Purity and no water, no kindness and no wind,
No light, nor fire, no spirit, no body.
Everything that is not everlasting
Is an occurrence brought into being.
But the occurrence cannot be denied,
Except by he who is ignorant, or without a mind."

For the people of the heart occurrences are manifestations just as are the waves on the surface of the ocean. As is said:

"The ocean is a sea in timelessness,
And all things that take place are like waves on the sea,
And like rivers that flow into it."

And know that Allah was, and that there was no other existence but His existence. As in the truth of non-existence, if you have looked upon it, and if you have witnessed it, you will find in it also the truth of the truths of Allah, Praised and Exalted is He. For the truth of the Essence is the Reality, and therefore it is referred to as the truth of the truths. And know that beneath every possibility, and unknown to the Creation, lies the Reality of the Essence which is the meaning of His words, Exalted is He, "Wheresoever you turn there is the face of Allah."

Furthermore, it can be seen that all things exist also in their opposites, because if it were not so *contraries* would not manifest. But this cannot be understood except by those who have witnessed the Reality of the Oneness of the Essence and its decrees. And also, that which is hidden can be revealed through the understanding of the Unity - that Allah is One. Meaning that His Essence has no composition, and that there is no essence that is like unto it. But this does not mean that the Oneness does not recognize what is at the lowest state, or rank, in existence; but that it forbids completely, and without any doubts, the existence of anything that resembles itself. So when has there ever existed anything that has resembled Allah? This is borne out, and confirmed, by His words, Praised and Exalted is He, "And there is nothing like unto Him," referring to the non-existence of things in relation to Himself. So do not think that this world is a *thing*, for it is nothing. And at the same time, do not think that it is anything except, or unknown to, the Divine presence; but rather that it is an occurrence from the occurrences of the presence of the Divinity, and a Secret from His Secrets, and a light from His lights. Allah, Praised and Exalted is He, said, "Allah is the light of the heavens and the earth." And He said also, "And We also showed Ibrahim the kingdom (*al-malakut*) of the heavens and the earth, and when he saw a star he said, "This is my Lord." He did not utter these words in a metaphorical, or symbolic sense; far from that. But Allah, in this, made known to Ibrahim how he could manifest His kingdom to him. Ibrahim uttered these words because it had not yet been made clear to him about the non-existence of everything which does not endure before the face of the Reality. But when the Reality of the Truth was revealed to him, Allah said, "But when it set, he said, "I love not those things which set." And it is this which is referred to in the holy *aya*, "Wheresoever you turn there is the Face of Allah." (*fa `ayna tawalu fa-tamma wajhu 'llah*). Ibrahim, may peace and blessings be upon him, proclaimed this Truth to his people so that they might fear Allah in everything; and this is an example of the deepest reverence (*at-taqwa*). So follow Allah in true fear and awe.

But when the minds of his people were not able to grasp this hidden truth it became as proof of their disbelief. And this is what is meant by His words, Exalted is He, "That is Our argument which We bestowed upon Ibrahim, as against his people. We raise up in degrees whom We will."

All this took place when Allah revealed to Ibrahim the kingdoms of the heavens and the earth, and he found them to be the Reality of the Creator existing in all the Creation. Ibrahim wanted to proclaim what had been revealed to him, but he only found hearts opposed to the Unity, the knowing of the Oneness of Allah and His Creation, which He (the All-Mighty) had given specially to him. So when he saw the people in this state, he said, "O my people, surely I am quit of what you associate with God (*shurk*). I have turned my face to He who originated the heavens and the earth - a man of pure faith; I am not of the idolaters."

And know, my brother, that the Reality, Mighty and Supreme is He, is beyond any pictures of *otherness* in the Oneness of existence, because the *other*, and this is anything which is not Allah, is non-existent in the existence of the Unity; and the existence of the Essence is that of Qualities and Actions; and there are no actions except those of Allah. The Oneness of Allah is the Essence of the Qualities and Actions, and if it were not for the Unity neither the existent nor the non-existent could be created, because if the Qualities were joined to anything but the Essence they would fall down and fade away, for they would be subjected to fatigue, exhaustion and depletion; but his Qualities are steadfast and powerful when a person is in the truth of the witnessing of the Essence, the Qualities, and the Actions of Allah. Action is not close at hand but it is one of the manifestations indicating the appearance of the Qualities, and a revelation for the manifestation of the Names. The world, as it is, comes to nothing when the Names and the Qualities manifest. And even if the Names and Qualities were to be removed from it, yet it would not be firmly fixed to your sight, because of its non-existence in material reality. Meaning that if these Qualities did not manifest in all that is created, it would not be possible for a person to see the world, because what can be seen of it is only the manifestation of the Qualities; and its very existence can only be confirmed through the witnessing and the realization of the Qualities. If it were not so the world would be transitory and void, and without any outer or physical state. Finally, the six Qualities associated with obligation are: capability, will, knowledge, hearing, sight and word, and everything that manifests which is not Allah is from the pictures and vanity. These six Qualities have been mentioned, but we have not mentioned the Quality of life although it likewise is a Quality of Allah and does not come from anything which is not He. Existence is confined to the manifestation of the Names and the Qualities, as has been said, and if existence did not have the quality of life, will, knowledge or capability you would not see a world, and it would not then be said that capability, will and knowledge were, in fact, Qualities, together with others which are associated with the *perhaps* and the *maybe* (*al-mumkinat*) not only now, but also as they were in the past.

Know, that hearing and sight are Qualities of the revealed Face of Allah (*az-zahir*) of what exists, and not of what is non-existent of His revealed Face, whereas capability, will and knowledge are non-existent Qualities belonging to His hidden Face (*al-batin*), and nothing can be added to this state, because what is potential has no place with its Lord and it cannot be anything but what it is. However, it has a degree, or rank, with Him, in which case it can be referred to as either existent, or non-existent. But anything that is empty of Allah is falsehood. Then, that which is possible, or potential, is that which passes away. And know, that if what is possible (*mumkin*) had the order for existence, and that order was for it to be not what is Allah, and at the same time it were possible to witness it, it would appear in any case, and it would be described as being either existent or not possible to have existence. But as for the Reality, it has no description, no Quality, nor Name, and no image by which either its disappearance or loss could be described. For this reason the Folk do not refer to it as being existent or non-existent, because if they affirmed its existence this would be idolatry and the making of a partner with Allah (*shurk*), and how could they give manifestation to what does not exist, for Allah is that which is the very Essence of existence, and everything else is nothing.

The Necessity of Knowing the Prophets
may the peace and blessings of Allah be upon them

Know, that it is necessary for every person, who is under obligation, to know the Prophets, and to be polite with them, for both when he is drowned in the witnessing (*ash-shuhud*) and when he penetrates into the knowledge (*al-ma`rifa*) he must not go beyond his limits, nor lay claim to anything which he does not possess, so that he claims to have reached something which he has not reached, such as the notion to have realized the same knowledge as the prophets, and such like things.

And if their goal is to reach the Divine Presence, and revelation from Allah is what they are seeking, the revelation will not be similar for all seekers, but it will vary from one to another, and it will come down in different ways and manners; yet the Secret of the Creation will be shown therein, in both its minute and its vast aspects. For Allah, Praised and Exalted is He, whose intention cannot be known, reveals Himself to each person according to his ability and capacity, and according to his capability for receiving the Revelation of the holy Beauty *(al-jamal)* for which no limit or ending can be ascribed.

If you know that, know then who it is who in the knowing of the Revelation of the Names, the Qualities and the Reality (*a-Haqiqa*) is in the rank of the Prophet, may the peace and blessings of Allah be upon him. It is not the desire of any of the believers to be the first of the Folk of Allah, because none of the first of the believers can reach that rank. Then, seeing that it is like that, and if you are aware of this apportioning, then know that the *states* that manifested with some of the foremost of the knowers, laying claim to, and imagining themselves to be in a rank higher than that of the Prophets and Messengers, were not from the Truth. Some of their *states* led their owners to give voice to such sayings as that of Abu Yazid al-Bistami, may Allah be pleased with him, who said, "We have dived into the sea on whose shores the Prophets stood." And the words of the Shaykh `Abd al-Qadir al-Jilani, may Allah be pleased with him, who said, "O Prophets, you have the title of Prophets, but we have reached to something which you have not reached." And the saying of "Ibn al-Farid, "I have dived into the sea on whose shores the seekers before me stood, from respect towards me, and the elevated station (*maqam*) that I have reached." And he, may Allah be pleased with him, also said, "So great was the station (*maqam*) I was in, in the past, and that which I have reached to now, that I found the seekers before me, and of my time, as children whilst I am as a giant." And he said, "All those who are beneath You loved You, but in reality they loved You through Your manifestation."

And some of the knowers have said, "The end for the feet of the Prophets is the beginning for the feet of the Saints (*al-awliya*)." There is a *hadith* of the Prophet Muhammad, which answers the utterances of some of the knowers in their *states*, for he, may peace be upon him, said, "There are times when no one but my Lord suffices me." But in the *state* where the annihilation (*fana'*), the drowning and the destruction (*istikhlak*) fall upon the knower and he emerges, through them, from the circle of his senses and the sight of his *nafs*, and he is released from all awareness of *self* and his own existence, and he is annihilated in the Essence of the Reality, Praised and Exalted is He, and is granted the likeness of the Reality of Allah through which he can lead people, then he no longer sees by himself, but he sees through the Essence of the Reality. Then, in this *state* he says, "Praise be to Me, there is no God but I alone," and suchlike words as, "My greatness sat down to worship My glory." In this case he is excused for that, because the mind with which he would distinguish, and know how to use, what he sees, and the means which would allow him to distinguish the ranks of the Qualities, by the knowledge which each one possesses, has been annihilated from him. Then, when he loses his mind by which he would usually distinguish and judge, the Secret of Allah takes possession of him, and he begins to utter such expressions as we have mentioned.

However, through this, Allah makes him an inheritor and His representative *(khalifa)*, because he speaks with the tongue of the Reality, and not with his own tongue; and his voice is not his own, but it is the voice of the Essence of the Reality speaking through him. From this rank, and station, come the words of Abu Yazid al-Bistami, may Allah be pleased with him, who said, "Praise be to Me! How great is My nature!" Or the words of al-Hallaj, "I am the Truth (*ana al-Haqq*) whose nature does not pass away in time." And his words also, "There is nobody inside my garments but Allah." And the words of others, "The earth is My earth and the heavens are My heavens."

And the words of Ash-Shashtari, may Allah be pleased with him, who said:

"I am something wonderful.
For the One who saw me, I am the lover,
And I am the beloved, and there is no one but I."

And there are many sayings attributed to 'Ibn al-Farid, coming from the annihilation (*fana'*), which resemble these, and which are in accordance with that *state*. But, by this, we are not to understand that those, who speak like this, are in a higher rank than the prophets.

Therefore understand that everything, which you have heard, or read about, of such a nature from the Shuyukh, was expressed by them in their state of annihilation from themselves, and their drowning in the magnificence *(ta`azim)* of their Lord.

Then, if you are in that state of awareness, and you have reached to the end of the knowledges, because of your maturity and your understanding, it is not for you to compare yourself with one of the prophets. But, above all, know that one of the conditions of obligation is that the mind should be sound, and that he who is under obligation will be punished if he abandons all manners and politeness, with the exception of those who are possessed and overcome, and who are referred to as helpless, to the extent that in the remembrance (*ad-dhikr*), they utter such sayings as those we have mentioned above. In this case there is no blame attached to them, but if they were *awake* it would be impossible for them to say such things, because every knower knows, in himself, that since he has been brought forth through obedience, and with the help of purification, he is far removed from the rank of the prophets, and that in his *nafs* he can find many qualities which are not like their Qualities.

Moreover, the saints have a protection which comes to them after they reach to the rank of a Saint (*al-wali*) and which varies from one to another of them, and this is not like the veil of purity and restraint which was granted to the Prophet either before his Prophethood was revealed to him, or afterwards. Therefore, the following Qualities are obligatory for the prophets, but not for anyone else.

The first of these is honesty which, for the Folk, means to be truthful in words, actions and states, bearing witness to their Lord in both His revealed and His hidden Faces, so that nothing comes from them except what pleases Allah, Mighty and Supreme is He.

The second Quality is of commitment, the preservation of which is a duty upon the prophets and the special friends; and there are few people who can carry the burden of it, and keep its secrets, except the prophets. Allah, Praised and Exalted is He, said, "We offered the trust to the heavens, the earth and the mountains, but they refused to carry it, and were afraid of it; and man carried it." For the People of Allah, what is meant by the trust (*amanah*) is the Secret of Allah which is only for the prophets, or the special ones of the Muhammadan Community (*'ummah).* For Allah has ordered them to keep it to themselves, and not to speak about it to anyone except the Family of Allah. So the prophets, may Allah bless them and grant them peace, kept it to themselves, and they safeguarded this Quality perfectly. As for the saints (*al-awliya*), some of them fell down and revealed what should not be revealed, but the preservation of the trust is a Quality which is obligatory for the prophets, but is not so for the saint.

Also, it is the duty of the prophets, may peace be upon them, to transmit (*tabliq*) and announce, for a prophet has the duty to proclaim all that Allah, Mighty and Supreme is He, has ordered him to give to his people, and not to keep back anything because he fears the hostility or insults of the people. Even if they seek to destroy him, and do not answer him, nor follow him, he must not care, because he is with Allah. So the prophet, at all times, delivers the message of his Lord, and this is different from the case of the saint who, in comparison with the prophets, may the peace and blessings of Allah be upon them, is sometimes silent and prevented from speaking because of an incapability, in a certain case, or because of a lack of determination, or of the necessary diligence, which is never the case of the prophet.

The prophets were also commanded to give their message in accordance with the capacity of understanding of their people, but the Prophet Muhammad was commanded to, "Judge by the outside, and Allah takes care of the secrets."

In this respect, the story of al-Khidr and Musa (Moses), may peace be upon them, suffices as an example. The prophets are endowed with what is an obligation for the saint, while the saints are endowed with what is an obligation for the ordinary believers. Briefly, the saint represents the generality, whereas prophecy is exclusive and special. Every prophet is a saint and a friend (*wali*) of Allah, but not every prophet is a messenger (*rasul*).

It is not possible, according to what is required of the prophets, may the peace and blessings of Allah be upon them, for them to have qualities contrary to those we have mentioned above. For example, falsehood and lying is one such contrary quality which, either by purpose, or through a lapse, cannot be ascribed to them. But this is not the case for the saints who may manifest this quality, albeit unintentionally, because a believer, and especially the knowers of Allah, do not lie.

Also, it is not possible for a prophet to be unreliable or irresponsible, so that he would speak about a matter for which there is no order; or he would reveal a Secret of Allah, because that would be contrary to being a custodian and preserver of the knowledge of Allah. This is something which, in the obligation of a prophet, is impossible. But as for the saint, he may be overwhelmed by the revelation of Allah to the extent that he begins to utter to others certain words and expressions which only should be spoken about with the Family of Allah who can understand them, and this is a shortcoming in his obedience and his trustworthiness in front of the prophets, may the peace and blessings of Allah be upon them.

Also, it is not possible for a prophet to conceal anything of the message which his Lord has given him, for this would be contrary to the order from Allah for him, even though it could lead to him being thrown into the fire, as was the case of our Master Ibrahim; or to his being put to death, as was the case of others of the prophets, may the peace and blessings of Allah be upon them.

There is no possibility of there being any disobedience in the obligation of a prophet, for disobedience does not enter into their Quality of safeguarding, preservation and protection, the Quality inherent in them, from the Unity, and essential for every prophet, but which is not essential for the saint. This Quality is like a garment for the prophets, and is known as protection (*hifdh*), for it is like a veil of purity which protects them both in their beginning and in their end. Regarding the knowers, their protection is, in the beginning, like a veil of restraint (*`isma*) which may change and be removed from them as a result of their actions, and of what has been decreed for them. In that case the boundary of protection must be surrendered to the One who is the owner of this limit of protection, and if Allah removes His protection the saint is returned to being an ordinary person again.

Concerning What is Permitted in the Obligation of the Prophets

Know that the prophets are human beings and that in spite of their obligation and duty, they have human qualities as is the case of all the creation. Therefore, it is not possible to ascribe only Divine Qualities to them, for they eat as we do, and they drink as we do, and they die as we do. Meaning that everything that happens to the human being happens to them, except for what could result from a shortcoming in their elevated rank, because this is not possible by nature of their obligation. However, other misfortunes and tribulations are possible for them, so that it is enough for us to mention what the Prophet, may the peace and blessings of Allah be upon him, said, "We, the Community of Prophets, are the most tried of all people, after whom come the saints, then those who are the nearest to them." For this reason you will find the prophets the most sorely tried of all people; all of which comes from their proximity to the Reality, and from their love for Him.

It is recorded that a certain man came to the Prophet, may the peace and blessings of Allah be upon him, and said to him, "I love Allah." He, may peace be upon him, answered him, "Make for yourself a gown of tribulation, and know that the prophets and the saints are under the rivers of destiny."

Concerning miracles (mu`ajiza) performed by a Prophet, and those (karamat) performed by a Saint.

Know that the miracles (*mu`ajiza*) of the prophets attributed to them, either through their words, their actions, or states, represent the proof of the existence of the Reality, Mighty and Supreme is He, in them. Miracles are sent for those who have newly entered into Islam, to help them to overcome their doubts, and to strengthen their belief in the Divine Transmission of a prophet. But, for he who is firm and strong in his belief, the witnessing, or not, of a miracle is in proportion to the prayer, or the asking, and it is an indication of the perfection of the saint, because Allah, Mighty and Powerful is He, makes the miracle manifest for His slave whenever He wishes; its Truth coming from Him. Allah also grants it to His slave, from Himself, as a gift and a blessing for him, and as a sign of the slave's sincerity. Also, sometimes the saint needs the miracle for himself, because he is not yet, in himself, spiritually perfect, nor is his *murid* fully aware of the Way, because this is the *state* of those of good intention who are, nevertheless, veiled. But as for the knowers of Allah, those who are firm and grounded in their witnessing, they do not need miracles because they have knowledge of the truth of their *state* in their *absence* in the witnessing of their Lord. Therefore, the Master 'Ibn `Ata'illah as-Sakandiriya, may Allah be pleased with him, said in his *Al-Hikam al-`Ata'iya,* "May those who are of the beginning (*bidaya*) see them in their beginning, and the people of the end (*nihaya*) abandon them in the end, for in abandoning them they do not then portray miracles for their students lest any one of them is tempted to stop with these things and to turn to worshipping Allah through the outside signs, instead of through inner devotion."

And know, that the words, *La 'ilaha illa 'llah Muhammadan rasulu'llah*, bring together all of the meanings; and what is meant by meanings is all that is of the Hidden and all that is of the Revealed; all that is absent and all that is present. Or, all that is sensed and all that is imagined; all that is known and all that is unknown; and if it is said also, "All that exists and all that is non-existent," then *La 'ilaha illa'llah* contains every one of these meanings; and Allah is the container of everything; and there is no end to Him. Say, "Though the trees in the Earth were pens, and the sea - seven seas after it (were ink), yet would the words of Allah not be spent. Allah is All-Mighty, All-Wise."

So if you come to realize that, then you will know that *La 'ilaha illa'l-lah* contains all the meanings, and there is nothing, only the Reality of *la 'ilaha illa'llah*. Or you say, as some beloveds said, "The knower, who lives in the Essence of the Creator, has no existence." He is a knower if he knows Allah not only in all faces, but also that for every face He is the One who faces it. Then, wherever you turn your senses to what is sensed, or your mind to all the possibilities, or your illusions to what is imagined, you will see the Face of Allah. Because in every *where* (*'ayna*) there is an essence, and all are *la 'ilaha illa'llah*. Therefore *la 'ilaha illa'llah* embraces all the meanings.

And know, that under these words of *la 'ilaha illa'llah* the whole of the Creation can be ordered and classified, meaning the totality of existence and the particularity of existence; or it can be said *true existence* and *relative existence*; or it can be said the *existence of the Reality* and the *existence of the Creation*, for the existence of the Creation comes under the meaning of *la 'ilaha*, all that is not Allah is falsehood. Meaning that it is annihilated from having existence of itself and by itself, and therefore cannot be ascertained or affirmed. Then the existence of the Reality is expressed by the words *illa'llah* (except Allah). So that everything that does not have true existence comes under the first part of the words of this saying, just as everything that in the Truth exists, comes under the second part. And Allah is the First and the Last, so that if you understand this and you know it to be true, then you know that there is no difference between the Beauty (*al-jamal*) and the Majesty (*al-jalal*), and that what contains them both is the Perfect, the Complete (*al-kamal*), and this is nothing but the Essence of Allah, Mighty and Supreme is He. These words of *la 'ilaha illa'llah* also refer to all the ranks of existence as contained in the world of the Unity (*at-tawhid*) which can be ordered into degrees and levels by the mentioning of the most noble of slaves, in the words, *Muhammadan rasulu'llah.* So, in this noble expression the three worlds which were revealed to `Isa (*Jesus*), may the peace and blessings of Allah be upon him, are brought together, and can be expressed by the Names of the Father, the Mother, and the Son. The pronouncing of these words contains the meaning of the message of Allah, which is that of the Prophet Muhammad, because in this expression lies the understanding that *Muhammadan rasulu'llah* means the mediator of the three worlds; the kingdom, the dominion, and the world of Allah (*al-malakut*, *al-jabarut* and *al-lahut*). The word *Muhammad* is a metaphor for the kingdom (*al-malakut*), which contains the hidden meanings of the universe of the secrets, and that he is the intermediary between the timeless *(al-qadim*) and everything that can be expressed by the Spirit, and the world of Dominion is a metaphor for the world of souls, which is the sea from which the senses and the meanings pour forth, each of the senses and meanings being some created thing; but as for the Reality (*al-Haqiqa*) there is nothing like unto Him. Meaning that He is everything. As to our saying that the word prophet (*rasul*) stands for the intermediary between what is contingent and what is timeless. Yes, this is true, for he is the intermediary, because without him all existence would become non-existent; for if what is contingent meets with what is timeless it vanishes, and only the timeless remains. But it is through the mediation of the Prophet that both sides are brought together, and the world falls into its rightful order. In his outer form the Prophet is from clay, but in this inner existence he is the Viceregent (*Khalifa*) of the Lord of all the worlds (*rabbil-`alamin*). Therefore he is the medium between what is contingent and what is eternal.

And know also, that the Messenger is he who is called *the interval* (*al-barzakh*) which is referred to in the *aya*: "He let forth the two seas, between them a barrier which they do not pass over." And if it were not for this interval (*barzakh*) which is the message of Allah, there would be no order for existence, and everything that bows down and worships would disappear into the existence of He who is worshiped, because if the word messenger (*rasul*) is taken away from the saying: *Muhammadan rasulu 'llah* (Muhammad the Messenger of Allah), the meaning would be *Muhammadan Allah*, but in the order of God this is not possible. Therefore when the interval is removed, what results is faultiness and imperfection; and this is the reason why Christianity falls down regarding the order, because in Christianity the intermediary, which is the spirit *(ar-ruh)* was removed from the words `Isa (Jesus) is the spirit of Allah. Then they began to say, "Jesus is Allah." Therefore Allah answered saying, "Those who say that Allah is Jesus, the son of Mary (Maryam) are unbelievers (*kafirun*)." And to now the true meaning of this expression has not been understood nor recognized, because the meaning and beneficence of the words can only be felt through the witnessing of the Essence, the Qualities, and the Actions.

As has already been mentioned, all this comes from the saying: "Muhammad is the Messenger of Allah (*Muhammadan rasulu'llah*)," which is some of the meaning relating to the deep understanding of the witnessing (*as-shahada*).

But what is involved in the grammatical form of this expression of the Unity (*at-tawhid*) is that it is said that the word *la* is the negation of every kind, sort or variety, so that it governs the mentioning of the Name, which is here expressed in the accusative form, as the state of bondsmanship requires, and its predicate is then placed in the indefinite case, or form, which symbolizes the world of freedom. This means that there is nothing in existence at all, except Allah, so that these words of *la 'ilaha illa'llah* negate all kinds, varieties, and all other possible things, because this sentence is the affirmation of the Unity, Oneness, and Singularity of Allah. And if anyone of the knowers says, *la 'ilaha illa'llah,* he will find only *illa'llah* (except Allah) in its true meaning, and not in its symbolical sense.

So my brother, do not be satisfied merely to repeat these noble words on your tongue, because if you are satisfied with that alone, then the reward and benefits which will come to you from repeating these words will only be from the knowing of the tongue; and this is not what is required. But what is required is that you should know Allah as He was: "Allah was, and there was nothing together with Him, and He is now as He has always been." If you know this, then you will rest from the necessity of having to use negating words, for that which is contingent and transitory will have disappeared for you into that which is the Truth; so that only what is the Reality will remain, and then you will only say, "Allah! Allah! Allah!"

But at present your heart is occupied with alterities, and your Essence is weak, and since the day you were born you need to deny and negate. Then when will you be free of this *state*? It will not leave you while you are still only denying with your tongue, but it is necessary for you to deny with your actions and deeds. Meaning that when you deny through your heart and thoughts, and through your innermost Essence so that everything disappears from your sight, and instead of seeing yourself and people, you find only Allah, then this *state* will leave you.

The People of Allah are those who have disclaimed the existence of anything else but Him, and so they are at rest, having entered under His protection, where they remain. But you are still denying and refuting, and you have been doing so since the moment you were born, and you will continue to do so until you die, because the human being dies in the same manner that he has lived.

But if you have been granted to deny, you have also been granted to affirm, and he who has been illumined in the beginning will be illumined in the end, because all things that come from duality are denied (*nafiy*) not only through the tongue but also through the eyes of faith and certitude (*`iqan*) until the station of eye-witnessing (*maqam ash-shahud al-`iyan*) is reached. And unto your Lord is the end of every matter. Then neither negation nor affirmation will be needed of you, because the existence of the Creator of the Creation has already been affirmed before you, yourself, testify to it. And the impossibility of a separate existence for the Creation has already been refuted before you, yourself, refute it. O human being! Why do you not find a Master who can teach you about the complete annihilation so that you erase every other word from the sentence, except the word Allah; and that He may take you into the state of awareness in which you find only Allah, exalted is He? Then you will live with Him, and you will die with Him, and you will be gathered together with Him; and you will live in a place of sincerity in the presence of a King Omnipotent.

All of which comes through the mentioning, reciting, and knowing of the meaning of *la 'ilaha illa'llah.* Now you only know about these words and the repetition of them, and your knowing is limited to saying, "Nothing is worthy of being worshiped except Allah." This is the knowing of the common people, so then, what is the knowledge of the People of Allah? I wish that you could know what the *special ones*, who went before you, knew, instead of only knowing what you know; but it is your own knowledge that has cut you off, because through error, you have turned away from your Lord, until you have arrived at the abandoning of the Truth. But deny everything then through the hand of a Shaykh who is well qualified in the knowledge of the Reality (*al-Haqiqa*), so that through the witnessing, and the eye-witnessing, nothing will remain of you, but Allah. Do not only stop with the Quality of faith or of certainty *(al-iqan*), because to *hear* the Quality is not like the *seeing* of it. But the knowers know of *la 'ilaha illa'llah* and they know of their bond with Allah, both on the outside and on the inside; for they have striven with the remembrance (*dhikr)* of Him and they have dwelt in the contemplation (*al-fikr*) of Him. They have found that *la 'ilaha illa'llah* contains every secret and every matter; and that it is the highest *face* of remembrance, and that there are no other *faces* after it. What is meant here by *faces* is all the forms of remembrance (*dhikr*) which are both possible and known, and which are also unrecognized. Or it can be said that, "It is the best of all forms of bondsmanship and reverence;" or "That which is given up and returned to Allah, and which is accepted by Him." My words, referring to the remembrance as being either possible or unrecognized, relate to the remembrance of all the worlds, and of everything which melts away in His praise, because every world according to its remembrance is either elevated or lowly. But the remembrance is accepted according to the manner in which it is witnessed, for there is no witnessing which does not mention the Name of Allah according to the *state* it may have in the creation, or whatever condition of remembrance it has been granted. The Reality, praised and exalted is He, is remembered by all tongues, both silently and aloud, and there are praises which are not known about, and others which are known. The remembrance which is *unknown* is that which goes out from those that are lost, and the *possible* comes out from the People of the Unity (*al-muwahhidun*), and all are gathered together in sincerity (*al-ikhlas*). The difference between them is that the first mentioned group (those who are lost) take the first part of the word *'ikhlas*, which is the denial without the testifying, and this cannot be considered as *dhikr* except when the second part, which is the affirmation is added. And if, in this case, there is a meaning which is hidden from the creation, it lies in His words, Exalted is He, "But you do not understand their extolling." And in every case the remembrance of both groups is the best of praising. So that, from this it follows that the mentioning of the Noble Word is the best of remembrances, and if he who makes the *dhikr* mentions and repeats *Allah* without giving its full meaning to this word, then the intention of his *dhikr* is limited in its witnessing.

On the other hand if it is the remembrance of the *possible* that is being spoken about, and which is the order for the People of the Unity, who in the mentioning of Allah with *the Noble Word*, reach to the make the complete *dhikr*, the unknown, or unrecognized or the possible, then everything that is in the existence of both denial or affirmation, and the extolling of all the worlds is contained in it. And this is the faithfulness to the Unity to which a person of the Unity has been led by his belief and trust in a face of His Faces, in the measure that each face of His Faces sees Allah in everything, and at all times, each according to its state, or condition.

And know, that everything in the Creation that is not Allah, if it obeys Him, is referred to as the *composition* and *material* of all that is in the heavens and the earth, which is in obeisance to the Mercy and is a slave in obeisance to the Reality in which there is no illusion nor separation, nor individual existence (*majaz*). However, the submission differs according to the various manifestations, as has already been mentioned; but the most Noble Word is that of the Oneness (*at-tawhid*), and this is reserved for the greatest knowers in the measure of their bondsmanship, and of their surrendering of their will to Allah, Mighty and Supreme is He, until through their efforts and endeavors they reach to their goal. And the endeavor of the knower, which comes from Allah, is not for himself but for his Lord, Mighty and Exalted is He, and to Him it returns. Therefore, this knower is not punished. Meaning, that because of his nobility he is not punished in this world, since the entire world and all that it contains is not the maker of even one good deed of those of this knower; for they come from Allah, mighty and supreme is He. It is difficult for this truth to be understood by the intelligence of the mind of any person, but only the mind of he who is of the Family of Allah is able to reach to this understanding.

The Conditions and their Meanings relating to the Remembrance of Allah (ad-dhikr)

Know that the owner of the *art of remembrance* can only be established in it through the following five conditions, of which if any one of them is neglected the order will not be fulfilled, and he will face destruction and failure. The first necessary condition in every case, is the pronouncing of the double *shahada* (witnessing) by which is meant that, in the first part of his witnessing, the owner of this station *(maqam*) has reached to seeing the Reality, mighty and supreme is He, through the unveiling (*kashf*) and that in the second part he should witness the Muhammadan presence, until he comes to possess both the inner and the outer behavior of it; his inner behavior being to see Allah and his outer being to ensure the well-being of the creation. For Allah, the Praised and the Exalted one, has said, "We have not sent thee save as a Mercy for all the worlds." He who combines these two states reaches to a rank higher than any other, because of the strength of his fulfillment in both these conditions. But he who witnesses one of these conditions without seeing the other, is like a person who has been annihilated in Allah but who has nevertheless remained in that state without having given due importance to the message *(ar-risala*) of Allah. What is missing in such a person's bondsmanship is that something else is required from the prayer. And likewise in the case of he who has witnessed the Muhammadan presence without realizing the Truth of bondsmanship, so that he possesses knowledge without giving proof of it, for the proof comes from witnessing and eye-witnessing which is also missing, and therefore he cannot be considered to be one of the knowers

What is required is he who is in command of both these states; which means the seeing of the Reality and the witnessing of the Muhammadan presence, and he whose qualities are sobriety and reliability. This means that his condition is that of bearing witness to the non-existence of anything else but Allah. It follows therefore, that these two states are necessary conditions for the other pillars of the Religion, for it is important for the knower to have been able to witness with complete witnessing everything of the states which he has left behind him in order to be able to understand, and to know everything that will come afterwards.

The second condition, or pillar, is the Prayer, which in the realization of the order goes side by side with the witnessing, because the knower only makes the prostration (*as-sujud*) after witnessing the One to whom the prayer is due, and the source of the prayer is the blessing bestowed in it, so that the knower is joined to Allah, and not separated from Him.

The third condition, or pillar, is the Alms-giving (*az-zakat*), the Truth of which is that the slave should know of all that has been bestowed upon him by Allah, through what He has created for him. For everything there is a *zakat*, the *zakat* of the knower being himself and what he possesses. About this, as well as what is, and what is not, considered as *zakat* we shall write later, if Allah wills.

The fourth pillar is Fasting (*sawm*), which means the denying of oneself, and for the People of Allah this means the denying of everything which is not Allah, and this we shall explain clearly later, if Allah wills.

The fifth pillar is the Pilgrimage, which means the journey to the House of Allah, and the circumambulation of the hearts in the Garden of the Presence of the Beloved. And His Words, "Whoever can, should perform the Pilgrimage;" and to witness in that whatever there is of the hidden Unity *(at-tawhid)* and the complete extinction (*fana'*) so that nothing remains of the performer of the pilgrimage; and we shall speak further about this annihilation in the right place also, if Allah wills.

In the Religion, the second degree, or rank of the states is faith or belief, and it means that the knower is consumed by the annihilation so that he is in a state in which the revelation from Allah overwhelms him, and he is taken out of himself and is removed from other human beings. "For when the trumpet is blown there shall be no kinship any more between them, neither will they question one another," for when Allah destroys all the pictures there is no human relationship that can provide either help or hindrance.

Therefore, this station of complete extinction is very hidden from the eyes of the seeker, because of the perfection of its annihilation. We have already said that the inner state of the seeker must be like that of al-Junayd, may Allah be pleased with him, and his tongue must not cease to mention the conditions of belief of the People of the Unity. In his praying he must embrace, to the utmost, accepted religious form (*mad-hab*), and follow the beliefs of one of the 'Imams of the Religion, for it is said, "The truth of the end is the returning to the beginning." For in this station he is requested to return to all the senses of subsistence (*al-baqa'*), because before through the unveiling of the Essence he had been annihilated from some of them, and from the material world *(ad-dunya)* and from the Hereafter, and from the stages and states. Also, he was absent from the creations and their states in the Hereafter, so that everything disappeared before his eyes, in the existence of the perfect Unity. And in that case he is extinguished even from the Unity itself, through the witnessing of something of *Uniqueness* and *Solitariness*, which cannot be named, nor can it be grasped through names, nor imagined by illusions, nor is there in it any non-existence, since the witnessing of both the Names and the Qualities is associated with created existence. This station takes place when everything has vanished from his eyes, and his mind also has disappeared in the Splendor, and his tongue has wearied of pronouncing the Names. Then if he were to make mention of the Creator it would be said to him, "Where is the Creation?" And if he were to make mention of the Maintainer it would be said to him, "Where is that which is decreed?"

Briefly, in that state there is no Hidden and no Revealed, and he does not find a single space which is empty of the existence of Allah; so that nothing but He manifests. This, for the knower, is the eye-witnessing, but if he begins with the feelings alone and he continues on to the awareness, he becomes of those who refuse to mention anything except the Reality, until maybe if the states of the Hereafter were mentioned to him he would deny their existence as being something that is besides Allah; and in his illusion he would deny the Resurrection itself, and other similar Truths; such denials being impossible to justify. In this case he denies all other existence because his eyes do not see things, and therefore whenever his feelings overcome him he pronounces such words; and this will be his case until he becomes grounded and reasonable in his faith, just as he was assured and certain in his eye-witnessing. Then he will look upon the states of the Hereafter according to the Law of the *shari`a,* and thus, through his conviction and certainty, which has come to him principally through the unveiling, he becomes an example for others. As to his state of being drowned in the Unity, in this case, because of his knowledge of the Hidden and the Revealed, and because of his annihilation and his return to subsistence he does not find anything, but Allah. He has found the Essence to be the source for the Names and the Qualities through his realization of the perfection of the Unity, so that he testifies to the existence of the creation because he has seen the truth of the Reality, and that he has, once more, been bereft of all needs.

The Master of *The Wisdom of the Universe* (*Al-Hikam al-'Akwan*) alluded to this, saying, "Steadfast is the Creation although it is erased through the Unity of the Essence." Therefore if the universes are annihilated they are annihilated in Allah, and if they are steadfast they are steadfast in Him. Then give all things their right, and due, and follow the wisdom according to its decrees, for the Names of the Creation are not absent from it, but they are derivations of the Beautiful Names of Allah (*Al-asma al-husna*). For this reason it is said that the Names of the Truth, Mighty and Supreme is He, are contained in the names of existence. Yes, each name of the names of the Creation has been ordered by a Name of the Names of Allah, because the realities of the names are not lacking in a Name, just as the realities of the qualities are not lacking in a single Quality, and the realities of the essences are not lacking in a single Essence. No name is empty of the Names of Allah, and no quality is lacking the Quality of Allah, and no essence is lacking the Essence of Allah, and so forth.

Therefore it is necessary for he who has been drowned, that when he awakens and wishes to return to a state of belief and faith, that he should restrict himself to what he has been informed of by the Law (*ash-shari`a*) concerning the manifestations of the Hereafter and the states of the Resurrection (*al-Qiyama*), and it is for the Master to teach the seekers when they return from their intoxication to reflect and reason about what they have witnessed, so that he does not pay attention to anything they say if he sees that their intoxication could lead them into a *non-Muhammadan state*, which is not praiseworthy according to the *shari`a*. For the Reality (*al-Haqiqa*) is the origin and the source of all manifestations while the *Shari`a* (the Law) is the authority granted from It. Therefore whoever is in contradiction with the authority of the *shari`a* is in contradiction with its origin and its source (the Reality); and the saint, in spite of his elevated rank, is not immune from that. For that reason the Master is concerned not to pay attention to what the intoxicated seeker asks for, nor does he act on what he says. Meaning if he asks for anything which is more than what the *sunna* allows, concerning the *states* of the Hereafter; for both the Master, as well as the student, is under obligation to the Law (*tashri*), since he is a teacher (*murshid*) for the seekers, and he is not a Guide for the Messengers, may peace and blessings be upon them. Therefore the Master believes only in the *shari`a* and what its people say concerning the words of Allah to the Prophet, "This day I have perfected for you your religion, and I have fulfilled My favor unto you, and I have chosen for you Islam as your religion."

For this, the knower, in the *state* of his beginning, is under the order of the beginning, until his Lord reaches out His hand for the order of the end, which is the opposite of that of the beginning. In which case he may become completely silent so that the ignorant will think that he has abandoned his state, but in truth his silence comes from the perfection and mastery of his station (*maqam*). It has been said that, "The beginning of the Path (*at-tariqa*) is madness, its middle is of alterities, and its end is stillness and peace." Then whenever the traveler returns to awareness it must be to the *shari`a,* with complete explanations and clarity of what he has witnessed.

And know, that faith means the intention to cut off the *nafs* whenever it seeks to inflate itself, and to become arrogant; because the yearning *(himma*) of the knower is very high when he carries what we have mentioned, since he has been removed from the existence of manifestations, and all that is contained in them. As a result, when he wants to speak about the states of the End he talks in a loud voice which it is impossible to bear, and he then becomes a trial (*fitna*) for those who believe in him, and also for those who do not believe in him. In this case talking is forbidden, but the more he surrenders, and when his surrender becomes deeper, so his proximity, and at the same time his assurance, increases. This station is called by the Folk, the station of subsistence (*maqam al-baqa'*). It may however, be a source of concern that the seeker, before mastering this station, is overcome by sadness and wretchedness in not being able to bear the station, and because of this it is said that after the annihilation (*fana'*) comes the subsistence *(al-baqa'*), and after the subsistence comes the hardship (*shaqa).*

Finally, it can be said that because the faith of the knower is in submission to Allah alone, and his heart which is the place of belief has been completely overwhelmed by the presence (*hadhrah*) of Allah, and because he has drowned in Him, and in His manifestation as a result of the depth of his drowning in it, his belief in it has made it impossible for him to see the existence of anything other than it. Then, if it were not for his obligation to the Law (*ash-shari`a*) and its precepts, he would not feel the necessity for belief at all, for he has now become a stranger to his knowledges, duties and intentions, and his heart is occupied only with Allah Himself. And know, that if the eyes of the heart of the knower are true, he does not need the second station (*maqam*) which is that of: "The Messenger believes in what was sent down to him from his Lord," because he is firm and certain in his belief. This is the belief of the saints (*al-awliya*) and the messengers, and of those who follow them, and which is not gainsaid by the existence of doubts and questioning. Meaning that these recur to them until they are called to return to Allah, after which they cease to exist. However, contradictions exist so long as feelings exist, and in the Essence of the Reality feeling and expression exist because belief is involved in, and is wrapped up in the creation, but when his belief is wrapped up into the existence of Allah and into the manifestation of the Reality, then through his belief his feelings disappear and in this case, he is exonerated from them. But as was mentioned earlier, alongside feelings there must be belief, such as belief in the Books that were revealed to the Prophets, may the peace and blessings of Allah be upon them, the belief being in the form of a Book or Tablets, so that when the Book is revealed to him, or when the remembrance of Allah (*ad-dhikr*) comes to him, then he speaks with the Voice of the Reality saying, "How long must He be worshiped until the revelation comes, or the mediation *(wasita*) between Him and His slave begins?" But the Reality is closer to him than he is himself: "And We are closer to him that his jugular vein;" so that the more he is strengthened in his belief the greater is his understanding; and the more the revelation will come to him.

Some of the knowers asked about the meanings of the revelations which are contained in the Holy Qur'an. I answered them that they are in accordance with a person's *state*; and I say, "O my brother, the words of Allah do not consist of letters, nor of sounds in the same manner that you know of words; for He is above that, and nothing can be added to that." Then they were satisfied with the manner of the revelation, even to it becoming a matter of letters and sounds. And this is the meaning of the manner of the revelation, because the Word becomes dearer to him than eye-witnessing itself, as was the case of the belief of the messengers, may Allah bless them and grant them peace.

And perhaps in the state of his intoxication, and when he is overcome by his feelings, he may say that he is Allah, or he may say, as `A'isha, may Allah be pleased with her, said when she was asked to thank Allah and His Messenger said, "By Allah! I will be grateful only to Allah." Or he may say, "I have been given what has not been given to the Messengers," for our Master `Abd al-Qadir al-Jilani, may Allah be pleased with him, said, "O Companies of the Prophets, you have been given a title, and we have been given that which you have not been given." All these sayings (*shatiyyat*) come about as a result of ecstatic feelings. Then he must return to his true rank and level. Allah says, "We have favored some of them above others." But if, in his state of annihilation, he takes these words, and if his feelings have the mastery over his reason, he then begins to say such things. But like the boy in front of his parents, he must return to his true level, because the Messengers (*ar-rasul*), may the peace and blessings of Allah be upon them, have a state *(hal*) with Allah to which the *friends* of Allah have not reached. And whenever their state is not clear to us, and if we interpret in it a lack of determination, or a state of weakness of intention, this is because of an insufficient reading or misinterpretation of their states, so that even the recalcitrance (*mas`iya*) of the Prophet, as illustrated in the Holy Book, shows us that it was not a result of lack of obedience, but rather that our minds are not capable of absorbing what lies behind such states. Therefore, it is important for us not to assign to seeming shortcomings, the label of failures.

Some of my brothers spoke to me about some doubt, which they had, concerning my Master Ya`qub, because of what overcame him of sorrow on account of Yusuf, may the peace and blessings of Allah be upon them both; and what is related about this in the words of the Reality, Mighty and Supreme is He, in the story about them: "And his eyes turned white because of the sorrow that he choked back within him." They said to me, "How could he feel so much sadness, and how could the beauty of Yusuf deprive him of seeing the beauty of the Reality?" I remembered then, the words of 'Ibn al-Farid, "If Ya`qub had heard of the beauty of Yusuf he would have forgotten the beauty of Yusuf." And I followed what he said, and I waited until my brothers had returned from their doubting state, then I said to them that our Master Ya`qub was not sorrowful about Yusuf for himself, but that he felt this deep sorrow because Yusuf was the manifestation through which the Reality revealed Himself to Ya`qub, in the same way as He had appeared to our Master Musa, may peace and blessings be upon him, while he was on the mountain (*at-Tur*), so that Musa came to his most complete proximity to Allah only on the mountain of At-Tur, although *He is in every place* and *He is with you wherever you are*. It was this same case for Ya`qub for whom the beauty of the Reality appeared in the image of Yusuf, so that he could not bear to be separated from him, for Yusuf was the *qibla* of the witnessing of his father Ya`qub.

In this same meaning the Prophet, may peace and blessings be upon him, said, "I have seen my Lord in the image of a beardless young man." And no doubt when the Truth, Praised and Exalted is He, had appeared to him in this young man, he would not have allowed him to leave him.

This is the reason why the Angels bowed down to Adam, may the peace and blessings of Allah be upon him, because Allah, Praised and Exalted is He, had created him in His image. And it is for this reason also that the Christian people prostrated before the Essence of `Isa (Jesus) in his lifetime, and that they described him with the Qualities of Allah. But the prostration of all of them was to Allah, and not to anyone else, for the beauty of Allah, exalted is He, appears with such power in some images of the *special ones*, that it removes all traces of the human being from their existence.

Those who possess complete minds, such as all the prophets and the special friends of Allah, recognize, and know, the revelation in its image, and they do not stop with the image itself, so that their knowledge *(ma`rifa)* is in the annihilation of the image which is not, therefore, a limitation for them; nor is it a similitude, copy or idol of any created thing. And if they see Allah in some such image their witnessing is associated with the revealed state of the Name, which is contrary to the case of the Christians, and those who follow them, who are lacking in mind. For whenever the Reality appears to them in the image of their Prophet, they stop with his picture, and they are veiled from the perfect manifestation of Allah; and it is He Who veils them from the true knowledge.

All these words go back to what happened to our Master Ya`qub, and about his sorrow over Yusuf, because his yearning for intimacy was increased by the sight of his son, so that when Yusuf's presence was removed from him, his witnessing became impossible for him; and because of that he was sorrowful. But he was never in despair about the *soul of Allah*, and so he said to his sons, "My sons, go and search for Yusuf, and do not despair for the soul of Allah;" and without doubt Yusuf was the soul of Allah for Ya`qub.

And know, that the Reality, Praised and Exalted is He, because of His manifestation to His slaves in certain images, is truly concerned that they should not, for that, be blind to Him in other of His manifestations, because the picture, which is attached to a particular presence, vanishes rapidly. Therefore, the Reality, Praised and Exalted is He, tests His beloveds in that, in seeing the image He immediately removes the picture in which He manifested Himself, so that His beloveds may see Him in all faces - and this was the case for our Master Ya`qub. However Ya`qub's fear was not calmed until Allah united him to Yusuf, in Himself, and lifted them to the Throne, and they fell down in prostration (*sujud*).

This was unlike the case of our Master Ibrahim, may the peace and blessings of Allah be upon him, who did not want to stop with seeing Allah in any picture that vanished away; for to him Allah *was* without His having to be seen in every picture. Therefore Ibrahim said, "I do not love things that disappear." Meaning that he did not want to know Allah through one thing and not through others, so that if that thing vanished He would be forgotten. But he turned his face, and wherever he turned it he saw the beauty of Allah. Ibrahim showed some preference for his son Isma'il so Allah ordered him to kill him, and he was obedient; and his sincerity, and that of his son, was clear, because Ibrahim was perfectly surrendered to the order of Allah, as was his son also, for he said, "O my father, do what you have been commanded, and you will find me, if Allah wills, to be one of those who are patient." So Isma'il saw his father as one of Allah's instruments. And He, Praised and Exalted is He, said, "You were not the thrower when you threw, but it was Allah who threw. This day the truthful shall profit from their truthfulness."

Ibrahim, may the peace and blessings of Allah be upon him, was not veiled by the manifestation of his middle name *the Friend* (*al-Khalil*), because he was with Allah in all his states. In this case it is enough to remember what happened to him when he was thrown into the fire and it was made to be a Garden for him, because of his Trust in Allah and of his knowing of his Lord in everything.

Finally, the behavior of the Messengers is not without wisdom, nor are their actions devoid of obedience and bondsmanship. And we have but to have faith and trust in all of them, and to follow their actions, and to surrender to their states and stations, may the peace and blessings of Allah be upon them all.

In the same way we should believe in the Angels and that they are chosen and obedient soldiers, who do not disobey the orders of Allah; and who carry out what they are commanded to do, being occupied with things in accordance with the decrees set out for them, as we have been told by He who is their Law-Giver.

What is meant here is that the state of annihilation is beyond all this, just as the state of drowning is that of being removed from the creation, as has already been mentioned. Then if existence is seen, it is seen in its hidden manifestation as the Omnipotence of Allah, and in its revealed manifestation as the Wisdom of Allah. And if the kingdom has been confirmed in the knower and the doors of the *malakut* have been opened, the existence of the Angels is revealed to him, and unveiled through eye-witnessing. Meaning certain bands of the Angels; and as for the others, all are to be believed in, may Allah bless them and grant them peace.

And then it is to believe in the Last Day, which means the resurrection from the graves. What is meant by this is that the person who is not firmly rooted in subsistence *(al-baqa')* may, because of his intoxication, only see the sea moved by the waves from its surface to the inside; and then from the inside to the surface, so that he is in delusion about what lies under the surface, and so the past, and what has gone before is obliterated for him, and has passed away and disappeared.

Also, it is to believe in Destiny. Meaning that a person should conform to its boundaries through the understanding and the knowledge (*ma`rifa*) which he has gained, firstly by means of feelings, and then by his mastery over them. Otherwise, if this mastery is not gained in the state of drowning, he will say, "I am the Secret of Destiny, and the overflowing sea." Or: "I am the doer, and I am the influencer (*atar*) and the *marker out*." In this case the more he feels, the more he is overcome by his feelings; and so he continues expanding until Allah shows him the limits that He has decreed. Then He takes him, and leads him, from one stage to the next of his stages, pausing at each one so that, in this way, Destiny becomes the unveiling, for him, of the manifestation of the Might and Power of Allah in all things, both in their Revealed and their Hidden faces, as well as in all His actions. Thus he comes to accept Destiny, whether it is sweet or bitter, whether it is Islam or unbelief (*kufr),* because there is nothing in this world that is not influenced by it.

Therefore, the knowers have found rest from the burden of the necessity of making plans, and they have rejoiced in participating in Destiny, and have surrendered themselves to their Lord, being content with what He has destined for them, because they are no longer with matters, but with He who decrees all matters. They are absent from the Creation in the witnessing of the kingdom of the Reality. They turn with the Will wherever it turns. As some have said, "Surrender to Salma, and walk where she walks, and follow the wind of Destiny, and turn in the direction that it turns."

And also it is to believe in the Path (*sirat)* and that through walking on it, according to one's state, the traveler is raised up out of the Fire. And know also, that the Folk have a special swift Way, and an immediate Way, so that they do not have to wait for a time in the future because they can walk on the Path *now*. A great band of Sufis has walked on this Path, who traveled on it, station after station, through the strength of their yearning *(himma*); for some of them walk and some of them fly.

The Path is raised up from the Fire of the *nafs*, and its end is the reaching to the Holy Presence; or it can be said that the Path is a journey from the world of pictures to the Secret of the Secrets; and from there it is the Garden of the knowing. But this Path is very difficult, and it is full of problems, ruptures and obstacles, and it is more arduous than the journey in the Hereafter, as likewise the Fire is stronger than that which is promised in the Hereafter. This Fire has caused suffering to most of the ascetic and self-denying travelers; those who are obedient. "Faces then humbled obedient," because of the strength of the fire of the love.

Also a matter of belief is *the scales* on which all actions will be weighed on the Day of Judgment, according to the knowledge of the doer, about which only Allah knows. So that the knower might be in a state of absorption, absent from the existence of the Creation, but if he recognizes the Creation he would say, "He created you, and what you do. So how can actions, of which He is the doer, be weighed?" However, when he is able to understand the meaning of actions, and the meaning, with exactitude, of their place in the Creation, he sees that the actions of the knowers are weighed before their death. Then, the Reality, Praised and Exalted is He, does not find any actions which are their own, because these do not exist in the witnessing of the doer. Therefore, the Truth (*al-Haqq*), Mighty and Powerful is He, says to them, "Where are your deeds?" They answer Him, "Where is our existence?" Then He says, "How did you call to Me, and approach Me?" They answer, "Through You we called to You, and through You we approached You, and through You we know You." So He receives them, through their strivings. And how should He not receive them when they have abandoned everything, through the knowing of Him; and they have lost their existence in what they have witnessed. May Allah not condemn them for what came to them!

As you already know, the knowers die before their death, as the Prophet, may Allah bless him and grant him peace, said, "Die before you die," for this is the true death, and nothing else; because it is only the changing, and the moving forwards. Death for the Folk is the annihilation (*fana'*) of the slave, and his disappearance and passing away from sight, for he is dead to his self (*nafs*) and to the entire world; and he lives only in his Lord. So, if you ask him about his existence, he will not be able to answer you because he no longer sees his own qualities, nor does he see his *self.* Abu Yazid al-Bistami, when he was asked this question about his *nafs* answered, "The nafs *(al-'amara)* of Abu Yazid al-Bistami has died, and may Allah not return it to him, for that is death."

As for the normal death, if on the Day of Judgment you were to ask the dead person, "Who are you?" he would answer, "I am such and such," because he is still *alive* and has not smelt the fragrance of death, but he has merely moved from one world to another. But the death, such as that of Abu Yazid al-Bistami, is known only to those who have died the true death.

And it is established that the knowers have an *account* before the Day of Reckoning. The Prophet, may the peace and blessings of Allah be upon him, said, "Know yourself before you are called to the reckoning." Therefore, make your reckoning with yourselves, so that you may see your Lord; for the knowers are brought back to life before the Day of Judgment (*yawm al-qiyama*). As the Prophet, may peace and blessings be upon him, said, "He who is annihilated, and who is expanded through the annihilation, *dies*; and whoever *dies* is resurrected."

What is meant by *expanded* is increased in meanings, for whoever is increased in meanings dies to the senses, and he who is expanded in the presence (*hadra*) of the Reality, dies to the created presence; and whoever dies to the created presence is raised up in the Presence of the Reality. And he who is raised up in the Presence of the Reality is he who is *by permission* to the Creation, for he dwells now in the Garden of ease and comfort.

It is necessary to believe in the *Water-Basin* (*al-hawd*) of the Prophet, may the peace and blessings of Allah be upon him. Also, it is necessary to believe in the Garden and the Fire, for they both exist now, according to what, of necessity, is known and experienced of them.

Know then, that for the Folk of Allah, the Water-Basin of the Prophet refers to the *Handful of Light* or the *Muhammadan Fist*, in which everything in the Creation is held, and is given its life, in accordance with the decrees of Allah. The knower will not reach to seeing the Reality, nor will he enter the Garden of the knowing *(al-ma`rifa)* until he drinks from that Water of the Unseen. Meaning, until, through it, his Reality is revealed to him; when he will arrive in the Holy Presence.

It is said that the Water-Basin of the Prophet, may peace and blessings be upon him, is surrounded by *Cups* which are as numerous as the stars. From this vine, which is also a symbol for the Handful of Light, all the essences of the stars and the other heavenly bodies are cups of both high and low degree, because the Muhammadan fist is divided into two parts - the Right Hand and the Left Hand. Or it can be said, the Majesty and the Severity *(al-jalal)* on one hand, and the Beauty (*al-jamal*) on the other. How great are the followers of the Right Hand and how poor are those of the Left Hand!

And know that the Water-Basin of the Prophet encompasses both the Garden and the Fire. It is necessary to believe, in the outer manner, in the outer meaning of the Water-Basin, and in the Garden and the Fire; and as for the inner meaning of the Water-Basin it is also divided into two parts - the Garden and the Fire. He who is the owner of the Water-Basin, said, "Allah took a Handful of Light and said, *Be Muhammad*!" So Muhammad was. And from him, all that *was to exist* came into being. Meaning that all that was separated off from the word *Kun!* (*Be!*) was from his Water-Basin, and all that *is* is only what *was*; and nothing has been added, or taken away, from this, but everything is from his *kind*. Likewise, the Message of the Prophet Muhammad, may peace and blessings be upon him, comprises the Garden and the Fire; "For we lived in suffering until we were sent a Prophet."

Know, that the seeker on the Path must have more faith than normal people. Meaning that he must believe in the knowledge of the Folk of Allah, both in its generality, and in its particular details. And he must also believe in all that comes to the seekers of Allah in their states of traveling to the Presence of Allah, after they have tasted the first death, in the remembrance (*ad-dhikr*), because everything that comes to their senses in their dying to their senses, is also contained in the meaning of the true death. He who does not believe in what is sent down to the Folk has not smelt the fragrance of their knowledge, because in both deaths there are clear indications of what happens to them in the true death in the Spirit, and on the Day of Resurrection, for the Resurrection, the Path, the Scales, the Water-Basin, the Garden and the Fire, these are signs. Meaning that all that happens for he who dies the death of the senses happens also for he who dies the death of the Spirit. Therefore, they all reach to see the Truth *(al-Haqq)* because he who does not die cannot see the Truth, nor the Angels, nor the souls of the Prophets and the Messengers. Yes, they have died and they have been annihilated according to what was said to them, "Die before you die, and know yourselves before you are brought to account." So they have died to the Creation, and to their desires and the *nafs*, and from security in this world, and from the material world (*ad-dunya*), and other things. It was said to them, "Enter it in peace and safety;" and they do not taste of death, except the first death, for that is their death; and their Fire is that of the *nafs* which is stronger than the Fire which is promised in the Hereafter. And surely there is no one of you who does not pass through it, because this is the Truth of the Creation, although it cannot have any effect upon most of them, because Allah protects them. Their Garden is that of the deep knowing (*ma`rifa*) which they have *now* in this material world, and good tidings in the Hereafter.

Their Path is the Straight Path, and it is the Law *(ash-shari`a)* of the one upon whom are the best of prayers, and the sweetest greetings: "This is My Straight Way, so follow It." He has walked with them on the righteous Path until the end: "And unto your Lord is the ending." Then he descended again to them with the Divine knowledge in which is the Boundary (*sidrat al-muntaha*), the boundary beyond which no creature may pass, bringing back to them the delight in the manifestations of the universe in which He appears to them in witnessing and eye-witnessing (*shuhud al-`iyan*); "The sight did not turn away;" and his gaze remained steady. Meaning that he did not remove, or turn away his eyes from the sight of his Lord; for they see with Him in the subtle state of vision and shadows (*tashbih*) just as they see with him in the state of non-delimitation and incomparability (*tanzih*), for wherever they look they see the Face of Allah; and wherever they are, they are in the Presence of Allah.

Concerning this state it is said to them, "From it We have created you, and in it We shall return you, and out of it We shall bring you forth again." In the Presence (*hadhra*) of Allah you are brought to life, and in it you will die, and from it you are sent out again. Man dies according to how he has lived; and he is sent back again according to how he has died.

Finally, it is for the seeker, who is at the beginning of the Path, to believe in everything that the Folk have affirmed, because their knowledge is beyond that of the mind. And know, my beloved, that if you want to know of the state of sincerity, excellence, and good conduct (*al-ihsan*) on the Path, this is as he, may the peace and blessings of Allah be upon him, who knew about it, and who lived in it, said, "It is that you pray to Allah as if you see Him, and if you do not see Him surely He sees you." This is the first step of the sincerity and excellence (*al-ihsan*) which can be seen when true witnessing is reached, and seeing with the inner Eye, and this is the beginning of Certainty (*al-iqan*) whose end is eye-witnessing (*al-`iyan*). In the beginning the walking is with the seeker, and in the end it is with Allah, as He, Praised and Exalted is He, said, "And My slave continues to draw near to Me with supererogatory works so that I shall love him. When I love him I am his hearing with which he hears, his seeing with which he sees, his hand with which he strikes, and his foot with which he walks."

So He made the beginning of the Path to be from the slave by the Love and Compassion from Allah. It is necessary for he who seeks for this *state* to be sincere and devoted in his awareness of the Reality towards what is Hidden of It and what is Revealed of it; both in solitude and in manifestation, until the existence of everything that is not Allah is erased from him. And if Allah so wills, and gives him honesty and sincerity in his bondsmanship, He, All-Mighty and Supreme is He, will be manifest to him in His Divinity, because the Reality, Mighty and Powerful is He, is not far distant. The Prophet, may the peace and blessings of Allah be upon him, said, "Be mindful of Allah and you will find Him before you."

So be attentive, O seeker, in your praying and in all your other states; and worship Him as if you see Him, and hold steadfast to good manners, because you are always with Him. For it is not existence with Allah which veils you from Him, but it is your blindness of Him in the fringes, or outlines of what He manifests of Himself to you. 'Ibn `Ata'illah al-Iskandari said, "What veils you from the seeing is that you do not remain within the limits of what Allah decrees." Therefore O seeker, abide with the rules that Allah has laid down, and do not stop with your own existence, and do not attribute your efforts to yourself, but ask for help from Allah in observing His bondsmanship, for so long as you attribute your actions to yourself, then through your regard for yourself, you will be cut off from the attentiveness to your Lord. As the Folk, may Allah be pleased with them, say, "Whenever you exist Allah is not present, but when you disappear Allah exists." It is said in the *hadith* that Musa, may peace and blessings be upon him, said to the Reality, Mighty and Supreme is He, "How can one reach to you, O Lord of all the worlds?" He answered, "Leave yourself and come!"

So come beloved, and turn away from yourself and your existence, and the people not of your *kind*; and come to your Lord. You will find Him nearer to you than your existence. But so long as you have an existence without Him, you will not see Him, and only when you live with Him will you see Him.

Therefore, if you say, "How can I see Him if the *I* has no existence with Him?" I answer you, "You see Him with His eyes, and not with yours, and with His existence and not with yours, because you are a contingency, and what is contingent, and ephemeral, does not see the timeless and the eternal. Your eye does not become His eye, and your ear does not become His ear, but your eye is His Eye, and your ear is His Ear, and through them you will see Him and hear Him. Allah sees Himself through Himself, and He hears Himself through Himself, and by Himself.

For this reason it is said in the *hadith al-qudsi* which was quoted above: "My slave does not cease to draw near to Me through prayer until I love him, and when I love them I am his hearing and his sight." And when this eye is His eye, it is the eye of the Reality. And what is meant by the eye (the Sight) is eye-witnessing, which is the seeing of the Reality through the Reality, and not through the *self,* for when the ephemeral meets the eternal it vanishes, and only that which is timeless remains.

Finally then, only Allah can see Allah, because the human eyes cannot see Him, but He sees the human eyes. And how can human eyes see Him when He is nearer them than themselves? Is the eye able to see itself? No, but it only sees other eyes.

So my brother, if you want to know the Unity (*at-tawhid*) do not make for existence any partners (*shurk)* with Allah, but descend through the ranks of existence to the level of the lowest; and if you can do that, then the knowledge of Allah will come to you. Then you will find happiness instead of suffering and sorrow. Then, do not be satisfied with an inferior state, and do not be satisfied with anything but what Allah gives you. Then you will say, "Islam is enough for us." But Islam without the state of *al-'ihsan* will not be perfected in you, because this is the final goal of all that comes before it; and it is the completion of the Religion, and of belief. For that reason it is called *al-'ihsan.* And this means, to arrive to the end of the matter, and to be certain about it. So that he who has no part in the state of *al-'ihsan* has not completed his Islam in the same manner as those who have knowledge of this station. It is the best of springs, which means that it is the highest point in the raising up of the decrees of the Religion, and the reaching to a state than which there is none higher. The owner of this station is under obligation to carry out three duties, namely: that he has a duty towards his Spirit, a duty towards his Soul, and a duty towards his Secret, each of which has an obligation which it is necessary to fulfill. The obligation to his Spirit is Islam, the obligation to his Soul is Iman (belief) and its decrees, and the obligation to his Secret is al-Ihsan, and the observance of it.

الله

بسم الله الرحمن الرحيم

Al-Wudu'
The Ritual Ablution

Know O beloved, that ritual purity is brought about by water of absolute purity which is the *Water of the Unseen*. It is necessary for the knower, through his witnessing, to reveal the clarity of this water, for although it manifests in numerous ways and places, yet its nature, which is pure in its self (*nafs*), is unique and hidden with respect to its obligation, because of the strength and the absoluteness of its manifestation. This immutable water is the source for the ritual ablution.

"Make ablution with the water of the unseen if you carry the Secret
Except when you make tayammum with earth or sand.
Follow an imam and you will go forward to become an imam.
And pray the fajr prayer at the beginning of fajr.
This is the prayer of the knowers of their Lord;
If you are of them wash your righteousness with the ocean."

This is the Water of the Unseen through which the ritual ablution (*al-wudu'*) and everything associated with it, can be realized and confirmed. Earth or sand are not used except when water cannot be found; and it is necessary for this special purification that the water used should be free from all possibility of change, or alteration of state. Neither the water of the World of the Kingdom (*al-mulk)* nor that of the World of Dominion (*al-malakut*) possesses this quality, for both of them are in their nature subject to changing to a state opposite to that of their origin, thus being incomplete in their created state for the special requirements of the ritual ablution of which we now speak. However, so far as the water of the World of Spirits (*al-jabarut*) is concerned, it fulfills the requirements, for it is absolutely free from change, and it is limitless in its original state, not mixing with any other thing or substance, nor forming a compound in any mixture; nor is it bound to anything, nor is there anything either beyond it or below it. This is the Truth of the Absolute and the Unique One, Whose water can truly be called *water* without any doubt or reservation, and which is the only water that can be used to bring about the ritual purity which is necessary for absolute existence.

Know then, that the springs from which this water flows are the hearts of the knowers of Allah, and if a *murid* (follower) desires to reach to completed purity, it is necessary for him to direct himself to their dwellings and to humble himself at their doors. When he finds this water he will be shown its soundness and flawlessness, then that which he is searching about and aiming for will be completed and perfected in him.

If, however, anything which differs from its original nature is found in the water, inasmuch as a thing is capable of interfering with it, and of mixing with its original decree, for example, some change in its physical state, this is referred to as impurity, for it is a change brought about through the existence of self (*nafs*) in it. If the *nafs* is able to mix with this water, it will take on an existence similar to that of the self (*nafs)* which is referred to as being ephemeral, and therefore, being a contingency, is non-existent in the Truth. In this case the water is of no use to serve either for daily religious tasks or for the purpose of the ablution of Bondsmanship, and therefore it will be rejected and cast aside. But if, on the other hand, any change which is not in disobedience to its decree, should occur to the physical state of the water, so that any, or all, of its qualities are changed, it is nevertheless suitable for daily religious tasks; but not for the ablution of Bondsmanship. What is meant here by *daily tasks* are those which are concerned with obedience to the orders, and the performing of deeds of piety, such as the prayer, as well as abstention from what is forbidden; and similar matters. However, this is not the worship which is a means for entering into the Absolute Purity, which is the Presence of Allah and His Witnessing, because this Absolute Purity cannot be realized except through its existence, and its presence in the seeker of the first-mentioned absolute Water.

Briefly, water of which we are now speaking, is divided into three kinds: impure, pure and absolutely pure. He whose water is impure, is he who mixes it not only with love for the material world (*ad-dunya*), but with an excessive love for it. He whose water is pure, is he who mixes it not only with love for the Hereafter, but with an excessive love for it, and who, because of this love, turns away from the love of his Creator. But he whose water is of Absolute Purity has not mixed it with anything, nor does he desire anything, nor does he wish for anything except his Master; and he is not satisfied to be with anything, but Allah; for his prayer and his bondsmanship are for Allah, through Allah, as some have said:

"Everyone prays to You for fear of the Fire,
And he sees his saving from it as good fortune.
Or they ask You for the Garden,
Then they appear in the Garden,
And they drink from the spring of Salsibar.
But I have no desire for the Garden or the Fire,
And I do not need my beloved
For anything except Himself.
The Way of the spirit has permeated me,
And through that the friend is called the Friend."

This is the truth of the purity of the Absolute Water, and of what results to him who uses it for the ritual ablution; but he who cannot find this Water is prevented from realizing the Absolute Ritual Purity. But if he has a mind and intellect he will not be content without it, and will strive to find it, and will search for it wherever he can, even if he has to buy it with all his possessions and his very self.

Regarding the alterability of the state of water, for example, its ability to turn from liquid to solid, then to melt and to return to liquid, this is an exception in the case of the water of the World of the Kingdom *(al-mulk*) and of the Dominion (*al-malakut*) because there is permission for this change of state, since the potential for this change has been decreed in its origin, and therefore it is permitted to be used for daily religious practices, and for performing the prayer of bondsmanship, provided that the absolute water is not available. This water is then acceptable for an absolute ablution and purification because its decree is from He Who is the Absolute One, its source, and its origin, and the source of the entire universe. Therefore, a return through such water is a return to He who is the Absolute, and Who is the Origin. For this, Sidi `Abd al-Qadr al-Jilani, may Allah be pleased with him, said:

"What is the creation in its solid sculptured form,
Except like snow of which You are the water,
Which is the origin of everything.
But with the melting of the snow, this decree is removed,
And another is laid down for a state of water.
In the Reality it is thus indeed."

And it results from this that the decree, which governs shortcomings and imperfections, will not be removed from the state of ritual impurity, except when the above-mentioned Water enters into it. And what is meant by ritual impurity is everything that is transient, contingent and non-existent. In other words: all that is not Allah, and which has not been removed from the heart of the knower, and which cannot be cleansed from it except by the seeing with the Eye of the Truth; after which the sight of the Eternal One will replace his seeing; and this only takes place through this Water existing within him, and his ablution (*wudu'*) and purification with it.

How impossible, then, it is for the human being to pass judgment by means of that of which he has no knowledge, upon the truth of what is revealed *(zahir)* through created things. For until the seeing of shortcomings and evil has been removed from his eyes, and in a purified state he comes to know about created things, how can he see them in the pure way when he is still in a state of seeing duality and pictures, contrariness, disobedience, unbelief, hypocrisy, idolatry, separation, and suchlike qualities? How can he replace this way of seeing with something which he has not yet experienced, nor realized? Is it right for someone who sees the letter *shin* to call it *zin*? Definitely not, because the individual must give expression to what he sees; and vessels only leak out what they contain. So he judges the majority of things to be bad; and this condition will not leave his heart until he purifies it by means of the Absolute Water. But when this purification takes place, and when, with this Water, he purifies all existing things that manifest to him, and he comes to see that the Revealed face of the Creation is pure and perfect, this means that he has washed his eyes with the Unseen Water of Absolute Purity. For then he sees that as far as existing things are concerned, they are already pure before he has completed his own purification. In that moment, when he is cleansed from the decree for his limiting characteristic (*hukum*) of seeing evil in created things, his eyes will begin to see what before was hidden from him, as it is said:

"Wash you eyes with tears seven times,
And ask Him for forgiveness,
Then you will see what you have not seen before."

Know then, that there are two kinds of purity: the lesser purity, which is required, and frequently found amongst Sufis generally; and the greater purity which is only granted to the special ones - the prophets and the great and elevated saints.

Know that the obligations which the traveler on the Path of Allah must observe for the lesser purity are seven, and not more than that. These are related to the Eternal Qualities in which the knower must make *fana'* until, through purifying them, he becomes completely pure. These qualities are: power, will-power, the Pen, life, hearing, seeing and speaking, and they are the Qualities which it is necessary for the *murid*, by means of his ablution *(wudu')*, to purify. Meaning that all those who seek to purify themselves must make the *fana'* in them. In this way each of these qualities existing in him is annihilated, and destroyed in the truth of the Quality of his Lord, until complete purity comes to live in him. This is what the Folk of Allah mean when they say, "O you who purifies yourself, make true your qualities with your Lord, then He will cover you with His Qualities."

It is essential, and there can be no doubt about the fact, that the person making the ablution must pass his hands over the parts of his body which are involved in the ablution. The intention of this is that the Absolute Water should reach to every part of his body in which these above-mentioned seven qualities are found, so that there may be nothing remaining of his own individual qualities, and no obstacle between him (the murid) and Allah. Then he will be freed into the Absoluteness of his Lord. It is required of the murid to hasten to make the ablution with a firm intention, and without any sign of weakness, such as, of being fearful of dying, or any other state which veils him, and cuts him off from his Lord. "For he dies in the manner that he has lived, and he lives in the same manner as he dies." May Allah protect us, and all Muslims!

Because of this it is necessary, when making the *wudu'*, to have a pure and sincere intention in one's heart, for this is the source from which one finds the strength and the yearning (*himma*) to enter into the Presence of one's Lord. This is the nature of the ablution with which the murid must intend to destroy all things in himself that are contingent and transient, and therefore non-existent in the Reality; and that is everything which is not Allah; for any claim, which he makes to have individual existence, is an obstacle for him, and a hindrance on the Path. Then, while he is still seeing with the eye of non-existence he cannot enter into the Presence of his Lord, because the existence of anything that is not Allah is falsehood, and therefore it is forbidden, for there is no foundation for it, because it is sheer illusion which is an obstacle for the slave in his reaching to his Master. For this reason, it is said that it is important for the murid to have the intention to remove the veil, which can be done when he, when making the ablution, ensures that it penetrates into all parts of his being, starting with his outward bodily members, and passing into his inner qualities, and to his spirit within him.

As far as the slave is concerned it is necessary for him to strive with, and to work on, his obligations relating to the lesser purity and the cleansing of the qualities mentioned earlier namely: power, will-power, the Pen, life, hearing, seeing and speaking, which he will achieve through the remembrance (*ad-dikr*) of his Lord, because He loves the slave who draws near to Him through the fulfillment of these obligations. About which he, may the peace and blessings of Allah be upon him, spoke when he mentioned the words of Allah, Mighty and Supreme is He, to him in the *hadiṯ al-qudsi*: "My slave does not cease to draw near to Me with anything more beloved by Me than the religious duties which I have imposed upon him. And My slave continues to draw near to Me with supererogatory works so that I shall love him. When I love him, I am his hearing with which he hears, his seeing with which he sees, his hand with which he strikes, and his foot with which he walks, until he becomes a slave in the station of his Lord; then when he says to a thing, "Be!" It is.

This is the ultimate of purification, both outwardly and inwardly. The slave must work with the obligatory duties of purification of the above-mentioned seven qualities so that when he reaches to proximity with his Lord He will take possession of his hands, his feet, and all his organs.

Know, my beloved, that the practices (*sunna*) for the lesser ablution are seven, the aim of which is to purify seven parts of the body, namely: the hands, the feet, the eyes, the tongue, the stomach and the private parts.

By this I mean that the murid should, within himself, make the real *tawba* about these parts, followed by the promise not to use these bodily members (eyes, mouth, hands, etc.) in the wrong way; and this intention should be a prelude for the making of his outer and his inner ablution (*wudu'*). For that, it is said that the cleaning of these seven bodily members is the beginning of purification, and that the heart of the matter is that the necessity for their purification is from the *sunna* of the People of Allah, for he who desires to purify himself must cleanse the organs of his body from doubtful matters, and all vices. Know, my beloved, that what is meant by *doubtful matters* is that they are a similitude for what the murid, by nature, possesses in some of his bodily parts. For example, the mouth and the nose, and the vices which are associated with the tongue and the mouth, such as malicious words, lying, anger, etc. which can be likened to unpleasant odors which affect the nose. It is therefore necessary for the murid to abandon any such behavior, and not to allow himself to hold onto it, nor to let it persist in him.

Those who have gone before us have laid down the right order for the ablution, such as the rinsing out and cleaning of the mouth, and the nose, etc., and this is what the People of Allah have chosen for the manner of the outside ablution. It is considered desirable for the murid, before making the ablution, to pronounce the Great Name (In the Name of Allah, the Merciful, the Compassionate) and to make the *fana'* in it, so that following this, the *fana'* in the Qualities can be made without effort, and without causing fatigue.

The second requisite is a pure place in which the murid can mention the Name of Allah, and make the retreat (*halwa*), because in order for the remembrance (*ad-dikr*) to be pure it is necessary for the body of the murid to be pure for it is the place in which he makes the *dikr*.

The third requirement is to use only a small amount of water for the ablution; the meaning of this being that the murid should not plunge headlong into the realities before they come to take possession of him, because if he hastens himself to them before they come to him, or if he takes more than he is able to carry from them, he will be overwhelmed by foreboding. Therefore, the murid needs to humble himself, and to subdue himself, and to be absent from his body by letting the water flow gently over him.

The fourth requirement is that the murid should always start the ablution from the right-hand side of the vessel; and what is meant by the vessel is his body which is the carrier of the Secret of Allah, and that Secret is the Guide, and those who follow him. Therefore it is said that the murid should respect, revere, and honor any of these vessels because they carry the Secret. He must not belittle them, but should regard them as mighty and esteem them highly, realizing what lies hidden in them.

The fifth requirement is that of the second and third washing of the above-mentioned parts of the body, the inner meaning of which is the making of *fana'* in the Names and Actions. As to the *fana'* in the qualities, this, as we have explained earlier, means the obligations which the murid must fulfill for the lesser purification.

The sixth requirement is that of observing the rule of conduct and polite behavior which favors the *beginning from the right-hand side*, so that when the murid is sitting, he greets his brother on the right-hand side, with his right hand to his brother's right hand, for if he observes this favored rule he will not become proud, nor will he be led to consider himself higher than they are, for this practice, when performed with its deep meaning in the heart, brings honor to each one, as is pleasing to Allah.

The seventh requirement is to use the tooth-stick (*siwak*). The murid should use this stick in order to clean his mouth from all impurities, and to give it a wholesome refreshing fragrance.

The eighth requirement is that the murid, concerning the obligations of purification, should carefully follow the sunna so that he cleanses his bodily parts by beginning with his head - his eyes, his ears and his tongue. It is said that no other requirement of the purification is like this one, because all the vices which manifest, originate in the head. Therefore, the other bodily parts, which are also involved in the ablution, need to be protected every day from the harm and contamination which can come to them from the head. For example, a deadly poison, which can be likened to an arrow which pierces the heart, can come to the eyes if they gaze upon what Allah has forbidden. But if the human being lowers his gaze and restrains his tongue and his hearing, it is easy for him to purify his other bodily parts. For this reason it is necessary for the murid to begin his purification from his head downwards.

The ninth requirement is to wash the toes of the feet, the aim of this being that the murid does not leave any of the vices, which originate in his head, from entering into even the very extremities of his body. This means, to permeate his whole body with the above-mentioned Water. Therefore it is said, "The beginning is the passing of water from the top of the head to the toes of the feet." In this way, the murid does not neglect anything that could bring dishonor to his ablution.

Know my beloved also, that it is strongly disliked for a murid, when making the ablution, to try to go beyond the obligation laid down for the purification of the seven qualities mentioned earlier. For he must restrict himself to these and not try to work with any additional quality, for example, the *reaching* and the realization, because in his beginning, the mentioning of them, and the requesting for them, could bring about an undesirable picture, for he could not know the meaning of what he says, nor of what he asks for. Therefore, it is strongly disliked, even abhorrent, for him, until he is required to do so, to go beyond the obligations for purification, and that is the fana' in the Essence, through which he finds the Truth, Mighty and Supreme is He, by Whom he understands things in a manner in which he did not understand them before.

It is also not pleasing for the murid, when making the ablution, to exceed the washing beyond the requirements that have been set out by the rules of the People of Allah, which, for the lesser ablution, are the washing of each bodily part three times. In the deep meaning, this is the fana' in the Names, the Actions and the Attributes, and there should be no washing, of one's own accord, a fourth time; for that would be an illusion concerning the fana' in the Essence, since it would mean that the murid is desiring this without the mediation of a Shaykh. The Prophet, may peace and blessings be upon him, said, "Look at the Shaykh before you look at the Way." And this is especially the case in this mighty station (*maqam*) and important order.

As has been said, it is required of he, who at the beginning, or in the middle of the ablution stops, and is unable to complete it, that he must return to make the real repentance *(tawba)*, and then to perform the ablution as laid down, thus continuing with what he has already carried out. An example of a person, who is unable to perform the complete ablution, is the murid whose Shaykh has died, or for whom an excusable separation has come about between him and his Shaykh. In this case he should reunite himself with his Shaykh, or with someone else of the knowers of Allah, and he must continue with his ablution which he was performing before. For example, if he is in the fana' in the Names, he continues to complete that. Or if he is in the fana' in Actions, he must be ready for that, and then he must aim for, and direct himself to move forward, to make the fana' in the Qualities.

This is the manner of he who has become temporarily incapable of completing the ablution, on condition that his separation and his *cutting off* came about through there being, in that, no blame upon himself. However, if it has happened because of slackness, laziness or neglect on his part, then what he has already achieved is of no use to him, and he must recommence with another ablution; and he must ask Allah to accept this from him, because he began like one who was not serious in his intention and actions.

Know then, that the murid, who is permitted to continue with his original ablution, is required to fulfill an added condition - which is that he does not prolong being in a state of separation, and that he should always be conscious, and aware of, both his proximity and his separation, so that when he is no longer separated from Allah, and when he has returned to Him, then there is no objection for him if he continues on from the *place* to which he had already reached. But, if he has wandered far from Allah it is not possible for him to rely upon, and to return to, what he had reached to before his separation.

The state of separation which we mention here can, by analogy, be compared to the degree of drying out, parching, and hardening of the parts of the body and of the heart, for lack of water. When the murid making *wudu'* performs his ablution in a state of incomplete surrender and submission to Allah, it as though the water of his ablution dries quickly from the surface of his body, and does not penetrate inside him, thus having no effect upon his heart or his self (*nafs*), and consequently he returns immediately to being in the same state in which he was before he made his ablution. But the murid who makes the ablution in a state of obedience to Allah, the Mighty, the Supreme, and whose heart which has not been conquered by disobedience, continues to be his spiritual guide and counselor, allows the water of his ablution to penetrate himself deeply. And this is a measure of his proximity to Allah; so that, in this case, he can rely upon, and continue with, the purification which he has already realized. If, however, the qualities of rebellion, intransigence, and of hardening prevail in him, and persist in his heart and his bodily members, then the murid cannot rely upon, nor return to, what he may have realized before, in which case he is obliged to make another ablution at the hand of a knower who has knowledge of the rules relating to purification. And all perfection lies with Allah.

Next we will explain about the rule for the murid who has abandoned one of the obligations for the ritual ablution, but who, nevertheless, knows about the rules for observing the perfect ritual ablution, and whose intentions and words are seen to be true and sincere. This is the case of he who has purified some of the qualities but not others; in which case he must complete the purification of the qualities which he has neglected; and he must do this without delay . If he remembers them, within a short space of time, then in a state of ablution he must continue to complete what follows after, not covering up his walking with outside distracting actions.

If the person who claims to be in the *prayer of union* (*salat al-ittisal*) yet neglects the obligation of purification for this prayer, then it becomes null and void. However, as soon as he remembers the unfulfilled obligation of purification, it is necessary for him, in order to make the prayer sound, unblemished, and free from error, to complete his purification, and to start the prayer a second time. This is a rule for he who has neglected an obligation for purification, and if the bodily part, which has been omitted from the ablution, has been omitted unintentionally, and it is subsequently remembered, the murid should finish the prayer and not interrupt it; but having finished it he should hasten to purify the part of his body that he has omitted. But if he has intentionally omitted a part of his ablution his prayer is void and worthless, and he becomes like a person who is pretending; for how can he leave a part of his body still clothed in disobedience when he is in the Presence of the All-Merciful? May Allah protect us from that! The knowers of Allah are those who, both outwardly and inwardly, purify themselves with a complete ablution.

Know then, that what destroys a person's state of purity is the persistence of the self (*nafs*) when it repeatedly returns after the *fana'*, for when this happens the purity is removed. The existence of the *nafs* manifests itself by certain signs, because everything that is evil comes from it. For example, the *nafs al-'amara* can be compared to the waste products, or impurities of the body, such as urine and feces and suchlike things; and in using this analogy there lies a deep meaning. The People of Allah consider their *nafs* to be the worst of all bad qualities, because they know that all vices come from it.

Know then, my beloved, that the ablution is a promise between the lover and the Beloved, and if he breaks his ablution it is necessary to renew the promise. Some of the qualities which nullify the ablution are known to human beings from within themselves, whilst others manifest outwardly; but whenever the ablution is destroyed, the purification must be renewed, and it is necessary then for the murid to make the intention not to repeat his mistakes, for without this intention his ablution will not be of any use to him, because it would indicate that he has become someone who is not serious, nor is his intention sincere. It is always necessary for the murid to be careful about his purification, and if something happens to remove it, he must waste no time before he renews it, because without it, he is turned away from the Presence of his Lord, and he will be driven back to himself. He, who has once purified himself must not be content with any separation from the Presence of his Lord, for if this is the case it is a sign for him of the persistence of his *nafs* of which there are sixteen kinds.

The first of these is everything that manifests from the murid at the beginning of his walking on the Path, such as the words and expressions which come from the mouths of people ordinarily, before they are taken by the Path; and which are normal until people become followers of the Way. Therefore, it is very necessary for a murid to change these habits and to purify himself from everything of his past life, because if he does not do this these qualities will return to him, and will reveal what remains of *nafs* which are not in keeping with his station (*maqamahu*). In that case he will be obliged to recognize that whatever manifests to him of *nafs* is not only coming from something outside himself, but it is indeed a manifestation of what lies inside him. The example here is that of a vessel which only spills out what is inside it. In the same way everything that comes from the tongue of the human being is a result of what lies in his heart, for the tongue is the interpreter of the heart. The six qualities of the *nafs*, which lie in the heart and which manifest on the tongue, are: lying, slander and the bearing of false witness, insults, cursing, ridicule and mockery, and quickness to show anger. These qualities without any doubt are a strong indication of the existence of the *nafs*.

The second sign for the *nafs*, which wipe out the ablution is the manifestation of hypocrisy, envy, hatred, hostility, fraud, lethargy, pride and laziness in obedience. If the murid finds signs of any one of these in himself it is necessary for him to be truthful and sincere about them with his Lord, and he should hasten to purify himself so that he does not return to a closed door, nor fall down to where he was before - meaning to where the ordinary people sit.

Thirdly, the ablution is nullified by *nafs* which has an excessive love of material riches. For that, everyone, for whom the *nafs* makes demands upon him in this manner, must hasten to purify himself in order that he can return to his Lord in humility and submission, having broken all his pictures, and bringing with him everything that he has of purity and love; thus returning to the state in which he was before he lost his ablution. And Allah, Mighty and Supreme is He, accepts everyone who truthfully returns to Him. However, if he, wishing to purify himself and to return to Allah, has not cleansed himself of all his shortcomings as it is desired of him to do through making the true repentance, and if he tries to keep something of himself, secretly in his heart, then this only increases the extent to which he destroys his ablution.

I will now, therefore, speak about the means for removing all weaknesses and shortcomings, or the *how* of the ablution, so that the purification of a person becomes firm and reliable, as is necessary for he who desires to enter to Allah. He must empty himself of whatever sins and vices that he has, not leaving anything of them to remain, either inwardly or outwardly, because the *nafs al-'amara* is the most destructive of all existing things, and even worse is the person who is a slave to its demands. Therefore, he who desires to purify himself must destroy all his shortcomings to rid himself of this unpleasant state, exchanging it for a pleasing and praiseworthy one, in which he is freed from all his faults. About this, it is said, "O murid! If you desire to reach Allah, beware of holding onto any characteristic of your *nafs*."

Know now that we are going to speak about the person who *reaches*, and who arrives at his goal. We are also going to speak about he who is like a woman hidden behind a veil, and who imagines that by wearing a veil she can conceal her shortcomings, and that her veil will remove her impurities in the way that she wants. In fact anyone, whose case is like this, instead of using the water of purity to cleanse himself, replaces it with his own qualities, but "Those who are godfearing when a visitation of the Devil troubles them, remember Allah, and then they see clearly." (7:201). Then, whoever is aware of his shortcomings must rid himself of them in the way that he is capable of so doing, because no shortcoming originates from the Essence. On the other hand, he who is veiled and incapable of reaching the station of *manhood* can only rid himself of his shortcomings through using the Absolute Water, as we have mentioned. If he finds that shortcomings continue to plague him and to increase, there is no doubt but that the murid needs the Absolute Water, otherwise his existence will become like that of the ordinary people.

Know O beloved truthful one, that for the People of Allah, the truth of the greater ablution (*ghusl)* is the withdrawing totally from everything that is not Allah, until the person purifying himself has no existence except His existence. Before this ablution the slave is impure, and is separated from Allah, and it is impossible for him to enter into proximity with Him unless he performs this ablution. But when he completes it he will be granted proximity; and it is through the knowledge, which comes from proximity, that he will be able truly to understand, and to perform this ablution, because this greater ablution, of which we are now speaking, is about revelation just as the sitting in the Presence of the Truth is revelation.

Know then, also, that the true ablution is the *fana'* of the slave from himself and from human beings, for this *fana'* is made in the existence of the Essence of Allah which is what he desires to reach. It is necessary for him to be in the Presence of Allah, and to follow the example of he who has purified himself; for it is through him that he makes the *fana'* from his *nafs* until he comes to the subsistence in which there is no *he.* Some of them say, about this, "I have come out from the *fana'*, and from there I have remained without any *I,* for who am I, O I, but I?"

If the slave is in this state and he has realized the entering into proximity *now*, since nothing remains to veil him from his Master, and if Allah has granted him the direct and true seeing (the vision of the hearts), then the One Who has been his aim brings about that which he has aimed for, and from this comes the vision of the Truth, which manifests to him immediately after he has emptied himself through the *fana'* of this ablution. His seeing is then completed, neither isolating his *self* nor cutting him off, nor does this come to him through some of the faces of existence, and not others, but the Truth manifests to him the order of the revelation so that, through this, he knows the truth of the words of Allah: "Wheresoever ye turn your face, there is the face of Allah." (2:115). And this means that the splendor of the Truth encompasses all existing things, both the lower and the upper ranks, as well as all the *jamal* and all the *jalal*. At that moment he has reached the station of the Friend (*halilal-maqam*) which means that he has reached the station of the complete Unity, so that the love for his Beloved is intermingled with his blood, his flesh and his outer and inner being. This means that the knower is now entirely permeated with the Love of the Truth and of the Complete Ablution, just as the roots of the hairs of the head are permeated with the water of the outside ablution. As it is said:

"The spirit has penetrated into my Way
And through this the friend is called the Friend."

The person, who has made this Ablution, cannot allow anything of his individual existence to remain for he has had to walk in completion and totality through it, and has left it behind him; and this he has done by means of the Water of the Absolute. But if he cannot reach to this state, this is because his ablution has allowed a residue of his own existence to subsist alongside with that of his Master, and as a result of this he becomes separated from Allah. If he allows only a single hair of his own existence, in which he has not made the *fana'*, to remain, and if he has not totally abandoned the greater impurities, then he is in that state to which the Prophet, may peace and blessings be upon him, referred when he said, "Under every hair of the head lies a greater impurity." Meaning that every hair of your existence, O murid, separates you from your Lord if you do not make *fana'* in it, and if you allow yourself to remain in a state of impurity. And the truth of this state of impurity is the truth of your distance from Allah. We seek refuge in Allah from that!

So, O murid, examine whatever of your existence you are concealing, and whatever keeps your from your true ascription and existence. Do not be forgetful of anything, and destroy anything which you are keeping to yourself, because it separates you from your Lord. And if this is difficult for you, then achieve it with that which is not your *self*, and I mean that you should realize this through trusting in, and relying upon Allah, that He will help you. Allah guides us on His Straight and Unique Path, and He suffices us; and He is the best of Protectors.

الله

بسم الله الرحمن الرحيم

As-Salat
The Ritual Prayer

Know my beloved, that the prayer, which is the most elevated of ranks, is the means by which the seeker can reach to proximity. The Arabic word, *as-salat*, comes from the stem *silla*, meaning connection, link, bond - a bond being that which connects one thing to another; and there can be no doubt but that the prayer is the bond between the slave and his Lord, which can be expressed as *the reaching*. If the slave reaches his Lord then he will have gained the mastery required for the Prayer of Union (*salay al-ittisal*) after which there is no separation, as it is said:

"Since they reached they have not returned,
And since they made prostration (sajda) they have not stood up."

In short, it was about this prayer that the Prophet, may peace and blessings be upon him, said, "Prayer is the cooling of my eyes." It is the *cooling of the eyes* of the prophets and the highest rank of the knowers. Anyone who reaches to a part of it has the possibility of reaching everything. The search of the knowers has no end, nor do the tongues of those who seek the Unity stop moving, for the yearning of the *muridun* to ascend to this rank never leaves them, but remains with them until they die.

The knowers of Allah are those who have reached this prayer, but as for the rest, they have no knowledge of it, nor do they walk with elevated thoughts, for they are ignorant of them. These are the people who, if they do not know about a matter, will dislike it, and reject it. For example, a group of learned Egyptian men *(ulama)* visited some knowers of Allah with the intention of arguing with them. The knowers said to them, "Is there anyone amongst you who has stopped praying?" The *learned* men were astounded at hearing these words, and replied, "Is there anyone amongst us who has stopped praying?" The knowers answered them, saying, "You are those about whom the Truth, Mighty and Supreme is He, said, "Truly man was created very impatient, fretful when evil touches him, niggardly when good reaches him; except for those who pray." (70:19-22).

Hearing these words of Allah, the learned men became silent, because they knew that they could not perform the prayer about which Allah had spoken. This prayer is a Secret of Allah, by means of which He bestows distinction upon whomsoever He wills, and to which He guides those to whom He grants strength. Therefore he, may peace and blessings be upon him, said, "The cooling of my eyes has been made for me in the prayer," for it is the place of proximity and the ultimate of desire. Its outer form is prayer and its inner form is *reaching,* for it is the bond between the one who worships and He Who is worshiped. Therefore it is said that its outer face is worship and its inner face is witnessing.

As a result of its power and the nobility of its rank, it is divided into practices (*sunnan*), on the one hand, and orders, or conditions, on the other, and it is important for any beloved of Allah to be very careful not to fall down, nor to make any mistake, nor to give way to doubtful actions; but to be knowledgeable in what is ordered. Those who are ignorant of the Order of Allah, concerning a thing, are separated from it, as it is said, "A man is not permitted to carry out any action until he knows the Order of Allah for it." This applies especially in this mighty and important matter, about which only a few people know, and of which most people are ignorant, except for those who truly pray and keep the prayer, and turn away from foolish talk. And for the knowers of Allah, foolish talk means everything that separates us from Him, because they are the ones who know the meaning of this prayer and what it requires of them, and who perform it in accordance with the practices (*sunnan*) which are its due; those that are pleasing to follow, in keeping with what was habitual for the Prophet. It also has obligatory requirements, or preconditions, which are necessary for every person who prays, to fulfill. The practices are related to the very nature and inner meaning of the prayer.

Know that the preconditions can be subdivided into two kinds, namely: those which are obligatory, and those which are pure and which originate from the Truth. An obligatory condition refers to any matter which the *murid* cannot, of his own free will, choose to perform or not. It is something that he gains, or loses, in accordance with his yearning and remembering, or his forgetfulness and idleness; and which relates to his proximity, or separation, from his Master.

There are five obligatory preconditions, the first of which is Islam, and which is uniquely concerned with the surrender to Allah, so that the person desiring this station should have a pure and unblemished tongue, a clean heart which is surrendered to whatever the Merciful One wants of him, and which is moved wherever the power of Allah moves him. This is with regard to the knowing of the prayer, but does not refer to its outer movements.

The second precondition is that the person performing the prayer should have reached the age of fifteen years, thereby attaining the station of reason, insight, and ability of speech, being firmly grounded in, and being capable of penetrating the knowledge of the People of Allah, and of being able to *drink* from them.

And they said, may Allah be pleased with them, "Whosoever has not penetrated to this, our knowledge, dies persisting in the great sins." So that whoever does not reach this station is not ordered to perform this special prayer, so that his prayer, so far as anyone of the Folk is concerned, is like supererogatory praying, and his knowledge is ignorance.

Then know that the *youths* of the Path are the people of the *fana'* in deeds and actions, and also those who seek to have knowledge of the *fana'* in the Qualities and the Names, and who are still veiled from what is required for the *People of the Essence*, which is the complete annihilation in the Essence from all created things. The youths are those who are slack or negligent in their striving for Allah, but those who are veiled from Him are neither men nor youths, because they are still wrapped up, and enveloped, in the folds of non-existence. And when will they reach to true existence? If they manifested in existence they would witness He Who is the Creator of existence, whose manifestation in His existence is like the appearance of the sun in the middle of the day, as it is said:

"You manifested and You are not hidden from anyone,
Except from he who is blind and does not see the moon,

But You became hidden, being veiled through You manifested.
And how can the One Who is hidden by might, beknown?"

Briefly, the Truth, Mighty and Supreme is He, is veiled from some, but without a veil existing, for He draws near to them in a manner which unites the opposites of proximity and separation. And this is the case of the *men*, and all other cases are an illusion, for they do not even reach to the rank of *children*, because the truth of the child is that he emerges from the bondage of the womb into the vastness of the world. And therefore, with the People of Allah, the truth of the child is that he leaves the bondage of material existence for the unlimited freedom of the witnessing. And if he reaches to the knowledge of the Essence of Being, then his existence comes from the Merciful One (*ar-Rahman*), and through the help of the Hand of Allah he finds the *lap* of the Merciful One, and he begins to be taught and made knowledgeable between the *jamal* and the *jalal* until he rises to the rank of perfection (*kamal*). Then it becomes clear to him that instead of being the one who desires, he becomes the One Who is desired. Briefly, he is the one for whom this prayer is made obligatory.

The third obligatory precondition, or stipulation, is that the *murid* should have a mind (*`aql*) which knows that everything that is not Allah is without intelligence, and is therefore described as foolishness (*batil*) so that if an intellectual person is lacking in this precondition he is not one who is put under obligation.

The fourth obligatory precondition for the performer of the prayer is that he should be in a state of greater ablution (*ghusl)* as well as that of lesser ablution (*wudu'),* so that what is required of him is that after he has been annihilated from the existence of his *nafs*, he should then cleanse himself from those impurities necessitating the greater ablution, for he will be forbidden to enter into the Presence of Allah and to stand before Him, if he is not in a state of Absolute Purity.

The fifth obligatory precondition is that of a respect for the times of the prayer. Meaning, that he, who prays the prayer, should be in readiness for the times of the witnessing of the revelations of Allah; but he who prays in a state of veiling, and until the Truth, Mighty and Supreme is He, is manifest to him, is not under obligation to perform the prayer.

However, as soon as the Truth is revealed to him, this prayer, of which we speak, becomes an obligation for him, because the time of revelation demands prostration, so that what is desired from it can manifest. The Shaykh Muhammad al-Buzaydi, may Allah be pleased with him, said:

"When the perfection of the Truth is truly established then prostrate before it.
For you mount up so long as you are obedient.
So the Truth manifests the Beauty (jamal) happily,
And its lights are sent down upon you shining, brilliant."

There are, in addition, four preconditions relating to supererogatory prayers. But now we wish to speak of the obligations (which are sixteen in all) which concern the prayer.

The first obligation is that of pronouncing the words *Allahu Akbar* (God is Great), and this is the *takbir* which opens the prayer and which should enter the performer of it into the state of consecration (*ihram*) so that his heart is filled with the awareness of the Magnificence of Allah; and that he should express this with his tongue, "Until he is lost in the Might and gazing at the Magnificence." Then, with all this, he enters into the holiness of the prayer. But if he does not make the *fana'* in these two Qualities (the Might and the Magnificence), he may be distracted in his praying by what is not Allah, and if he pays any attention to this, he cannot enter into the sacredness of the prayer, nor will it satisfy him to say, "Allah al-'Ajal!" Because if he enters the prayer with the Quality of *jalal*, or Omnipotence, then it is necessary for him to perform the prayer in that manner; and in that manner he is required to pronounce the *Allahu Akbar*!, so that his tongue and his heart are at one with each other.

If however the heart, of he who prays, is surrendered and attentive, but his tongue fails to speak, then this is enough so far as the witnessing of the Merciful is concerned, for when Allah straitens the breast then the tongue is silent. The Prophet, may peace and blessings be upon him, said, "Whoever knows Allah his tongue becomes tired."

Briefly then, the prayer of Allah is beyond the understanding of people generally. Al-Jili said:

"I pray when all the people pray.
However my prayer is that I surrender to Your Glory.
I say Allahu Akbar! declaring Your Essence holy above any other thing;
And with Your Name I say my Bi-smi-llah when I humble myself.
I stand and I pray. Meaning that I stand faithfully.
For You are the One uniting excellence and perfection."

The second obligation for the prayer is in the manner of standing for the pronouncing of the *takbir* (Allahu Akbar!), and what is required in this is to stand with the truths of the Magnificence of Allah, Mighty and Supreme is He. It is important, therefore, for he who prays to stand in the prayer with the necessary politeness, the ultimate of which is his *fana'* and his extinction, so that he becomes as *a thing not mentioned* before the manifestation of the Magnificence of Allah, Mighty and Supreme is He. And if he desires to stand in a manner, which is not like this, he will be rejected, because this means that he is lacking in the proper feeling.

The third obligation is in the intention, or in the murid's setting out to reach Allah, because everything that he possesses is like scattered dust, as it is said:

"Is not everything not Allah falsehood?
And, without doubt, every comfort and ease goes."

This is the case of those who proclaim the Unity, and who desire to reach to the Lord of all the worlds, and who do not follow the rest of the Creation, as it is said:

"They do not desire the Garden of Eden,
Nor the beautiful rivers nor the tents and dwellings.
But the Face of the Beloved is their fate.
This is what the noble-hearted aim for."

And he who desires this in the beginning of his Way no doubt will reach his Lord, because of the soundness of his intention and the perfection of his love; and the intention is in the spirit within the deed.

The fourth obligation, which concerns the reciting of the *Fatiha*, requires that it should take the form of an intimate conversation from he, who is praying in the special Presence of Allah; for now he stands before his Lord, as the Secrets of Allah are poured out upon him. For he, upon whom the Divine revelation comes down, and upon whom the lights of the holy Presence shine, is in the station of proximity with nothing wanting or lacking; after which only the intimate dialogue remains. The People of Allah call this the station of intimate discourse. Is there then anything remaining of proximity, O knowers, when your ears are delighted with the discoursing of the Lord of the worlds, and the nobility which your Master casts upon you? And they say, "This is the station of he who drowns in the lights of the witnessing." Yes indeed! Praise be to Allah the Lord of all the worlds. This is when what happens to him has not happened to anyone else, and he has reached to what he could not have imagined, with his thoughts, to reach, as it is said:

"I was given what I aimed for, beyond what I could have wished for,
If this rapture would be completed and last me forever!"

The fifth obligation is in the standing for the reciting of the *Fatiha*. This means the standing for the intimate discourse, in the Truth, because Allah, Mighty and Supreme is He, speaks intimately to the heart of he who performs the prayer, when he recites these words of the *Fatiha*, which satisfy him; and it is not right for him to use any other words than these, because in the Presence of Allah nothing can exist except Himself, and no other words than His. For if he speaks in Allah's Presence with only His words, it is the Truth, Mighty and Supreme is He, Who speaks to Himself, from Himself, because the slave, who existed before he entered into the Presence of his Lord, has been annihilated by His Presence, and he has vanished completely, and has come to nothing, as some have said:

"I have come out now after the fana',
And from there I have remained, without I,
And who am I, O I, but I?"

The sixth obligation concerns the bowing down *(ruku`)* which is the complete immersion which the People of Allah call annihilation (*fana'*), and which they describe as the obliteration of actions and qualities, the desire for the material world (*ad-dunya*) and the Hereafter, and the ranks and stations *(maqamat*) until the slave is left without any station as He, Exalted is He, has said. "O you men of Yathrib you cannot stand (the attack) therefore go back." (33:13) The meaning here of *go back*, or the return, which is the seventh obligation, is the rising up from the *ruku`*, but with his Lord, and not with himself, so that all his actions, deeds and words become those of Allah. This means that they originate from Allah and are intended for Him. In this station some of them have said, "When the knowers stand they stand in Allah, and when they look their eyes look with Allah; and Allah has turned about their affair." Then if a good deed comes from them they do not ask for any reward for it, and if something bad should originate from them, then the blood-money must be paid from the one who has killed, because they know that every action, whether from themselves or from others, comes, in the Truth, from Allah. Very few people *own* this station, for it is a difficult one, because no one can speak about it except he who has *tasted* it, and realized it.

What he, who is setting out on the Path, has to fear most is the extent of the interference and hindrance of his *self* (*nafs*) which is still hidden from him, for no one is safe from it except he whom Allah takes by the hand, as they, may Allah be pleased with them, said:

"After the fana' in Allah to desire to be as you wish,
Is not your knowledge ignorance, and your action falsehood?"

For this reason one has to be fearful for he upon whom the help of Allah has not yet descended.

The eighth obligation is in the prostration (*sujud)* which is the utmost that is desired of he who is performing the prayer, because it is the equivalent of the plunging down from the ranks of existence to the lowest rank of non-existence. The People of Allah refer to the plunging down as the extinction of the essence by the Essence, so that the state of prostration in the prayer is the measure of his proximity to his Lord. And from here the Truth, Mighty and Supreme is He, speaks to he who has this station, and He says to him, "Prostrate! And draw near to Me." The Prophet, may peace and blessings be upon him, said, "The nearest that the slave can be to his Lord is while he is prostrating." And if the worshipper reaches this rank of prostration, and he makes *fana'* from his existence then he prostrates a second time, which is the ninth obligation, to make *fana'* from this *fana,* so that his prostration may be the *eye* of his rising up from it. This is expressed as being the *baqa',* or the subsistence in Allah and for Allah, as it is said:

"He makes fana' and then fana' and then fana',
And his fana' is the eye of the baqa'.

This means that he makes the complete annihilation from his *nafs*, and from everything that is not Allah. Then he makes the annihilation from this annihilation, so that his subsistence (*baqa'*) is in Allah. And if his *fana'* and his extinction is in the Might of Allah, then after it he will remain without *he* because his prostration has been in the Eye of the Truth, and his ascent will be in the eye of the Creation, having made *fana'* from the Oneness, and being in the *baqa'* in the Unity, since the prostration of the knowers is that of those who *reach*, and their reaching is not cut off, as some of them said:

"I prostrate so that I make fana', and I make fana' from the fana',
And I prostrate again, and the one enslaved by love catches fire.
My heart's fortification is Your goodness.
In it are the greetings, and from You to You they hasten."

And how will the return be for the people of this station, when what is other is forbidden? Only there is the fear that they may return to their selves (*nufus*) and to seeing things as they used to be, but if they are still prostrating, making *fana'* in the existence of He who exists (their Creator), then there will be no individual trace left of them, and there will be no *news* of them. They existed in the days gone by, but now they are in Allah, and with Him. The Truth, Mighty and Supreme is He, made them die a hard death. Meaning that He brought them back to live in Eternal Life; which means that, after this, there is no death. They died to their *self* (*nafs*), their nature, characteristics and desires, to be resurrected in their Lord, so that their existence is with their Lord. On that day there is nothing which exceeds this both for he who makes the prayer, and He Who is worshiped. For with His Secret they worship Him, and with His Eye they witness Him, and if you called the knower, his Creator would answer you. This is the meaning of the proximity of the slave to his Lord, until he no longer manifests his own essence but only the Essence of the Truth, for now he is absent in Its witnessing, as some of them have said:

"When the love between us became pure
We began to love like one thing.

I did not cease to draw near to Him,
Until He became my seeing and hearing, and my help wherever I was.
When I look I only look through Him,
And when I strike He does not cease to help me.
If I want He wants, and if I command, my command is His order
For I have reached everything I aimed for."

After this, everything that happens to them is from their entering into the station of the shining presence, following which all created things vanish and are extinguished in His eyes. The Lord is the Truth, and the slave is the Truth, and there is ever more Truth to follow; and understand this!

The tenth obligation concerns the greeting at the end of the prayer, from which the return to the Creation is required, after the person praying has been consumed by the Presence of the Truth. In this station he must turn his face to the Creation with his Revealed state, but not with his Hidden one, and he must talk to the Creation with his tongue, but not with his heart, for his heart has only one face, and that belongs solely to his Beloved. For, so long as he is witnessing only his Beloved, he cannot return to anything except to Him. Therefore, his return is with his revealed heart, and not with his hidden heart, as is said:

"My heart is with my Beloved, talking to Him,
But my tongue is with you."

Because of this it is necessary for the person in this station to talk to the Creation with its tongue, and this is the meaning behind the words: "Peace be upon you" (*as-salam `alaykum*). It is the obligation for he who prays as one made *Single* in *the station of Union*, for he does not find, on any of his six sides, his right-hand, or his left, in front of him or behind him, above him or below him, any other with Him. This means that the Mighty One surrounds him so that, in every case, he is asked to return to the *world of the wisdom*, and to be present with the

Truth of the Names. Therefore he says *as-salam `alaykum* as if there were large numbers with him, although he is alone in his prayer; then his greeting is to himself from himself, as some have said:

"When I return my greeting is upon me, for myself."

So that whoever does good, it is for himself, and whoever does evil, it is against himself.

The eleventh obligation is that which exists in the sitting for the greeting, for the meaning in this is the necessity of upholding the mid-point in this station of returning to the Creation, so as to enhance his intimacy with it, because sitting is the position between prostration and standing. For if he were to enter back to the Creation in a state of prostration and annihilation in the *fana'*, it would be impossible for him to perceive it; and also it would not be desirable to be standing, or at a distance from the Truth, as he was before he made *fana'*.

This is the entering into the Creation through the Creation, and there is nothing more to accrue from that, nor from his return. For this it is said that if the worshipper says the *as-salam `alaykum* when he is in a state of hearing the prayer while, at the same time, he is with the Truth, then the Angels answer him, saying: *wa `alaykum as-salam wa-rahmatu 'llahi wa-barakatuhu*. However, if he is only with his *self* his prayer is thrown back to him, and he returns, after it, blamed and cast out. Therefore it is necessary for him to be in the very center of this station, for the best of situations is their mid-point. It is said, "He, who knows his rank and sits below it, is truly alive." For when the human being is annihilated he knows his rank, and then he is asked to sit in it.

Next, there follows the twelfth obligation, which is the order in which the prayer is performed, inasmuch as this order, or progression, cannot, in any way, be altered, nor is it permitted for any innovation to be added to it. Therefore, no request to enter to Allah can be made, except through the well-known Way of the People of Allah. How can you ask to leave the prayer before you have even entered it? And how can raisins be raisins before they have been grapes? No, he has to enter the houses by their doors, for it is not possible to ask for the *fana'* before it has been realized, nor the annihilation before it has been experienced. These are the firm foundations.

The thirteenth obligation is to strive for the right balance, or measure, in everything; and this involves sincerity and soundness of heart. What is needed here, is the right balance between the Reality *(al-Haqiqa*) and the Law (*ash-shari`a*). Sidi Ahmad 'ibn `Ajiba, may Allah be pleased with him, in his explanation to the words of Allah, Exalted is He, "Lead us on the Straight Path," said that it is the Path which brings together the Reality and the Law (*al-Haqiqa wa ash-shari`a*). Then, because it is an obligation to maintain the correct balance between them, the owner of this station must balance these two sides. Meaning, that he must give equal importance to what is Revealed and what is Hidden, and he must not put one above the other, or be unbalanced in this; for Allah commands us that there should be a balance between them, and therefore He orders the performing of good deeds, in order that the Reality *(al-Haqiqa*) should be witnessed in a knower's hidden face and the Law (*ash-shari`a)* should be heard from his tongue. Then, if you wish you can say that his Hidden is the witnessing and his Revealed is making the *jihad* (the battle or struggle). Or, if you wish you can say, "His Hidden is freedom and his Revealed is bondsmanship," but not the opposite. He, may peace and blessings be upon him, said, "O Allah! cover me, but do not make me obscured."

If the person, when praying, does not keep the balance in himself in his prayer, but allows one part of him to rise above the others, then it becomes as 'Ibn al-Qasim said, "If he does not balance his parts, and in rectitude and sincerity ask Allah's forgiveness for his shortcomings then He, the Exalted the Supreme, says to him, "Go straight as I have commanded you." And only the *owner* of this station, may peace and blessings be upon him, can complete this.

The fourteenth obligation is to have a state of peace, or tranquillity, which comes from the heart which is silent under the backwards and forwards flowing of Divine Destiny. This is the effortless, untroubled silence about which it is said:

"With what You want in Your passion, test me,
For I choose that in which You are pleased."

To some of them it was said, "What do you choose?" And the answer came, "I choose not to choose," and this is a noble *state* which does not come as a result of yearning, nor through ability; but He favors with His Mercy whom He wishes; and Allah is the One of Blessings and Might.

The fifteenth obligation is to follow the *'imam* into *the station of holiness*, which is that of the entry into the Presence of Allah. When the *murid* has been granted to enter this station he must follow the Shaykh in the greeting, which is the return to the Creation in the *baqa'* (subsistence) and to hold onto the Muhammadan Law (*shari`a al-muhammadiyyah*). But if he does not follow the Shaykh so that he can *cast* him into the Presence of the Truth, and if he does not return with him to the Muhammadan presence, so that he can help him, then his prayer is of no value. This case, of which we now speak, is that of he who is aware and conscious of himself and his actions. But for he who is not aware that he is not obeying his Master and following him, either into the station of *ihram* (sacredness) when he pronounces the *takbir* (Allahu Akbar!) at the beginning of the prayer, or when he gives the greeting of *as-salam `alaykum* at the end of it, then his prayer is not worthless. This is how it is, except for the case where the murid has done something forbidden, because Truth, Mighty and Supreme is He, is not pleased with anyone who desires to approach Him in a forbidden manner.

As for the People of Allah, there is nothing in this station which is forbidden for them, except anything that leads to a state of separation, as it is said:

"Nothing is forbidden for us except a glance
That brings about for us a veil."

For it is said that the reason for chastisement lies in the existence of the veil, and that complete happiness is to gaze upon the Face of Allah, the Generous One.

The sixteenth obligation is the intention of the *murid* to follow the example of his *'imam* because he is the Master, who in all the affairs of the Religion and of the material world *(ad-dunya)*, guides to Allah; and the obligation is that the *murid* should not oppose his Shaykh, whether in his heart or with his tongue, nor should he neglect him, nor pay only slight attention to his orders. The intention of the *murid* should be to move with him wherever he moves, and to follow him wherever he goes, and he must not, in the slightest degree, be tired nor dissatisfied with him, for the *'imam* is the mediator for his followers, as the Prophet, may peace and blessings be upon him, said, "Your *'imams* are your mediators." Therefore is it right for the follower to be in contradiction with his leader? How can he know the *how* (*kayfa*) of the Way of Allah if he does not know Allah? The *murid* is the follower, in order that he may be guided; therefore is it right for the follower to turn away from the Guide? If that is the case then no doubt he will be destroyed, without his being aware. No, for he must be like the body of the dead person in the hands of those who wash it. Briefly, there are numerous conditions laid down for the followers of a Shaykh, but the intention lies with the *murid,* and with Allah lies the lifting of the veils.

Then know, that it is necessary for the *'imam,* who guides to Allah, to make the intention of guidance. Meaning, that he makes the intention that he will guide all those searching for Allah, and that, in the case where he does not have any followers, the favor *(fadl)* of bringing together *(jama`)* will come to him, and he will be one of those who make the *du`a* (supplication) to Allah on the Day of Judgment *(yawm id-din*). But this is on condition that he has been granted, from Allah and His Prophet, the permission for this. He is then known as *'imam ar-ratib* (the appointed leader) for a mosque, and he is the only one who is officially permitted to lead the prayer in the Mosque; and if he does not find anyone to follow him in turning his face to Allah, Mighty and Supreme is He, then it is his obligation to make the intention of guidance, so that the blessing of the group may descend upon him. And with Allah rests the perfection. However, if he is alone or solitary, it is not necessary for him to make this intention. It is not required, nor is it acceptable, for the *'imam* who is in the station of *the ultimate of the absolute*, and who is guiding to Allah, to make the intention in a state of awe and fear, or because he has been chosen as the appointed Inheritor (*Khalifa*). The weightiest matter for him, in his remembrance of Allah *(ad-dhikr*), is his obligation to announce to his followers the impending awesome revelations, which tighten and restrict the breast, since on the Day of Resurrection he will have to stand in front of Allah, Mighty and Supreme is He, and see himself as the *'imam* with all his followers behind him. He, Mighty and Supreme is He, said, "A day when We call every people with their *'imam*, and he contemplates his ignorance beside Allah," and in that, as He, Mighty and Supreme is He, says, "Either We, or you, are upon the right guidance, or We are in manifest error." (34:24).

Then know, as has been mentioned, that there are four qualifications for reaching to Allah, Mighty and Supreme is He. The first one is a recognition and acceptance of the *qibla* (the direction of prayer), the meaning and the intention of this being that the traveler should turn his heart towards the Presence of Allah, Mighty and Supreme is He, for this is necessary in the beginning of the Way, and ever afterwards. Whoever wants to *reach* must turn to face the Ka`ba, which is the symbol for the existence of Allah, and His Might. But the traveler can only turn to the Eye of the Ka`ba if he is in close proximity to it. For example, this will be if he is in the station of the *eye* of certainty *(`ayn al-yaqin)* and the truth of certainty (*haqq al-yaqin*). However, if he is only in the station of the *knowledge* of certainty (*`ilm al-yaqin*), it will not be possible for him to reach the Eye of the *qibla*, because of the veil which marks the distance of his separation from Allah. In that case he must turn to Allah making the *jihad* (the battle and struggle) until he reaches the point where were he to stray slightly from Allah, no judgment would come upon him, because a slight deviation and straying does not harm the person who is still veiled. An example of this harmless deviation is what comes to someone, who is fighting on the Path of Allah, Mighty and Supreme is He, and whose struggle is justified because, through it, he is striving to *reach*. His struggle, then, becomes the means of his *reaching*, and it is from his truthfulness that his return to Allah is truly a return to Allah, and not to anything else; and this is the only goal that brings no harm upon the beginners. Therefore it is referred to as *a slight deviation*, because it originates from the person who is still veiled from the complete knowledge of Allah. But if the deviation originates from a person who is in proximity to the Essence, as symbolized by the Ka`ba, for example: the person who is in the station of the truth of certainty *(haqq al-yaqin*), then it is called *flight* from the Eye of the Ka`ba. So, if I say that an action is a deviation from Allah when in truth, its aim is to reach to Allah, what about the aim of an action which is to have a reward? I say, "This is something unimaginable," in the search for Allah, and on His Path, for the person in that station cannot be counted as being of those who are traveling to Allah, because he would be on a Path which is not Allah's. But he is of those of the Way of the Garden, for his goal is the Garden, and not the Lord of Paradise.

He, may the peace and blessings of Allah be upon him, said, "He whose migration was for Allah and His Messenger, his migration was for Allah and His Messenger, and he whose migration was to achieve some worldly benefit or to take some woman in marriage, his migration was for that for which he migrated."

Know then, that this *qibla*, in which a deviation may occur, surely comes about because a traveler raises his glance to what is not Allah. But this is not possible for those who keep their eyes on their goal and who reach and come to witness Allah, to turn to something which is not His *qibla*, for it surrounds them and they are drowned in it, so that even if one of them intended to flee from it, it would not be possible for him to do so. How then would it be possible for someone, who is inside the *qibla*, to turn to anything else but it? Even if a traveler, through his prayer, only sees the material Ka`ba it would not be possible for him to turn to anything else. How then, is it for he who is in the station of seeing the hidden Ka`ba, which is a metaphor for the holy Presence? Some of them said, "If I intended to see anything which was not Allah I could not do so. The Sultan of poets, 'Ibn al-Farid, said:

"They are planted in my eyes manifestly, wherever I travel,
And they are hidden in my heart wherever they adorn and grace."

In these lines the word *they* refers to Allah, the Mighty, the Supreme.

Briefly, if the person who drowns in the truths of the Presence is not hindered, in any way, by his *nafs* it is as though he emerges from the Presence and says, "I am its Eye."

The second qualification for the prayer for reaching to the Presence of Allah is the destruction and elimination of all faults, and this is a condition which is required both at the beginning of the prayer and continuously afterwards. He who prays and turns to Allah, must be clean and purified before the Mighty, the Exalted One, both in his garments and in his body. What is meant here by faults is the existence of all contradictions, from wherever they may come. The purity of the *place* of the prayer is a metaphor for what is revealed, and the purity of the *garments* is a metaphor for the heart and what is hidden, and the purity of the body represents the Secret and what is hidden of the Hidden. What is revealed is purified by the Law (*ash-shari`a*) through obedience to the Order of Allah, and the avoidance of all that is forbidden. The Hidden, which is the heart, is only purified by clothing it with the Path, and by relinquishing the influences of the *nafs;* for example, envy, hatred, arrogance, hypocrisy, vanity and every blameworthy characteristic which is not compatible with purity. The purity of the Secret lies in the existence which is free from everything that is not Allah, the Truth, Mighty and Exalted is He. For this, He, Exalted is He, says, "And your garments purify." If such a purification is required for the garments, which represent the heart, how then would it be for the purification of the heart of the heart, which is the House of the Lord? Whoever is in this station must stand guard at the door of his heart so that the power of the perfect Unity can always return him from everything that may come from what is not Allah.

In all cases he who seeks to enter to, and to meet with his Lord, the Mighty and the Supreme, must be pure in his *self,* and he must not at any time, think of turning away from the *qibla* of his prayer, nor from the two conditions which, in the beginning and always afterwards, are necessary for it. In other words, he must not turn his face to the Master and then turn away from him, nor in the beginning purify himself then sully himself again. But he must stand firmly on the roadway of his heart always turning to his Lord, and being aware of the impurity of the world, and all its vanities. And it is important that if anything of the afflictions of the world should befall him, that he should purify himself immediately from them, because Allah, Exalted is He, has said, "Surely Allah loves those who repent, and He loves those who purify themselves." (2:222).

The third qualification, for those who seek for the right conduct in the prayer, is the veiling of everything that it is necessary to veil from the imperfections of the world; and this is the concealing of all matters of the Path that have to be hidden. The person, who wants to enter to Allah, must veil from all outward eyes whatever of the Secret has been manifested to him. And this is necessary in order that the Secret of Allah may be magnified, which it cannot be if it is not concealed from all those who are not His People. It is said, "Gratitude for the Secret is shown in its being protected from all those who are not from Allah." If a person does not protect the Secret it will expose him amongst the people, for every person who speaks about what should have been concealed only reveals his own imperfections, as it is said, "Whoever speaks about the Secret of Allah, Allah makes to speak about the defects of his *self,* and he is cut off from his *time*, because he has not respected his promise which was given, and witnessed in the special Presence of Allah, into which it is not possible for a stranger to enter." Therefore, whoever is careless about the Secret of Allah will, no doubt, be thrown out from His Eye, because he did not safeguard the Secret, but he only bore out his betrayal of it, and therefore he severed his bond with Allah, and he returns himself to be as nothing: "And your Lord is not the oppressor of His slaves." It is necessary for the *murid* to veil everything that is of *the right-hand side* from the minds of the Creation. And his reward for this is that Allah will return him to Him; for if he safeguards the Secret then his own imperfections will not be revealed, but if it is revealed then his imperfections will also be uncovered.

Know then, that this condition of being able to protect the Secret only comes about through the extent of the *murid's* remembrance and his magnification of Allah. However, in this station, the prayer of the person who is overwhelmed by the revelation so that he loses his ability to keep the Secret, is not worthless, and his Path is not cut off, but he is excused of his lapse; which is the case of the *majdhub*. For, in this case, the intellect and mind, with which the witnesser distinguishes, separates and classifies the ranks of the Creation, has been taken from him in his annihilation, so that the Order for protection of the Secret does not apply to him, because Allah does not *ask* the person, who has lost his mind about his actions. From this example it can be seen that every fulfilling of the Order depends upon the *state* of a person's intellect, and is there not beauty in he who has lost his intellect? Some of them said:

"Do not interfere with the state of he who is drunk
For the command is lifted from us in our drunkenness."

And therefore it is not a qualification for the proof of his truthfulness that whoever is overpowered by the revelations of Allah, and who has lost his awareness, must in all cases conceal the Secret. And this, together with the remembering, the potentiality and the ability, applies to all the conditions laid down for right conduct for the prayer, as has already been mentioned. An exception to this is the last qualification, which is the fourth one, and which concerns the cleansing from all ritual impurity. This condition is for those whose prayer is not with the remembrance and the magnification of Allah, because they are beginners on the Path. However, this condition, which applies particularly for the beginner, is also applicable for the *muridun* throughout the Path.

What it requires is that the *murid* should engage himself in the battle with any shortcomings that are ritual impurities (everything that is not for Allah), because he who desires to enter the Door of Allah, must destroy the veil of ritual impurity which prevents him from entering the House of his Lord.

Earlier in this discourse we have mentioned the means by which these ritual impurities can be removed, together with any weakness and forgetfulness on the part of the murid, so that he knows that the destruction of such veils depends upon his remembrance and upon his magnification of Allah, which, in turn, come from his general capacity and capability. However, the person who enters to the Presence of the Eternal One in purity, and who is free of the doubts coming from his humanity (*nasut*), but who nevertheless afterwards experiences something in his witnessing which reveals new shortcomings in him (new desires), must then renew his purification if these shortcomings gain the mastery over him; and he must not belittle these obstacles which hinder him from being able to stand in front of Allah, the Mighty the Supreme, Who does not accept any action which makes a partner with Himself. How then, will it be for a heart which makes a partner with Him? No, this is not possible, for it is not conceivable for shortcomings to exist together with the Eternal One, as 'Ibn `Ata'illah, the Master of *The Hikam* has said, "How can a heart, in whose mirror are imprinted the images of existences, ascend?"

Know my beloved, that there are four worlds: the World of the Creation (*an-nasut*), the World of Allah (*al-lahut*), the World of the Spirits and of the jinn (*al-jabarut*), and the World of Fear of Allah (*al-rahbut*), for it is the World of the Mighty Fear of the Truth, Exalted and Supreme is He.

And know also, that it is not possible to unite opposites such as, for example, trying to unite movement and stillness, or the darkness of existences with the lights of knowledge.

O you who claim to have knowledge, where is your witnessing and your seeing when you are still with existences? O you who claim to have the deep knowledge of the World of Allah, from where then in yourself, have you discovered still further shortcomings? How many times have you purified yourself only to return again to your shortcomings? How many times have you sworn, by Allah, and then have broken your oath? When you have made the Promise with Allah not to see anything but Him, how then is it that you have found new shortcomings? O you who claim to know the World of Fear (*alam ar-rahbut*), do you not listen to He who said, "How can Eternity be revealed by existence, or how can shortcomings persist in he who carries the attribute of the Eternal?" Briefly, the Presence of Allah, Mighty and Supreme is He, is above everything which is not Himself, and everyone who, in this station, circumambulates Him, must be attentive to the remembrance of His Name, and to his purification of himself; for He, the Exalted One, said, "The god-fearing, when a visitation of Satan troubles them, remember, and then they see clearly." (7:201). For every time that a shortcoming manifests to the murid it removes him from the Presence of Allah; and there is, in this, no difference between the shortcoming which is intentional, and that which is not.

Al-'Adhan The Call To Prayer

For a Sufi, the meaning of the call to prayer is: "You are what is decreed." Meaning that you have looked for, and have found, one of the *unrivaled ones* of the time, and this is the Perfect One of his age, and he is the owner of his time; and he is of those who have been chosen to announce the prayer for all those who, in their truths, are seeking for it, before its time has ended. For he, who observes the prayer in its *time*, which is short, is the best of the world and all that is in it. And our words *the Perfect One* exclude all that is not in keeping with the rank of perfection. He is the example of blessedness of the people of blessedness and good deeds. But as for the people who only perform supererogatory prayers and supererogatory actions, there is no necessity for them to have a call to prayer *(adhan)*. In the Truth of Allah there is no call to prayer except from the one of this station who is the Perfect One of the time. This means that he is living in this world, and not in the Hereafter. A sign of the fact that he is the Perfect One is that it is he who possesses the highest knowledge of all those who derive their source from him. This also means that he is absorbed into the rank of Uniqueness, and that his answering to his Lord is that of the obligation of the Perfect One who brings down the complete knowledge. And which knowledge is the greatest? Who is in proximity to the Promise with Allah; and with whom is belief renewed? It is only renewed through meeting with the People of Allah - the beloved People, about whom it is said, "Your faith is renewed through meeting with the beloveds." These beloveds are not the people whom you love with your self (*nafs*), and your ordinary nature, or because of the good things which they do for you; for the people whom you love in that way are not those who feed you, nor do they renew your faith when you meet with them, for they only speak to your *self*; and the *self* is fashioned to love only those who are good to it, even if they are unbelievers. But the beloveds, who when you meet with them renew your faith, are the beloveds of the Prophet about whom he, may peace and blessings be upon him, said, "Send greetings upon my beloveds." And he, may peace be upon him, said, "You, who are my Beloveds, are my Companions."

So strive to know one of His beloveds, and endear yourself to him until he loves you; and when he loves you, then know that it is Allah Who loves you, and Who has chosen you for Himself.

In short, the Perfect One of the time is rare; but whoever meets him meets all things, because for the knowers, the noblest station is that of perfection, since he, may peace and blessings be upon him, said, "For Allah is the Unique, and He loves what is Unique." He, may peace be upon him, also said, "Follow those Perfect Ones who went before you." When they asked him, "Who are the Perfect Ones, O Prophet of Allah?" he answered, "They are those who always have regard for whatever of the world is Hidden, just as the people have regard for whatever of it is Revealed."

Yes, they look at what of the world is Hidden so far as the Secrets, the knowing, and the lights, are concerned, because they look upon it with the Eye of the Truth, and they are annihilated before it, finding it like a mirage and seeing it just as the thirsty person sees a mirage and thinks that it is water, but when he reaches it he finds nothing there except Allah alone, Who is with him. Then, when in this way he finds Allah, he comes to rest with Him, having reached Him, and having left the material world (*ad-dunya),* and the Hereafter (*al-akhira*) behind him; for he leaves everything for Him, and he does not return wholly to the Creation, because although his outward form returns to it, his Spirit remains with Allah.

Know then, that the call to prayer also demands of the knower, if he enters a waterless desert (meaning any place which is parched and thirsty because its *earth* is empty of the knowledge of the existence of the Secrets), if he does not find there anyone in this station of knowledge, he should speak about what he has. But if he does find there such a person with the knowledge, to which we refer, he does not himself need to speak. He, may the peace and blessings of Allah be upon him, said in praising such people, "Through them the rain comes to the Creation, and through them it is nourished." As it is said:

"Through you every earth is revived where you set foot,
As if you were rains upon the earth.
For the eye desires in you a beautiful picture,
As if you were in the eyes of the people, flowers;
And your lights guide the traveler to see,
As if you were moons in the darkness of the night."

The Prayer When Traveling

Traveling is of two kinds, both the traveling in the body, and the spiritual journey; or it can be said from body to body, or from the material to the material, or the journey of meaning to meaning. Just as the object of speech is to convey meanings through words, yet it is not the words themselves which are the vehicle which convey meaning, likewise the material world is an outer illusion and an image of which the true meaning only begins to emerge when the traveler sees, by means of his imagination, what exists in the Essence of his image. The journey of the People of Allah is from existence to He Who creates existence, whereas the journey of the people of the material world is from existence to existence.

You may ask then, if it is permitted for he whose goal is the Creation, to shorten the prayer, how can it not be permitted for he whose goal is the Truth? No, for if he is asking for a shortening of his obligations, he is, in his Truth, asking for the cutting short of the steps of his Way: for example, the remembrance, the reflection and the contemplation, and similar practices, which are like the *buraq* which carry him to the object of his desire, leaving behind everything which is not it. Since the

Shaykh and Master is the doctor, who knows how to heal his community, his journey with him is swift, and almost instantaneous, so that he does not perform either too many, or too few, supererogatory actions. In addition to that, and while on his way, the traveler should not pay attention to anything except the object of his desire, which is to *reach* to his Beloved. And how could he work, or walk, without Him, for everything that is not the Beloved, regarding what is still hidden within him, is a veil over the Beloved, just as worship is a veil for He Who is worshiped, and the remembrance is a veil for He Who is remembered, and the Name is a veil for He Who is the One who is named.

Know then, that in the case of the murid who is traveling to Allah, everything that is not Allah Himself is a veil for Him. Therefore, it is necessary for the traveler to dispense with all the generally, acknowledged and accepted actions, which nevertheless have not been ordered for him to perform, so that he should not turn to face anything which is not He; nor should he see anything but He in any thing; nor should he stop with anyone who is not He, until he comes, through Him, to be He. Then, with respect to his Beloved, both darkness and happiness are the same for him, as it is said:

"In her love I bought happiness with difficulty and pain,
Being astray, because my mind was not with my beloved."

Briefly, in his walking the murid does not stop with the intellect, nor with the traveling in itself, but he leaves aside these things that should be left aside.

A long-distance journey, in Islam, is represented as being a distance of at least four *abruda* (*barid*), or stopping-places, each *barid* being approximately eighty-five kilometers. In the deep meaning a *barid* is a metaphor for the four ranks of existence; namely: *al-mulk*, *al-malakut, al-jabarut* and *al-rahbut*, and in this last station the murid makes *fana'* even from the Names, Qualities, and Attributes (*nu`ut*). This is the meaning of their words: "The murid makes fana' from his Lord in the same way as he makes fana' from himself, so that there is no Lord (*rabb*) and no slave (*`abd*), but only Allah, which state is referred to as blindness or obliteration." In every case this is the highest goal of the traveler, and it is the journey for which a shortening of the prayer is both desired and permitted; but the condition is that, from the outset, the traveler should aim for his journey to be swift and sure, so that he will then reach its goal, in the same manner in which he has traveled its Path. But when a person travels from the World of al-Mulk, then to the World of al-Malakut, then to the World of al-Jabarut, he travels step by step, and if he does not intend to complete his journey in one time, it is not necessary for him to request a shortening of his prayers, because he will not be over-tired from his traveling. He who is tired from his journey is the first one upon whom hardship befalls because he has cut himself off from the resting-places, and therefore he will encounter difficulties and deprivations until he comes to a state of the most complete exhaustion. About this he, may peace and blessings be upon him, said, "The journey is part of the punishment, and especially the journey in which the complete destruction of the *self* (*nafs*) does not take place."

On the other hand, he who is in the station of the true traveler is required to cut short and to ease his journey; this cutting short beginning after the destruction of his humanity, his idols, and his bondage and imprisonment by the desires of his *nafs*; but not before. While he is still in that state of bondage he should not cut short his prayer, because the stages of his journey have not been sufficiently long nor arduous for this to be necessary. But in his case he should strive with many supererogatory actions, and he must carry all hardships, and everything that he finds to be a burden upon himself, and against which he must stand firm. And he must be diligent in seeking out everything that will set him free from his *nafs*, until he rids himself of them completely, and his walking brings him success. Meaning, when he has abandoned the frivolity of his *nafs*, so that freedom from it becomes his true dwelling-place. Then, from this point, begins the cutting short of the prayer, and not before it. This is the outside meaning of the condition under which it is permitted to shorten the prayer, but the inner meaning of this is that while, in the beginning the person praying is traveling in his Spirit, his prayer is shortened until he is returned to *the station of descent* after his traveling and witnessing, and he returns to his physical dwelling-place, which is his body.

The condition for shortening of the prayer also states that when a person on a journey has remained in any one place for more than fourteen days, he is required to pray the full prayer. This is with regard to the outside ritual prayer, but the inside meaning of this is the example of the traveler on the Path of Allah who remains for a period moving around in one particular station, either because he is fatigued from the walking, or because he is seeking refuge from traveling on the Path, and he is far away from the presence of his Shaykh and thinks that he (his Shaykh) does not see him, or does not know of his case in his journeying. But, in truth, the Spirit of his Shaykh sees him and embraces him, for the spirits move freely although the bodies are fettered, as Allah, the Praised and Exalted, has said, "And thou shalt see the mountains that thou supposeth firm, passing by like clouds." (27:88). Therefore, the murid who remains in this case, is in truth, in his rightful dwelling-place and therefore he is required to perform the complete prayer, because the obligations of he who desires to know can never be forgotten, and in truth his only real resting-place is in Allah.

But whoever hears the call to prayer while still traveling should perform it, because so long as he is called to perform the prayer he has not been granted the right to do as he pleases, since he lives constantly between the fear of the Way and the hope in Allah; for although his Spirit moves freely his body is still fettered. Then he who remains in this case is always in his true dwelling-place wherever he finds himself, and therefore he is required to perform the complete prayer.

The Declaration that the Truth is Above Everything Else

Know then, that when a murid becomes completely obedient, and when the sun of knowledge enters him filling his heart with the lights of subtlety, he should then become this light and shine it upon any vessel that is revealed to him as a container of the light, as someone has said:

"He who has wine has containers for His wine
No-one tastes it who is ignorant,

Only the one who knows the meaning,
And who reaches in the love."

Know, that when the murid pronounces the Glorification *(tasbih)* when bowing down and prostrating, and he declares that the Truth is above every other thing, this means that he declares that the Truth, Mighty and Supreme is He, is beyond anything which is not befitting to Him. The manifestation of this special Quality, which is the noblest of them all, only takes place in the *ruku* and the *sujud*; which means in the *fana'* in the Qualities and the Essence, as was mentioned earlier. In making the *ruku`* the murid declares that the Truth is above all qualities of contingency, and in making the *sujud* he declares that the Essence is above the essences of created things, and beyond their descriptions and sides. If, in making the bowing down (*ruku`*), he only declares with his tongue that the Truth is beyond anything, yet duality and comparisons still exist in his heart, this means that he has not yet abandoned his individual characteristics, returning them to the Qualities of his Creator. As for the prostration (*sujud*) how can he declare the Truth of the Essence to be beyond everything when he still sees, and is manifesting, his own individual existence, because his testifying to this only veils him, and leads him away from the Essence of his Creator? Only when he bows down, prostrates and makes the *fana'* from all created things, does his Reality then reach to declaring the Essence to be beyond all things. No one can know his own Reality unless he is in that state of prostration, for his Reality will only be revealed to him when he loses his material existence, as the words of the Exalted One proclaim: "Everything perishes except His Face;" and that is His existence, so that if a person is separated from this existence he will continue in that state until he comes to see, through his existence, another existence for which there is neither individual existence, nor any manner of material non-existence. So far as non-existence is concerned, it remains separated from the Essence, which is a shining light, and a clear truth in which we cannot see any possible existence for, nor any acceptance of created things, as Allah, the Praised and Exalted One, says, "Allah is the light of the heavens and the earth." So far as His majesty (*jalal*) is concerned, there is in it no picture nor fantasies; and as far as His beauty (*jamal*) is concerned, listen to, and understand the words of one who said:

"Every jamal is the jalal of Allah.
There is no doubt about that.

Is it not a sign of denial
That doubt was victorious over them?

The Essence is the Eye of the Qualities,
And there is no doubt in its meaning."

This means that when, with respect to His majesty *(jalal)*, the knower sees how he stands in the Eyes of Allah, then he is careful with respect to His beauty *(jamal)*. In both stations he does not find anything except Allah, and then when he prays he puts his hands at his sides, as he stands before Allah; which means that he does not turn either to the right or to the left, and himself he does not see anything that either benefits him or that keeps harm away from him. However, if he does see anything besides Allah which helps him, then he is not a real *faqir* for Allah, nor can he have the good fortune of knowing His Grace. "The freewill offerings are for the poor." So the murid must say, as regards help or harm, "I am not my own Master, but I have what Allah wants for me." Then he remains in this state with his hands by his sides; and this means that he does not rely upon anyone except Allah, and he does not see for himself, that he can turn for help to anyone, but to Allah. But whenever something comes to him from Allah, and he thinks that this is from himself and what he has earned, and he acts accordingly, this is like the person who aggresses against the order of the World of the Kingdom (*al-mulk*). Therefore the murid is asked to remain in the state of relying and depending only on Allah, until the Truth comes to him, and it becomes, "His hand with which he strikes, and His foot with which he walks." Then he strikes with His hand, and he attracts blessings to himself, and he wards off harm from himself, so that there is nothing now which can deter him, because his hand has become the Hand of Allah. If something advantageous comes to him he knows that, in truth, it is Allah, and no one else, Who brings this to him. It is the Mighty One Who speaks in the words of those who declare: "With Me strike!" Then, when the knower strikes, it is Allah who strikes, for the Truth, Mighty and Supreme is He, has no partner in His actions, as some of them have said:

"If I say kun, it is.
My order is the order of al-wahid, the maker of Oneness.

My tongue is My Eye,
And My Eye is My hand, which is unique.

My hearing is in my heart,
And it manifests.

There is no power for me, and no strength
Except in Him, the all-sufficient One."

When the knower comes to realize this station, and that there is no doer in existence except Allah, then he must not be in ignorance about what He has done, so that each time that he comes to know Him as the One Who strikes, he also has to know Him as the One Who is struck. And at the outset of every action, he has to be aware that it is Allah, the Mighty, the Exalted One, Who is acting. Then he praises the Truth, Mighty and Supreme is He, for he sees that only His Power and His Might exist in every action. This means that in every action, either of eating or drinking, he must be aware of Allah in what He (Allah) wants, and not what he himself wants. He, the All-Mighty, said, "Eat Me O My slave, in the food, and drink Me in the drink, and clothe Me in the garments, and ride Me on what you ride," and so forth until the end of this *hadith al-qudsi*. The knower is required to witness the authority (*sultan*) of the Reality in all the Creation, both in the *doing* and in what is *done*, in the known and in what is not known; and everything else that has a similar meaning.

"Allah, the sun has not risen and has not set
When I did not remember You with every breath.

I did not sit with the people talking to them.
While I was talking with You and sitting with my companions."

As it has been said before, the He-ness of the Truth exists in the Essence, which is hidden from the Creation, and therefore cannot be witnessed in created beings. The word *huwa* comes from the pronoun he (*huwa*), which is also used to mean the person who is absent, or hidden, and for the knower there is no state of being separated from the Essence except when it becomes hidden after he stands up from his *fana',* and having been drowned in the center of the He-ness, he returns to the witnessing, and to *be* in it. In this manner it is necessary for the knower to gather together, and to unite in the prayer, the three states of standing, bowing down, and prostration; for this is the bond and the connection from which he must never become separated. The outer meaning of this bond is in *islam*, *'iman,* and *'ihsan*, and the inner meaning is in surrender, certainty and eye-witnessing. In every case of action it is necessary for the knower, as has already been mentioned, to return to his first state of knowing that Allah alone is the *doer* of any action, and not he himself. He must leave all the outside manifestations of the Creation and its people, so as to be able to *eat* and *digest* the meaning of these three states, and at all times to live and act from their mid-point, in order to keep the balance (*al-mizan*) between them. If the knower does not have this balanced state to help him when he witnesses the lights of the beauty which constantly come to him, then the Master of witnessing may overwhelm the person who is absorbed with the *jihad* until it appears to him to be impossible to unite these contradictory opposites. If this is the case the traveler must walk in the Way of the witnessing of the Truth, and abandon whatever is not of it; and he must return to his Path, safeguarding it, and remaining in its center, so that he is able to protect, with the firmest preservation, the bond between the bowing, the prostrating and the standing; and this is the mid-point of the prayer, for which the metaphor is the middle prayer about which Allah, the Mighty the Supreme, has said, "Maintain and observe the prayers, and the middle prayer." (2:238). The owner of this station is required to join these three right-hand states, and if he cannot do so he should take whatever is of the witnessing and leave aside whatever is not of it. By this we mean that he should walk the Path of the *tasting* and witnessing of Allah and leave everything that is not of it, regarding which it is said:

"In my heart were varying desires,
But since my eyes have seen You I have united them,

And I have left the people to their religion and their world,
Being busy with You, O my religion and my world.

Those whom I envied in the past began to envy me
For since You became my Master I have become the Master of existence."

Know then that he who knows this station possesses the noblest of them, for whoever has witnessed the *dwelling-places* is not content with the rubbish dumps. Meaning that he is not content to be in the witnessing of what is not Allah. But in all cases it is required of him to be mindful of the Creation just as it was asked of him, in the first place, to be mindful of the Creator. The meaning of this can only be seen from the fact that the pronoun *ha* is used both for the Creator and for the Creation, so that, on the one hand, the word has the meaning of *gather-*

ing together, and on the other hand, it has the meaning of *separation*; and in both cases the knower should, if possible, be the mediator between them. But if this is not possible for him, he should then take what he can from the witnessing, and leave everything else.

There are many things that veil a person from Allah, and whoever is halted by them, stops with what is not Allah. We will mention two of these because they are the most important. The first one is that the murid, who has reached the stature of *manhood*, must shun his inner desires by withdrawing from them, and not carrying his yearning (*himma*) in his stomach, otherwise he will become weak with his Lord. Therefore his words, may peace be upon him, "The standing with Allah of he whose yearning *(himma*) comes from his stomach will be from where he sets out." And this is especially the case of he who is traveling to Allah, for how can someone reach his Lord if his *himma* comes from his stomach? No, and Allah asks him to abandon his stomach because His People are, of necessity, aware of its evils, and therefore the murid is advised to avoid them.

Likewise the murid is advised to abandon all his former companions. Meaning that if he desires to follow the Path of Allah, he must leave everything else, and everyone else except for Allah. He must, as far as possible, avoid his former friends and companions, and this is specially the case in relation to his *fana'* which he demonstrates by his prostration (*sujud*). In that (his prostration) he must be annihilated from his *self*, so that how can he, then, have any relationship with fellow human beings? No, he must avoid them because separating oneself from the Creation is a condition for entering into the Truth, until the murid has left his fellow human beings behind him. Then, in Allah's Grace, the Truth, Mighty and Supreme is He, opens a door for him because He, Praised and Exalted is He, has said, "When he left them and what they were worshipping beside Allah," referring, by these words, to Ibrahim, may peace and blessings be upon him, who, when he turned away from his family and left his friends behind, Allah, Praised and Exalted is He, then granted the gift of his sons Isma'il and Ishaq, and after them, all the prophets whom came from them.

Therefore the knowers of Allah have to be diligent about leaving their former friends because keeping company with them is a deadly poison, as it is said, "To mix with the ordinary people is like a poison." The murid cannot walk if he depends upon them, and listens to their advice and to what they say, for if he does this he will be returned, unawares, to where he came from; and this happens to many travelers. We do not see anything, in the beginning, more distasteful than keeping company with former bad companions who are the *qarin*, or devilish friends. How can a person be a friend of someone with whom he does not agree? If he is a friend of such a person, and if he does not bid good-bye to him, there is no doubt but that he will be cut off from the Path of Allah. Meaning that he must leave behind every relationship, that he had before, with ordinary people.

Briefly, when the murid enters the Path he will enter it as a stranger from the people, in as much as he does not ask for a Beloved except for He whom he loves. And if, in his search, he turns away from the people they will not accept him for this, and his close relatives, and his tribe, will not have anything to do with him. But if he does not refuse to have anything to do with them, you will see that he will become more unpleasant than he to whom Allah, Exalted is He, referred to with His words, "To whom We grant long life We bend (distort) him in the Creation; will you not understand?" As it is said:

"I did not want to enter to Him
Until I had humbled the place of the slave ,

And I had cast down my eyelids upon its partners;
And the nafs was silent about why? or what?

And the slave had humbled himself to his Master
And he became rich.

And, how rich he is,
For his intention is for the long Journey."

It is said, "Whoever does not become a stranger to the Creation will not become intimate with the Truth." So leave all others, except the highest Friend, to be with Him, and to observe and follow his politeness in all that is revealed, and in all that is hidden, for whenever, in your hidden being, you are not polite with Him, you will be chastised for it in your hidden, and whenever, in your revealed being you are not polite with Him, you will be chastised in whatever of you is revealed, since your revealed and outer politeness is in respect to His Name, the Revealed, and your inner politeness is in respect to His Name, the Hidden.

The sitting position in the ritual prayer, as has been mentioned, is the expression for the worshipper's leaving the praying to return to the Creation, at which time he is careful about what is required of him in this station and his politeness in the sitting position will result from his uninterrupted remembrance. If it is not thus, then the person praying has not understood the meaning of the sitting position; and likewise it is for all his standings still, and all his ritual movements.

Thus he is required to observe politeness at all times, but the station of the sitting is more demanding for the murid than that of the bowing down *(ruku`)* or the prostration (*sujud*) because his politeness in the prostration is a result of the Divine nature of the revelation of the Truth upon the slave since he makes his annihilation (*fana'*) from himself. But in the case of the politeness required in the station of the sitting, the slave is asked then to have the politeness which is due to the Truth, whilst, at the same time, he is looking upon the Creation.

Here therefore, I will mention to you some of the polite observances required in the station of the sitting, and I will say, "The body does not hide how the slave sits before He Whom he worships, so that if he does not empty himself of his own human politeness, he cannot reach the truth of the politeness which is due and proper before Allah." He, may peace and blessings be upon him, said, "I sit like the slave sits, and I eat like the slave eats." So he, may peace be upon him, himself realized, through his Reality, the One Whom he worshiped, so that there was no difficulty for him, the Prophet, may the peace and blessings of Allah be upon him, in this; but we will not enter into the details of this here. So far as anyone, except the Prophet is concerned, it is difficult for him to observe all the politeness, in the manner that he, may peace and blessings be upon him, would have done, let alone to realize it. And if the Truth did not look upon us with His Eye of Subtlety, in which there is no censure, we would perish altogether. Sari as-Saqati said, "One day, after the prayer, I sat in the *mihrab* to perform the *wird*, and being by myself, I stretched out my legs, when behold I heard someone call out to me, saying: 'What is this? Is this the sitting of the fuqara?' So, hearing that, I drew myself up in fear, and I swore, by my right-hand, that I would not stretch out my legs again, as long as I lived." Al-Junayd, may Allah be pleased with him, said about this, "And, by Allah, I did not see him stretch out his legs, until we stretched them out when we washed him." All of which results from a continual awareness of Allah, for so far as his witnessing is concerned this awareness, on the part of the slave, brings about his extinction when He Whom he worships is revealed to him. This politeness is then followed by that of the politeness in the station when the Qualities are revealed to him, and which is symbolized by the bowing-down, followed by the politeness in the station when the Essence is revealed, which is symbolized by the prostration. Similarly is the case of the station symbolized by the sitting, which is the return to the perceiving of the Creation.

Next we draw attention to what is required of the murid when, at the very beginning of the prayer, he desires to enter to Allah. It is necessary for him to raise his hands as he pronounces *Allahu Akbar,* for this is when he is standing with Allah; and what he needs now, by the raising of his hands, is to *reach* to Allah, and that he should not conceal his belonging to the Path, nor, once he has entered into it, should he be neglectful of it. He should raise his hands as an expression of his bearing witness to having turned his face to Allah, until he comes to know Him, both in the particular and in the universal sense; and thus to show that he is not ashamed of belonging to those of the Path of Allah, and that he is not cut off from his Lord. Then, in the beginning of his order, he should set out with everything of which he is capable, and therefore the Order for him is to announce this publicly by saying, "Allahu Akbar," as he enters into the *state* of holiness. This is his affirmation in words, and at the same time, he is ordered to raise his hands so that that action becomes the manifestation of his affirmation; and in this, both words and action are brought together.

Know then, that it is also expected of he, who seeks to reach that, in the beginning of his affair he should manifest that he belongs to the Path of Allah, and at the same time, he is required, until the very end of his Order, to conceal that to which he has reached. Therefore, the lights of revelation will appear upon he who establishes the prayer and who truly enters into its sanctuary, and he will, little by little, and step by step, be *rolled up* and concealed. The sign for the beginning of his rolling up is that after his hands have been raised to the level of his head, he then places them at his sides, and then folds them over his chest. This ritual action he makes to show that he desires to approach the Truth, so that each time that he draws nearer to Allah, the more he is rolled up in Him. Thus it is demanded of the worshipper to draw up his body and to raise his hands before the revelation of the Truth descends upon him. Then when the Union takes place, and he draws near to the Truth, his body, little by little, changes and his own existence fades away as he is rolled up, like a scroll, into the Truth.

All this now is because of his proximity to the Truth, and it continues for him until he reaches the utmost of nearness, which is in the state of prostration (*sujud*). Our Master, the Prophet, may peace and blessings be upon him, said, "The closest that the slave is to his Lord is when he prostrates." When the performer of the prayer prostrates he descends from material existence into the folds of non-existence. Every time that he prostrates and is folded up, so his existence is folded up in his folding up, for before the knower makes the prostration (*sajda*) he was standing up in his existence, but after his *sajda* he has become annihilated and non-existent. He is annihilated through himself, and he is raised up and becomes subsistent through his Lord. Those are the *men* who, in their conduct, are sincere with Allah, and it suffices them to reach to Him; and if they do not rise up their proximity is therefore unproved. But what confirms their sincerity and accelerates their ascent, in addition to their proclaiming of the Truth, is their following of a Shaykh, who is an *'imam* of the Path, until such time as you find one of them, may Allah be pleased with him, who follows his Shaykh, both in what he takes from him of his Secret which he keeps hidden, and openly in what he declares; and in whose heart there is no desire which is in contradiction with what his Shaykh desires of him. The evidence for that is in what, of the higher states of knowledge coming directly from Allah, falls upon the knowers; and all others, except such knowers, are referred to as *children,* for when they resist anything, does that not prevent their reaching to Allah?

Know then, that if, in his setting out, the murid desires anything except his Shaykh he will be turned back, and if after he has reached his goal, he desires anything except his Shaykh, then with regard to him, this is disobedience to his Lord; for if he who is sent back desires something which is not what the Truth, Mighty and Supreme is He, wishes from him, and he becomes like a person who has abandoned his Way, then what he desires comes to him because he has been neglectful of his witnessing.

However, for he who is in the rank of completion, moved between the *jamal* and the *jalal*, either of these states is the same for him because that is his rank. Then, since he is in this rank it is necessary for him to desire whatever Allah sends upon him, and not to ask for any other station *(maqam*). And this is while the sun of knowledge is still rising upon him, as it is said:

"If a desire, which is not You, comes to me,
The negligence is upon me and I ask to be sent back.

For Yours is the decree in my affair and for whatever You want use me.
For my desire is only for You, and for nothing but You."

This station comes from the desire of the knower to have the meaning of the Essence in material things, for as far as the human being is a copy of existence, existence is a copy of him.

When there are periods of time, hours of the day, and of night and day, of sunrise and the gilding of the earth, these are caused by the proximity of the sun to the earth, which proximity can be seen by what manifests from one to the other, or by their separation, as a sign of their distance from each other. In like manner the hours, and the times of the knower are marked out by the revelations of proximity, or of absence and of being sent back, or of finding or halting, or of losing. All these states result because of the rising of the sun of knowledge upon his heart, so that each time that he is in proximity to the rising Sun it is his morning-time, and when the manifestation becomes stronger, this is his noon-time. Then the lengthening of the *sura* for the midday prayer is required for the person in this station, for as in the analogy of the rising and shining of the sun in the morning and at noon, so his yearning *(himma*) is awakened, and then as the shining of the sun of knowledge falls upon him, and what his senses receive and is revealed to him through them, this quiets his *self* (*nafs)* because the morning only smiles when the day is near, and likewise the heart of the knower is illumined by the knowledge of the proximity of the Beloved. Every person, upon whom the lights have shone, knows that he is in proximity to entering the house, for no place is illuminated except when its inhabitants arrive. Then, which morning is dearer to the heart than the morning of the Beloved when He draws near, as it is said, with this meaning?

"The riders travel at night and You are with them.
On their way in the morning, shining from You.

The riders do what they want with themselves,
For they are the people of Badr who do not fear any difficulty."

This is the time for which a lengthening of the prayer is desirable, for there is nothing for the knowers, more longed for, more loved, more bewailed than this best of times. Meaning, when the sun of the Reality rises above the clouds of the Creation, and it is the time when the earth shines with the light of its Lord, the earth of the *selves (an-nufus)*, in the arrival of the Sun of the Presence of the holy One. It is the time when the part is united to its origin, and when whatever has been separated (*fasl*) is brought together again. This is the *time* and whatever is not of it, is odious *(maqt)*. And how could it be otherwise when the *breath of proximity* pervades everything, and the Beloved of the heart is at hand? Which soul would not be overjoyed, and which heart would not long for the protracting of this time? For, in the Unity, every long period is short, but in the separation, every short period is long. If the beloved longs to prolong the time of proximity with his Beloved, how could he then not desire to prolong it when He reveals Himself and the perfection of His Light? No, but rather he knows that even if it were from his own power that he was on the Path of obligation, the Truth would only manifest for him when the creation no longer existed for him.

Likewise his true noon-time is when the created *nafs* is annihilated; there being no doubt about its destruction. The Truth will not manifest to him, except when it can manifest from itself to itself in him; and the Truth is the One Who delights in seeing His appearance in His slave, through His Essence and His Qualities, and nothing else. Therefore, in this station, the knower is silent, especially about what he has realized of the singularity of Oneness. For if, when a person is with his *nafs* and he speaks in a loud voice and in a direct manner so that he does not need an interpreter in order to be understood, how then could he, who informs about the Oneness of Majesty, need an interpreter? So far as the Oneness of the Essence is concerned, it appears through created things, and he who makes it his goal is the Eye of what is aimed for, just as the Essence is the Eye of the existence in which all numbers vanish. In this station the knower realizes the Essence through the Essence, as they said:

"I did not cease to be Her, and She did not cease to be Me.
There is no separation, for My Essence loved My Essence.

There is nothing with Me, in this mulk, that equals Me.
And there is no companion nor companionship, only Allah.

This is My hand, which in my nafs I fear.
In the Truth there is no other only I, and for my good I ask Her."

If there is a difference in the lengths of times of the revelations in the prayer, this is because of the state of the heart of the knower with his Beloved. For example, in the desired length of time, already mentioned, between the dawn prayer (*al-fajr*), and the noontime one (*az-zuhr*), and also in the desired shortening between the afternoon (*al-'asr*), and the sunset (*al-maghrib*) prayers this is analogous with the distance of the sun from the earth at these times. For, just as the period between the morning and noontime prayers is long, thus representing the rising up of the sun and its climbing to its zenith, so the shortening of the time between the afternoon (*al-asr*) and the sunset (*al-maghrib)* prayers signals the departure of the sun from the center of the heavens, and expresses the sun of the knowing leaving the heart of the knower (meaning his innermost heart). In this case it is necessary for him to hasten on from these times, or moments, for why does it trouble you, O knower, if the sun intends to set; and when it sets? For know then, that these times, when the sun of knowledge sets in the heart of the knower, do not come from this sun itself, but from his heart. Every time that he turns his face away from the sun of the knowing he is required to shorten his prayer and to limit everything that is not the time of proximity which is symbolized by the dawn prayer, and to limit what is not the revealed, as symbolized by the noontime prayer. By this we mean that he is the *place* where the subtleties manifest, for in a state of separation he is, "But a handful of clay," but in a state of proximity he is the Caliph *(Khalifa*), "Of all the worlds." In other words, just as the earth changes its condition as a result of its proximity to, or distance from the sun, likewise the knower changes his quality according to his proximity to, or his distance from, the Truth. So that if you ask him about himself, at a time when he is in proximity, he says, "I am the One who remembers and the One who is remembered. I am the inhabited House. I am the overflowing Ocean, and suchlike things, and no number of lines of paper could contain what I want to say." All of that because of his being in proximity to the Truth, for no object is close to another without being given the meaning of its decree. But if you ask him about himself, when he has returned to himself, and when he looks upon his weakness in comparison with the Truth, Mighty and Supreme is He, he says, "I have been cut off after having reached. I have returned back after I had entered," until if you listened to his words you would think that he had never smelt the fragrance of acceptance, nor been answered by his Beloved. But what Allah wants from him, at all times, is that he should discard his veils so that he is able to hear his Lord calling him, and is able to see His refuge.

At the beginning of his Order, Shibli, may Allah be pleased with him, sometimes said, "Nothing exists besides Me." And sometimes he said, "My insignificance is greater than the insignificance of the Jew." The first words came from his being drunk in the witnessing of his *fana'* in the Essence of the One Who is worshiped, and his second words were a result of his return to being bound, hand and foot, because he was seeing only the boundaries, or fringes, of the Truth, as the Sultan al-`Ashiqin, 'Ibn al-Farid, said, pointing to the first station:

"I became the Musa of my time
When the part of Me became the totality of Myself."

This is concerning the *reaching* and the enfolding of the part in its Origin. Then, when he indicated the second station, he said:

"I am the humble, obedient faqir.
Have compassion upon my state and my insignificance."

See my beloved, how the stations came upon him and how he gave expression to the politeness in front of the revelations!

However, when I speak about the two states of proximity and of separation, I refer to the middle state between them; and I say that it is what is symbolized by the *`isha* prayer because it is between sunset and sunrise. He, who is so described by this evening state, or whose condition is between that of unveiling and veiling, is not required either to shorten or the lengthen his prayer, in this case, for he is in the center of, "the two bows-length and of the *barzakh* between the two seas." And the setting of the sun of knowledge upon him is because the eyes do not see Him, yet he possesses the knowledge, and he also knows, when it rises upon him, that: "Faces that day do not look to the right nor to the left, but to their Lord," as it is said:

"For, as a great beloved, I do not reveal Him to anyone.
I am afraid of the humiliation of my face on the day I meet Him.

And He is not absent from me, although I cannot see Him,
Except when I speak out, I say, 'He is Allah.'"

Know, that it is stronger, if they forget Him for a moment, for those whose station is that of remembering Allah with His Remembrance, than it is for those who are forgetful of Him, because the remembrance of the forgetful is not for His Face. For when the Essence of Allah is revealed to he who remembers Him and sits with Him while he is saying, *Allah! Allah!* he would stop if he were not annihilated, and he, may peace and blessings be upon him, said, "Whoever knows Allah, his tongue stops." And, from that, understand the words of some of them, who in intimate discourse at the time of their drowning, said, "If they knew You, they would not worship You," and suchlike expressions.

All that is with respect to the Presence of Allah. Briefly then, for the knowers there are times when they cannot utter any word while their eyes are fixed upon their Lord. Meaning, by that, the Eyes of the Beloved. Nothing then contains them, in that time, except their Master, which explains the words of the Prophet, may peace and blessings be upon him, when he said, "There is a time for me when only my Lord suffices me." From there it follows that he, who is of this rank, may peace and blessings be upon him, when the witnessing descends upon him, sometimes cannot be contained by anything except the Essence. Meaning that no created thing can contain him. Likewise this means that neither the earth nor the heavens can contain the Truth, only the hearts of those beloveds, may Allah be pleased with them all, who existed in the past, and who exist in the present. And they draw near to Allah, and He draws near to them; and they remember Allah until He remembers Himself. They remember Him in the beginning, but it is He Who remembers Himself in the end. They have left the bonds of the words: "Remember Me!" for the freedom of: "I remember You." Remember Allah, O you who do not see Him, and safeguard Allah, O you who know Him. He, may peace and blessings be upon him, said, "Protect Allah and you will find Him in front of you." When has He ever been far from you, so that you have lost Him; and when has He been absent so that you could forget Him? And know, that the knower is not known to the people.

Be aware then that no one should judge himself for not knowing this station, for only a few people know it; and they are the Perfect Ones who proclaim the Unity.

It is also disliked, for he who enters into the Presence of Allah, to seek refuge in Him. Meaning, that when he enters into the Presence of the Unique One, the Self-Subsisting One, in Whose existence there is no space and no end to His manifestations, how can he, for whom the where (*`ayna*) is non-existent, and who witnesses the eye with the eye, and who reaches to the clear Truth, in as much as the Reality of the Oneness is revealed to him, see the Devil in this? Meaning, does the one who enters into the Presence of the Merciful One, and seeks refuge from Him, when he is in the Presence of the Majesty, find yet another Path for himself? No, by Allah! there is no mentioning of the Devil there, and no experiencing of him, and no existence, or trace of him, for he is a figment of the imagination; and imagination has no Reality. Therefore, in that case he must not say *`audu* (I seek refuge) from anything, because nothing exists there; and if it did exist, then, without doubt, he would say, "I seek refuge from You, through You." The One from Whom you seek refuge is, in this case, the One Whom you ask for refuge. This is the ultimate realization for the knower, and he does not need anything else, after that. For this is what he has found, and this is what he has witnessed.

The Truth is the Eye of the Reality of the gathering together, in the Unity, of all that is praiseworthy and all that is blameworthy, so that, in this knowledge the beloved relaxes from the deceptions of the Devil (*ash-shaytan*) and he enters the group of those about whom He, exalted is He, said, "My slaves, you have no authority over them." Meaning, that: "I am their authority, and I am their Lord, and I am their Creator, and I am their Friend. I am the One Who whispers into them, and My dwelling-place is in their hearts. And I am them completely. You have no chance with them, either in their hidden or their revealed states." Some have said, about this:

"If the people have a whisperer who whispers to them
You, by Allah! are my whisperer and my khannas."

This is because the human being, who whispers thus, is absent and annihilated in the witnessing of his Lord; and he who knows the Compassionate One does not find, beside Him, either the Devil or the human being or the jinn, for: "He whom Allah leads astray, for him there is no Guide, and he whom Allah guides there is no one who can lead him astray."

Praise be to Allah in the beginning and at the end, and blessings and peace be upon our Master, the Perfect Man, Muhammad, may the peace and blessings of Allah be upon him, and his Family; and many greetings upon him until the Day of Judgment (*yawm id-din*). May Allah make us to be of His beloveds, and make us only to see, and to know, Him. He is my Sufficer, and He is the Best One in whom I put my trust.

الله

بسم الله الرحمن الرحيم

Az-Zakat
Almsgiving

Know my beloved, that Allah, All-Mighty is He, has given His Folk, the People of Allah, secrets and knowledge of the Essence of things, a knowledge which no human eye has ever seen, nor the human ear ever heard, nor the heart of the human being yet realized.

And when the Folk then came to realize the kingdom (*al-mulk*), and they were able to *reach* the meaning of this knowledge, so that it became uniquely for them, because they had withdrawn from the world and devoted themselves to their life with the Truth (*al-Haqq*), and had become as orphans in this world from their proximity to Him, then He gave them what they possess of blessings, and safeguarding their secret, He said to others, "Do not approach the property of the orphan save in the fairest manner." (17:34)

I say, "Who can speak about the secret of their station if he is not one of them?" So, avoid the knowledge of the Folk if you are not one of them, and do not approach the belongings of the orphans, for this will bring trouble and hardship to your self (*nafs*).

Then, when this knowledge was fulfilled in them, they were then asked concerning the duty of *zakat*, in accordance with his words, may peace and blessings be upon him, "Everything has a *zakat* so that people may prosper because of it." Thus, the knower is protected from losing this favor (*ni`amat*) in that the meaning of zakat is that by it a person is expanded and increased, as a result of which he is thankful for its blessings, and in this way, the favor is preserved. As it is said, "Secure the favor of Allah by giving thanks." And He, Mighty and Exalted is He, said, "If you are thankful We shall increase you." (14:7) And some said, "He who is not thankful for favors is in danger of losing them."

Generally speaking, this means that thankfulness to Allah is a duty placed upon a person because of all the well-being that comes to him. But if people have certain favors which cannot be counted or assessed, or if they are granted hidden blessings, of whose meanings they are not fully aware, then no zakat is required on these. And this also concerns their material possessions.

There are three groups of possessions which have been laid down by the outside Law (*ash-shari`a*) for the giving of zakat, and they are: money, including gold, silver and suchlike possessions, flocks of livestock, and crops of grains and fruits. This is the outside ruling, but the inner meaning of the zakat on these three groups is what we now wish to speak about.

And know that people themselves have also, for this purpose, been divided into three groups, namely: the beginners (*mubtadi*), those traveling on the path (*sa'ir*), and those who have reached (*wasil*); and each station and state (*hal*) has its special obligation in relation to it. Although possessions have evolved into many different categories, and their domain has grown, yet they can still be divided into the categories of either money (*`ayn*), livestock, or grains; or to be the owner of all of these, in which case such a person is referred to as *the universal Pole* (*qutb al-jami`*), who is the possessor of the healing medicine, for he owns everything that is in existence, from the Throne to the soil of the earth.

Know that, as has been mentioned in some *ahadith,* each of these categories has a particular zakat, as confirmed by his words: "Everything has a zakat, and especially anything as elevated as that." By which he, may peace and blessings be upon him, meant the person who is the possessor of everything that is between the Throne and the soil of the earth.

The zakat varies according to all the multiform manifestations of the Truth (*al-Haqq*), Exalted is He, some of which He reveals with His Names, and some with His Attributes, and some with His Essence. Because of this, the offering to Allah is also divided into three parts: firstly, that coming from the tongue, which is through praising, and by the mentioning of His favor (*ni`ma*) according to His words, All-Mighty and All-Powerful is He: "And proclaim the favor of your Lord." (93:11) Secondly, the thanking from the heart which is through its cleansing from everything that is not Allah, as revealed by the words of the All-Mighty, the All-Powerful One, to Musa, may peace and blessings be upon him, "I have chosen you for Myself" (*istana`tuka li-nafsi*); and this is the thanking of the *special ones.* Thirdly, the thanking of another kind, which is with everything that he has, according to His words, All-Mighty is He, concerning His Prophet and the first of His creation, Muhammad, may peace and blessings be upon him, "Be steadfast as I have commanded you; and do not follow their desires." (11:112)

The truth of this last-mentioned offering, or zakat, is that the slave gives his entire being - his body, his essence and his senses - to He for Whom he has been created. Then, he is the most precious object of existence for, through him, Allah is seen, as He, the All-Mighty, says, "And few of My slaves are thankful." (12:38)

And know that each of these three categories has varying ramifications, each one having its own condition (*hukm*) relating to it, but their meanings stem from the three categories mentioned earlier, which are: money (*`ayn*), livestock, and grains, or cultivation.

In the inside meaning the foremost zakat is on money and wealth which symbolizes the Essence, and is exactly equivalent to the Essence of the Truth, and carries the meaning of the deep subtlety. This is referred to as the Essence because the Arabic word *`ayn* has an inner meaning which is exactly that of all the rules, or principles, governing the People of Allah, and in fact, it comprises the meaning of everything, even of words, since every existing thing has an essence; and if it does not have an essence then it is non-existent.

The Essence (*`ayn*) gives Itself to every existing thing in obedience to the order of Allah, so that if It is not found in any thing, this means that that thing has no true existence, because the Truth is in all things except those, whether they be human beings, animals or material objects (such as stones, trees, etc.), which are in a state of ignorance, in which case they do not have true existence.

Thus, the Truth of the Truths is manifest, and he who has realized it becomes an Eye of its Eyes; or you can say an Eye of the Eyes of Allah; and the earth is not devoid of His Eyes. He, Praised and Exalted is He, said to His Prophet, "You are Our Eye." By these Eyes (*`uyun*) are meant the four *Hulafa,* may Allah be pleased with them. They are the Eyes of Allah, and all those who follow their Path partake of that inheritance. Meaning, that they have a part in the witnessing of the Divine Essence, the Truth of the Truths, which cannot be seen by the eyes of the humanity, nor by the heart alone. But only he who has an *Eye of iron* sees. Meaning, that such a one truly knows, and has become One with the Essence and the Source, and the possessor of the Secret. Then the seer becomes the essence of what is seen of the Secret, which, when it is the Essence of the heart, then this seeing is like iron and therefore very sharp and clear, and he becomes the Perfect in Insight and his vision, which is unlike any other, is the Truth, because he reaches to see Allah, Who then becomes the Eye with which he sees. And nothing can be compared to this, for he has arrived in that station from the Secret, and not from the place of normal sight.

But this is not the case when a person's eyes are for material, bodily things, which have colors and are changeable, and which take their *new creations* from what is not the Essence; for it does not change, but only the colors and the forms change. However, if a person is bound to the Essence, then there is nothing to say, in his case, for his roots are the Essence, and his branches and offspring, which come from him, are also from the Essence.

But when the person is not rooted in the Essence (*`ayn*), a veil (*ghayn:* spelt in the Arabic script with a dot over the *gh* but without the following *h*) covers his heart. This veil is dark and obscure, and we can show the meaning of what we are now saying by looking at the Arabic letter g (with a dot over it) where the dot is always written first, and is a symbol denoting beauty and goodness, whereas the remainder of the letter symbolizes what is neither beautiful nor good. And between these two is a veil of sadness and pain, resulting from the misdeeds of those who are neglectful, wandering, and lost. "And Allah does not punish them whilst you are amongst them." (8:33)

Let us now return to what we were speaking about earlier, and say that the Essence (*`ayn*) of the zakat is a recognition (*`irfan*) that has a ramification and inner dimension which is that of keeping silence towards the people who are not from this Way. And know that the zakat of the Essence, which is bestowed on the Folk, who are the poor and needy, should only be given to them. This is regarding the zakat on the Essence, the details of which will follow later, if Allah wills.

Secondly, in the outside Law (*ash-shari`a*), the zakat on livestock refers to animals, but in the inner meaning of the Reality it represents everything related to the body, and is equivalent to the blessings which Allah, All-Mighty is He, has given to His slaves (*`ibad*), and which are two bounties of the Essence, namely: *the blessing of creation* and *the blessing of subsistence*; both of which have their own branches, as will be shown. Firstly, the ramifications of the blessing of creation are symbolized by the seven extremities, or limbs. He who has the mastery over them, and who can use them, and control them as he wishes, and without being hindered by the influence of the Devil (*ash-shaytan*) or the self (*nafs*), is bound to acknowledge what he possesses, in this case, and to give zakat on it, which is what is owed for the blessings of the use of the limbs (*shawarih*).

The zakat on grains and fruits, in its inside meaning, is what is owed to Allah in return for His outpouring of the blessing of sustenance, or provision (*imdad*). This zakat is required of the knowers once they are rooted in this station (maqam), and when they have been annihilated in its meanings, which is an indication of their being established in the presence of Allah (*fi-hadrat illahi*).

Then, in the measure that the nature of this sustenance is known, and that the fruits and grains, which are the blessings of provision, come to fruition, the knower is asked about what is granted to him, and payment of zakat on them is required from him. And there is a rule for each time of payment for this zakat, which is one of the matters which it is necessary for the knower to be aware of; and for this reason the zakat falls due at yearly intervals, for which there is never any exception; but in each time for it, its payment is obligatory upon everything of this kind. The period of a year is the amount of time laid down for the giving of zakat, for before a year has passed the murid is not counted to be of those who have reached (*al-wasilin*) even if he is of the special ones, because until then, he is in a state of discomfort and inconvenience (*taklif*) on account of the variety of sacrifices that are required of him. For, during that early period of walking on the Path he still sees his provision as coming from himself, and belonging to him, so in that case, how can he be asked for zakat, as has been said. "I began to see possessions as mine, and time as my offspring." The prince of lovers, 'Ibn al-Farid, said about that:

"In a state of intoxication, and even for an hour,
You see eternity obeying you, and you are the ruler."

For, in a moment, the state of intoxication and complete fulfillment banishes all separation, so that it becomes Oneness in the Unity and freedom in the freedom; a Oneness which is complete and without struggle or imprisonment.

But ultimately, it is a duty for the murid to pay zakat once he has become grounded and strengthened in his walking on the Path, and when he has gained the ability to distinguish the stations of the Path, and when he comes to know of its different manifestations; for he then sees that although He, Who manifests to him, is One, yet there is multiplicity in the forms of the manifestation. When the murid is in this station then he is required to give zakat on the minimum amount of his possessions in relation to which he is liable (*nisab*) to pay it. But if the murid has been granted the Kingdom (*al-mulk*), as has been mentioned, and he is sincerely grounded in his work, it is a duty for him, always every hour and minute, to give zakat on the favors he receives. However, if he is not in that state no zakat should be given, because the freewill offering on favors is only for he who is ever heedful and attentive of Allah, and who, at all times, uses his body and his senses with the help of Allah, Exalted and Mighty is He, as He wishes of him.

After the murid gains obedience then the *meat* for this (as symbolized by any kind of food) should be eaten, as a sign that it is neither forbidden, nor is it reprehensible, to do so; but rather that in doing so, it is accepted as a sincere action for Allah, Praised and Exalted is He, for it is an indication that the limbs, or outer members of the murid, are not harming nor sullying his work. However, if he consumes only for the *dunya* and not for the Face of Allah, then all that he consumes is forbidden (*haram*); but any meat that is for the Hereafter (*al-ahira*) is acceptable to be eaten. The meaning of this is that it is consumed with the pronouncing of the Name of Allah, according to His words, All-Mighty is He, "And of that over which the Name of Allah has been mentioned, if you believe in His signs." (6:118); so that his action returns to him, for: "Whoever does a good deed, it is for himself." (41:33). And:

"Their flesh shall not reach Allah, nor their blood, but the reverence from you will reach Him." (22:37) For, in this, the action is for Allah; however, the All-Mighty does not accept deeds which have been performed together with anything that is not for Him alone, according to his words, may peace and blessings be upon: "Allah does not accept actions or deeds in which there are partners (*mushtarak*)." Because of that, zakat cannot be given on reprehensible, or forbidden ways of obtaining provisions.

A human being should therefore work on himself, and complete the purification of his qualities; and he should only accept work if he knows that it is pleasing to Allah, in which case he gives a zakat upon it; and when he gives all his work to Allah this is called thriving, success, or prosperity (*falah*), about which Allah, Praised and Exalted is He, said: "Prosperous is he who cleanses (*tazakka*) himself and mentions the Name of his Lord, and prays." (77:14). And, in this, there is a sign and an indication. And another clear sign (*aya*) is His word, Praised and Exalted is He: "Prosperous is he who purifies (*zakkahu*) it, and failed has he who schemes with it." (91:9)

To purify the *nafs* is to know its essence and its branches, and so by cleaning it, to know how it can be destroyed, not listening to what it says; for the carrying out of the Order for the destruction of the *nafs* brings about nothing but good, as has been said, "Whoever knows his self knows his Lord," because the knowledge of Allah is not far removed from the knowledge of the self (*nafs*). On the contrary, and generally speaking, within the *nafs* lies the knowledge of Allah. For that reason I say that, "The knower is of two kinds: firstly, he who knows himself, and secondly, he who knows his Lord; but he who knows his *self* most is he who knows his Lord the most." And he who knows his *self* has no choice but to use it for the purpose for which it was created. This is the zakat on the *nafs*, or also on the extremities, or limbs, which are the recipients of favors (*ni`am*).

In relation to the zakat on *grains* and *fruits*, this is only paid when both are ripe for harvesting, and when they can be consumed; so that the zakat is only required on that portion which is suitable for food, and which is clearly acceptable as such. As a result of this fact, the knower should not perform any action if the Order for it has not yet arrived. This is the meaning underlying His words, Praised and Exalted is He,

"And hasten not with the Qur'an before its revelation is accomplished to you." And say, "O my Lord, increase me in knowledge." (20:114) Albeit he has been ordered to proclaim it.

From this you can understand the meaning of the words of those who have wisdom when they say, "Things manifest according to their *times*, and beware not to reveal the Wisdom before the time for its revelation has come, but only when its *fruits* are ripe, ready and full of the explanation of the knowledge of the Secrets, in which case this is an indication that the *time* of this knowledge has come, and therefore, in respect of what it contains of the Divine Knowledges, the zakat upon it is due. In such a case it is necessary to remember, and to put into practice, his words, may peace and blessings be upon him, "He who conceals knowledge given to him from Allah, He will place upon him a bridle of fire;" and this is also indicated by another saying, namely, "I ask for forgiveness if we abandon our belief." Meaning, if we seek for some well-being, and in so doing, we move away from our faith. I ask Allah to protect us from that, for the true believer will not be silent with any knowledge which could be of use to the religion, or the material life, of the people of his time. But, at the same time, he is not asked to reveal all his knowledge, lest a dissension (*fitna*) should result from that. The Prophet, may peace and blessings be upon him, cautioned one of his Companions when he asked him, "O Prophet of Allah, should I speak about everything that I have heard from you?" He said, "Everything except what cannot penetrate the minds of the people." And this he said because he feared that, through some of it, conflict might result amongst the people. The wisdom and the benefit coming from that *hadiṯ* is that, in the case of hidden knowledge which has not yet reached the minds of the people, it should only be revealed to them when, in so doing, good will result for them. But, as for the knowledge which can reach the people, those who have it are ordered to give it in words which are precise and to the point. 'Ibn al-Farid expressed this as follows, "Behind the mind (*`aql*) there is a knowledge whose purpose is deeper than the minds of the people can understand, and there is yet another kind of knowledge which is so subtle that only some of it can be grasped, including by the most perceptive of people, except those of sound minds.

Thus, there is a zakat for everything when its time arrives, and which must be manifested and proclaimed, because the pure Law (*ash-shari`a*) has been sent to give the Community '(*umma*) the best of the religion, and of the material world (*ad-dunya*).

Therefore, the Inheritors travel with the sublime in its revealed or hidden state, until whenever the *time* comes for a knowledge of the knowledges to be revealed, in which case it must be revealed. If it is possible to speak about certain knowledge of the Essence, even if it be only in enlightening flashes of revelation, then from whoever hears it there is a zakat on it, even though the hearer is only able to catch fleeting glimpses from it. This can be said for he who is not a knower, but for the knower, it becomes a possession which cannot be taken from him, nor can it leave him. Meaning, that he can understand it, and realize it, as if it were a part of himself, and in such a case, zakat is asked of him on it; for zakat is only required on all that is preserved until the day of meeting (*yawm al-mi`ad*) for this is the eternal knowledge of the knower. The knowledge, which he must not reveal, is about all those matters which are preserved until the day on which neither money nor children will be of benefit, except for he who comes to Allah with a pure heart."

However, clear words which come from the knowers are beneficial for the hearts of those who hear them, merely by the pronouncing of them. And he is only asked to spread knowledge of the above-mentioned kind, and to make it suitable for others. But in a case when it is suitable and could be beneficial in the near future, and when it can be seen that there is a clear necessity for an exception to this, it is permissible to speak out.

But usually the knowledge of the knower, and what is in his heart is not useful for people normally, and is not always suitable to be revealed, except to people whose minds are of a different kind. The Wisdom is always the same, but sicknesses are not always so; and each sickness needs its own specific cure. For example, a person who, in the thirteenth century, announces knowledge which is more suitable for the fourteenth century, would in so doing act wrongly, and would make a zakat for a harvest before it is the time for its manifestation; and this is not right. The Truth said: "And there is nothing but that its treasuries are with Us; and we do not send it down except by a well-known decree." (15:21)

Then do not say, "Why have not those, who went before us, told us of that?" The answer to that is that they were not given the knowledge:

"And we do not understand anything of knowledge, except as He wills." (2:255) And added to that is the fact that they were occupied with what was more important than that. Meaning, what was useful for their period, and for the people of their own language, because each period has its own worship. Had they occupied themselves with what was good for the fourteenth century, who then would have carried out the work of their own period, the thirteenth century?

Know my beloved, that the Law (*ash-shari`a*) is a treasure, and that every human being gives of what he has been ordered to give. If a person is successful in his business and he is rich thereby, he can give of his provision, which is what Allah gives him; and he then gives what he can, and not more (*li-yatafiq du si`a min si`atihi wa-man qadura `alayhi rizqahu fa-l-yawfaq mimma 'atahu 'llahu*).

Some knowers have said that if the knowledges are of Divine Insight and Gifts which come without asking, these could not have been taken from books, nor from the tongue, because they are of a special nature, and should not be questioned about. If those, who went before, could not understand the knowledge, but those coming after them are given to understand it, then that is a Gift for them. Therefore, it is necessary to preserve the knowledge for future understanding, even though it may not be possible for it to be understood at the time of its revelation.

And know, that the knower develops through stages, and will appear, according to circumstances, with different *colors*; for: "The color of the water is the color of its container," and what each container manifests of the Truth. And it is natural that circumstances change rapidly, according to time and place, each superseding and overthrowing what came before. Therefore, you will see that the knower gives all his time to what Allah has given him of knowledge which helps the people, and not more; for he gives them the guide-lines of what has been correctly established and confirmed. For that reason he is called *the Pole* (*qutb*), because the stars rotate around him, but he, himself, does not revolve. He manifests himself to those who are worthy of his revelation, and he admonishes the people according to whatever they have done which is contrary to the Law (*ash-shari`a*). And thus the Truth is revealed by the tongues of the scholars of each time, according to what is suitable for its people. Therefore we see that the knower (*al-`arif*), in every time, also develops according to the needs of his people, and draws out of the deep knowledge what it is necessary for him to reveal. And this he does in keeping with the custom of the Prophet, may peace and blessings be upon him; for this is his victory and his triumph. For these knowers are faithful to the Secrets of the Law (*ash-shari`a*) with which they are entrusted, on condition that they reveal only what is necessary to be revealed, as mentioned earlier, and not to add anything more than what is absolutely necessary.

At the same time, it is said that there are ignorant people, such as some *majadib*, who are at the fringes of understanding, and who talk and gesticulate, sometimes revealing something of the Secret, but at other times keeping it, so that they can begin to talk about, and to share, although not fully, some of the knowledge which should be concealed. This is because each person drinks in the manner in which he is able, as Allah, Praised and Exalted is He, says, "All the people now knew their drinking-place." (2:60) However, if here we go into the details of this, it will demand a lengthy explanation. Therefore we say briefly that he, upon whom the knowledge has descended, can draw out of himself what is needed: "For there are stones from which rivers come gushing." (2:74)

Know that zakat is a duty only upon those who are richly provided with knowledge and true insight (*al-`ayan*), for there is a line (*intisab*) above which zakat must be given, but below which it is not required. For those who, in the inner meaning are very rich, then they should give on their riches, but for those who have little knowledge, how can they give, and how can they know the difference between the Law (*ash-shari`a*) and the Truth (*al-Haqq*)? And Allah, the All-Mighty, has said, "It is We who have sent down the remembrance, and We are the watchers over it." (15:9)

This zakat is not due from the person who does not possess the deep knowledge. Meaning, he who is only using pious words which he has learnt through what the Prophet, may peace and blessings be upon him, left behind; and if this is the case there is no zakat for that. But if he has the knowledge, which has come directly from the Prophet, then he must give zakat on it.

Next, we point to the zakat on the provision of our extremities, or limbs, known as *favors* or *blessings*. As has been said, the receiving of favors is symbolized as being through the extremities of the body which manifest what is concealed within them. Then the acts of the limbs stem from the self (*nafa*) which changes according to five stations (*maqamat*). For instance, there is the station of *'ammara* or *lawwama, mutma'inna, radhiya* or *mardhiya*, of which Allah, Exalted is He, has praised only three of them, with His words: "O soul at peace, return to your Lord well-pleased well-pleasing." (89:30). The provision coming from these three stations of the *self* is, in the widest sense, accepted. But whatever comes from *the self of al-'ammara* returns to its possessor, because in this case the extremities have consumed food, or provision, which is forbidden (*muharram*); so that no zakat is asked for this, and none can be taken from it. Also, all the provision coming from the *nafs al-lawwama* is not accepted because it is contaminated and impure, and the murid does not receive any benefit from this provision. Therefore, in this case, it is an obligation for him to work on the purification of his self, as is said: "Draw near to the self and perfect its qualities, for it is through your soul (*uruhu*), and not through your body, that you are a human being." Then, when the *nafs* is completely purified, it is ready to walk, and now its actions will bring it nearer to Allah, because through them it is now absent in Him, and therefore it rises up into the Presence of Allah, who is the pinnacle of the heart.

But, in all this, it is only in the metaphorical sense that actions of the limbs are connected to the *nafs*; and this is made clear by His words, All-Mighty and Supreme is He: "And some of them they ride and some of them they eat." (36:72)

We should mention here the foremost rank of zakat for the *nafs* as being like the benefits which the camel affords us, for it can be seen as a symbol for the calm assuaging self (*nafs al-mutma'inna*). If the *nafs* comes to be quiet and peaceful in what it does, then all manner of devotion, prayer, and yearnings can be imposed upon it, for it is stronger and more steadfast in its efforts, even than the camel; and this is because of the sweetness which comes from its obedience. As a result of the acceptance of its efforts it has the first rank of: "Whoever fears the station of his Lord, there is a Garden." (55:46)

So if you, O murid, are in the state in which it is difficult for you to change to another in a given time, put upon your *nafs* everything that you know of, which is necessary for drawing closer to your Lord, because the time is short, and you are asked to draw near, and with but one sign. In any case, ask of your *nafs* that it moves forward, and let it know of the higher stations. Lift up your head to what is beyond, because if your *nafs* lifts its head and longs for what is hidden from it, then everything will be easier. In that way you can reach the rank of contentment (*ridha*) and the self then becomes contented (*radhiya*). If, in this station, the self surrenders to Allah all illusion vanishes, then the decree is changed regarding its efforts, and zakat is required of the extremities.

So look, and may Allah bless you, at how He changes the order for the zakat of the well-pleasing self (*nafs al-mardhiyya*), and how He makes its task easier, for it now cannot carry distress or hardship; and therefore it can be compared to the cow, which even if it can carry hardship, cannot do so in the same way as the camel does. And, in addition to that, the work of this *self* is all from the heart, and therefore the extremities are relieved of their burden, for He, the All-Mighty, says: "Allah changes no soul except according to its capacity." (2:287) For this reason it is said that if work comes from the heart, the outer limbs will be relaxed, and an atom's weight of effort from the heart is better, in the sight of Allah, than the weight of a mountain of effort from the outer limbs. For this *self* has begun to yearn for the Judgment of Allah and is content with whatever is assigned to it, for, in this, it recognizes His Attributes, and being annihilated in His deeds, it does not see any effort as coming from itself, as is said: "And Allah has created you and your actions." When this station (*maqam*) is steadfast and becomes well-pleasing (*mardhiyya*) to Allah, this is then the self of the knowers and the slaves of Allah, of whom Allah, the All-Mighty, has said: "Then enter into My bondsmanship, and enter My Garden." (89:30) This *self* is not like the other self before, and Allah, Praised and Exalted is He, puts upon it all the burdens, except for those concerning legal formalities. Therefore its relationship with Allah has changed because its work has now become wholly for the Hidden (*batin*) World, and there is no trace left in it of the Revealed World. Its Inner (*batin*) life is bondsmanship and its outer Revealed life is what is customary. As 'Ibn al-Farid said:

"I returned to make bondsmanship habitual,
And the inner bondsmanship became my yearning.

I returned to my revealed bondsmanship after my total annihilation
In which the majesty and the beauty became One and perfect."

Since each station (*maqam*) has its own decree, or rules, the zakat for this *self* is different from that of the *self* before, because the further it progresses the easier it is for it in dealing with outside things. Since the order for this self is now different, then its limbs and extremities, through which it is provisioned, can be compared to those of sheep and goats (*ghanam*) because of the benefits accruing to the owners of such animals. For every action of the self, that has reached to this station, is useful to its possessor, and all the work coming from the well-pleasing self (*nafs al-mardiya*) is gratifying to Allah, because its owner has become complete in Allah, and he is of the righteous (*salihin*) slaves of Allah, whom He, All-Mighty is He, mentions with His words: "For enter into My bondsmanship." (89:30)

These are the righteous slaves and the knowers who are known, until they leave their own existence to enter into the existence of their Lord, Who is their existence. They do not find any trace of themselves that is mentioned, either for the *good* or for what is not the good, for the work of the owner of such a self is all benefits, from the beginning to the end. As is said:

"By Allah, the sleep of the knower is as rich as his "dikr"
So how then is the prayer of the knower as he prays?

The Throne has been reached
As he stands in proximity to Allah."

Here we have only touched upon these three stations of the *self* in a general manner so as not to prolong our discourse for otherwise we could speak about each one, letter by letter, as we have done in speaking about the prayer (*as-salat*).

A sign of the People of Allah is that they take something from everything that exists, so that, in themselves they do not possess a specific color nor an individual quality. And this is because the person, traveling on the Path of Allah, should be aware, and watchful to see His signs in everything, and let he, who is inexperienced take heed of the food of the People of Allah, so that perchance they will long for their drinking source, because of its clarity and purity, about which it is said, "This is the drink which all need ever to drink, like the drunken man who needs to be always more drunk."

We can then reveal another meaning for this which is: that some people of the knowledge of Allah are obliged to manifest their *zakat*. This means that they should reveal their hidden knowledge, whereas others should not do so; these latter being those who do not yet possess the level for which zakat on their knowledge is required. This is concerning the dissemination of the truths in a clear and open manner. This state is not given to all seekers, but it is a duty upon he who possesses the necessary conditions for it, and whose heart has realized the required order of the Truth (*al-Haqq*) for him. So that the knower, who is thus obligated to manifest the truths, accomplishes his duty, either because it is asked of him, or because he has been granted the permission for it in accordance with the rules of the Law (*ash-shari`a*). However a trial or temptation will result for any person, as well as for his followers, if he tries to give zakat on his knowledge without having the permission from Allah for this, as our Master Sidi Abu Madyan, may Allah be pleased with him, said, "He who goes out to the people before the Truth has asked him to do so, will be imprisoned," for maybe there was no necessity for, and no zakat upon, what he desired to reveal.

Therefore, we repeat our words: "He who has not yet reached his Truth should work with the Truth of another, about which it is said:

"Perfect your Truth which you have not completed,
And leave the body and its lower parts."

For nothing of the creation, which is not from the Truth, will be of any use to him, because such a person lives only in the illusion of his self, and he has not, therefore, reached to the least degree of obligation; in which case no zakat is required of him. Then understand!

The knowledges are of various kinds, and the insights are many, so that the listener might be concerned that there is a zakat on everything he hears. But know, that the knowledge of the sciences of Insight and Perception, which are still in the Unseen, have no zakat, but only the knowledge for which the *time* has come, or for which the *time* is due; in the sense that the time for it is close at hand, because it is not for the knowers only to manifest whatever is already known. As for time for the rest of the knowledge, it should be kept stored away until *the day of meeting* when it will be of benefit for Muslims.

This is with respect to the life of the material world (*ad-dunya*), but with respect to the religion (*ad-din*), and the recompense of repentance, and good deeds (*tawab*), zakat is required on them.

Also, as we have mentioned, there is no zakat upon *fruit* which is not yet ripe for eating or for provisioning. An example of this are certain unforeseen and rapidly changing manifestations, which are not from the Essence, and which therefore perish and cannot be preserved, and for which there is no zakat needed on any of them. In saying this we have disclosed the concern that the murid may be deluded by the multiplicity and the universality of revelations and spiritual insights and knowledges which he may be attracted to, and cling to, to the detriment of other matters, so that he will begin to think that they are the ultimate goal, in which case he makes ready to speak about this, and sometimes to write about it, although what he has is a knowledge which is transitory, and is not founded upon the Truth, but it is like the foam on the surface of water which passes away uselessly. Likewise it is said that the human being should not talk about what he has been shown on the *preserved tablet* (*lawh al-mahfuz*), because every minute Allah erases from it whatever He wishes, or He confirms what He wishes; and He is the owner of *the Mother of the Book.* However, words that come from the Folk are from behind the Tablet, and are the knowledge which was written down in Eternity, and therefore it will, most probably, manifest and come about. The words of the Prophet, may peace and blessings be upon him, do not change if they are a revelation, for they come as a result of a dream or an insight, but the time for their manifestation may come later, as is the case with pronouncements of the saints (*awliya*); but such pronouncements may be determined by haste, as Allah, Praised and Exalted is He, says, "Man was created in haste." (21:37) And also the words of the Praised One to His Prophet, may peace be upon him, "And hasten not with the Qur'an before its revelation is accomplished unto thee; and say: O my Lord, increase me in knowledge." (20:114)

Some of the Saints (*awliya*) do not only speak about what Allah has already completed, but they also proclaim what will surely come to pass. This is the case of *the red sulphur* and *the sweet-smelling musk* (names for the Muhammadan Inheritor and the Muhammad of the time). And if it should be asked, "How has he come to this great station?" we say, "He has reached this because he has been *increased* in the universal Essence from which comes the *eye-sight*, which gives him the knowledge of all essences, so that he can gather everything together, through his knowledge and understanding of every matter.

This state of being, which we have just mentioned, and which is not like any other, is only reached by he who has united the two kinds of knowledge: that of the Law (*ash-shari`a*) and that of the Reality (*al-Haqiqa*); the symbols for which are the elements of gold and silver. He, who combines the knowledge of both of these, is the trustworthy *holder* and *fastener.* And he who unites both the knowledge of the Law and that of the Reality, through *tasting* and through *state,* has taken his knowledge of them, as is done in the case of gold and silver, from their Essence (*`ayn*); and their true origin is the one who unites them in the Truth. He, who has not yet reached this state, cannot be regarded as being of *those brought near* (*al-muqarrabin*), although he is of the *special people of righteousness* (*ashab al-yamin*). He is, from a different aspect, a uniter between the actions of the heart and the actions of the limbs. Or you can say, a uniter between the words of the tongue and the belief of the heart.

We summarize here as follows: We have mentioned the uniting of opposites and branches with their origins, in which lies many eternal benefits, and therefore it is said that all things exist so that they can be made manifest, and that their origins are hidden in their branches. Meaning that the level of knowing for which zakat should be paid has not yet been reached, and that the knower is not complete if he has not gathered all things together, and united them, nor folded up the branches into their origins, nor gathered things together into a relationship with their origins. But when this has been achieved and fulfilled, and when all things are perceived with insight as to their hidden (*batin*) meaning, nothing will be difficult, because all will be united, one with the other. For then you will find that all the multiplicity is One in its Essence, just as the *doer* is One. "Your creation and your awakening is as One Soul." (31:28).

Because of this insight, it is an easy matter for you to know Allah in this world, and not to deny anything of that, because you now see all things as One, and the revelation as One, and that the whole world is inside you, as was the case of the mountain of Musa, may peace and blessings be upon him, "And when his Lord revealed Himself to the mountain He made it crumble to dust, and Musa fell down senseless." (7:143)

Because of such insight some have said, "I have become the Musa of my time, just as the parts of myself have become absolutely I." And this is because he now looks at everything with the Eye of the Unity, for had he looked at them with the eye of separation, he would not have reached, nor would he have seen anything. Thus it is said :

"Leave the mistake of separation
And unite so that you may be rescued

From the path of separation.
Through the Unity, walk to realize all things.

And say, when you are in the world of beauty, anything you like.
Only beware not to fall down into pictures, but remain in it."

So long as you see the branches, before you see their origin, you will remain veiled from the Creator, so that wherever the Truth (*al-Haqq*) appears to you, and you are also with the Creation, in the Creation there are attributes of multiplicity and opposites such as length and shortness, big and small, good and bad, Muslim and unbeliever, vanquisher and vanquished, deterrer and deterred, rememberer and forgetter, guardian and sleeper, grateful and ungrateful, patient and troubled, which can always be seen. Then, whenever the Truth, Who is the One Who is manifesting, appears in these contrary images, and when the attributes are in opposition so that He is not seen with the true sight, and you fail to unite His manifestations inside your heart and return them to their Origins, you do not have true knowledge; as is said, "Negligence will not attain it, but only if he is annihilated from all multiplicity, then he will see it shining and brilliant."

For the water is One, but the plants have varying colors. "Watered with One water, and some of them We prefer above others." (13:4) So, according to these words the Truth (*al-Haqq*), Praised and Exalted is He, is the Beloved in all things, and it is not the things in themselves which are loved, for their own individual qualities are lowly and abject, and do not in themselves possess any beauty to be loved. And if it were not for the beauty, which is loaned to them from Allah, they would vanish altogether and be non-existent, as is said, "Know, that if it were not for Him, you and all the universe would disappear and be non-existent."

O my brother and my sister, I say to you, "Do not let your eyes fall upon existences, nor be under the illusion that you have seen your existence existing in itself, or for itself, because this is something which is impossible, for all things are, in their being, subject to vanishing and being non-existent." But the true seeing does not perceive non-existence; only it sees the Creator Who alone is the true existence which He loans, from Himself, to all things; and unless you know that, you are in the illusion of seeing that things have existence. But, "Allah is the light of the heavens and the Earth." (24:35).

Know then, that this science, in whose midst we are, is the dearest of all that is dear, and it is only bestowed upon its People on condition that it is intended solely for its proprietors.

You should know that zakat is given for the poor and the needy, and also for he who has been appointed to collect it; and for those who have newly entered Islam, and for those who have *sold* themselves and who are slaves of Allah, and for the debtor who is requited on the Path of Allah. And according to the Law (*ash-shari`a*) this means those who struggle on the Path (*al-mujahidin*), and for the wanderer who cannot continue his journey, nor has he any means to take him to his country; and this is in accordance with the Law (*ash-shari`a*).

Concerning the Reality (*al-Haqiqa*), if it cannot be described by any one of the eight Qualities for it, then it is not known to the Secrets of Allah, and it should not be sought after if it does not concord with those mentioned. And in the same way, the person who can provide the zakat should only distribute it to its People, according to the words of the Prophet, may peace be upon him, "Choose those for your zakat as you would choose for your daughters." This is concerning the almsgiving, about the Secret of Allah which is a trust with the People, and which is confined to its People. It is said, "Do not give the Wisdom to others except to the Folk, otherwise you would commit an injustice; but if you withhold it from its People you will commit an injustice to them." If these words had been followed there would not have been any misunderstanding for the knowers about withholding the Secret, except that their state (*hal*) overcame them and they did not, in that case, recognize who were *the people of the Secret*. The Truth (*al-Haqq*), Praised is He, has given them the understanding, through that noble clarification, so that they will not be blamed for their mistakes. For mere existence is one of the Attributes, the right for which (existence) does not prevent them, or halt them, but they should give for each *right* what it deserves: "Verily, Allah commands you to deliver trusts back to their owners; and when you judge between the people, that you judge with justice." (4:58) And that means, according to the special ones of the People of the Path, those who are worthy of the eight Attributes which we will now mention:

The first attribute is that of being poor (*al-faqir*); he who is the one who truly possesses the attribute of the needy. Therefore, these are they whose hearts are empty of invoking favors (*da`wa*) for they do not see, for themselves, any knowledge, nor any station (*maqam*). It is the right of such a one to be given this *art* for Allah, Praised and Exalted is He, has said, "If they are poor Allah will enrich them of His bounty." (24:32) He has granted richness only to those whose existence is truly poor. Every person who can be described by that quality is worthy of the grace of Allah. And Allah, the All-Mighty, has said, "He who answers the oppressed when he calls upon Him." (27:67)

But the person who sees a state (*hal*) or a station (*maqam*) with the people, and especially with regard to his Shaykh should not give zakat for he does not have the *mark* of the Folk of Allah, because his heart is not full, and the Truth does not settle except in a *knocking* heart. For that reason it is said:

"Her love came to me before I knew love,
For she found an empty heart, and one that it was able to fill."

Of the second kind of *faqir* there are also specific categories. One of these is that of being poor, and by that it is not meant that he has empty hands in the material world (*ad-dunya*). But it is he with the *lowered wings*, who is humble, as the People of Allah say, that he sees himself as being poor, even as the lowest of the poor, and this no doubt brings about humility, in himself, towards Allah; and the help of Allah protects him, for victory only comes after humility, as His words, Mighty and

Supreme is He, reveal, "And when Allah helped you at Badr when you were humiliated." (3:123)

So look at how, after their humility, they were raised up by the caring of Allah. But everyone who sees himself as powerful, and not in need of Allah's help, the All-Mighty reminds them by His words: "The day of Hunain, when your multitude was amazing to you, but it availed you naught." (9:25)

And it is the case of the seeker (*al-murid*) that whenever he is seized by longing Allah takes him by the hand and brings him to a man of the Folk of Allah who rescues him, as in the story of al-Khidr, may peace be upon him, and the boat of *the people of poverty*, when by his hand he saved them, according to His words, All-Mighty is He, "As for the boat, it belonged to certain poor people." (18:79)

So, look at how He had described them as poor although they owned a boat, and perhaps they had even more than that. On the other hand, you might find someone with empty hands yet who does not have any humility, for he is a coarse creature like a giant in what he possesses, and he does not deserve to possess the Secret of the special ones, for he is not of the Folk of Allah.

The third kind of seekers are the travelers who walk on the Path. What is meant by this are the people on the Path, who follow courageously the Order of Allah, and to whom are attributed complete determination, and outstanding honesty. Because of their courage no obstacle can restrain them, and nothing comes to their hearts except for what they desire. They are those who deserve to be given this quality for they have unsheathed the *Swords of the Truth,* and with them, have cut away all the falsehood and injustice of separation; and surely in their actions are outward signs which shine from the Presence (*hadhra*) of the King (*al-Haqq*), for they have no resources for their deeds except their courage on the Path of Allah. And about that the owner of the *a`yun*, `Abd al-Qadr al-Jilani, said:[1]

"Be steadfast in what you wish,
For only the brave, who knock on the door, reach it."

The words of the All-Mighty One, in a Sacred Tradition (*hadiṯ al-qudsi*), are enough for he who has approached the Secret of Allah with honest seeking: "If My slave draws near to Me an arms length I am closer to him than his arm; and if he draws near to Me walking, I come running towards him." And the Prophet of Allah, may peace and blessings be upon him, said, "Honesty is the Sword of Allah upon this earth, and whatever it falls upon it cuts to pieces." So, if the human being is honest in his proximity to Allah, about which He, the All-Mighty, says, "And if My slaves ask about Me, I am near to answer the call of the caller when he calls," he will be helped by Allah, but if he is veiled from Him there can be no courage and little honesty in seeking for the Truth (*al-Haqq*). "For if they were sincere with Allah it would be better for them." (47:21)

Finally, we say that most of the truthful people are brave. Meaning, that they are people of courage in this *art*, and this is a quality by which they were known before they entered the Path, so that when they reach the state of being absorbed by the Path, this attribute remains, and He, the All-Mighty, says, "Their good works when in a state of ignorance, will be good works in Islam." The People of the Path say, "The special ones emerge out of robbers." So that the person who was courageous before entering the Path remains like that on It, because his self (*nafs*) always aims at his betterment in everything, and it does not want to remain in a state of duality and separation. For this station of duality is not a praiseworthy one, and Allah, Praised and All-Mighty is He, has condemned it for not being from the Prophet, as He said, "They are well-pleased to be those who stay behind." (9:87) And therefore they are not satisfied with this station (*maqam*), and because of their determination to move out of it they reach their goal, and achieve what they wish for.

It is said that what results from this has a double blessing. He, who has this quality, asks of Allah only to lead him to Him, in the knowledge that He is near at hand; and he begins to reach Him when he does not see any good deed that he could rely on, as coming from himself, nor any good deed, to which he is linked, but that he has found his destiny in Allah, and therefore he longs to grasp it; for surely this will come about because his opinion of Allah is the best, as He has said in a *hadiṯ al-qudsi*: "I am according to the opinion of My slave." And it is also said:

*"If he wants the Truth and continues towards it,
He will reach it even if it is as far away as the sun or the moon."*

The fourth kind of seekers are those who ask for the freeing of all creatures that are slaves in the clutches of their appetites, and imprisoned by their selves (*an-nufus*), the circumstances of the material world, and suchlike limitations. For each is a prisoner to the manifestation of jealousy, and other animal appetites. These are the qualities of the people generally, but the quality of the special ones is that they are prisoners of the manifestations of the Hereafter, and of their Lord. Because of that they are not concerned about *rights* in this world.

Then, if any seeker (*murid*) longs to free himself from his slavery and imprisonment into the true freedom, he will be taken by the hand of one of the special ones of the knowers of the Secret, who will rescue him from the slavery of being with *actions*, to the Spring of the Unity of He who is the *doer* of every action. So that he is taken from the slavery of seeing only actions, to seeing He who is the *actor* in every action. Then he will be free; and his reward will come to him from Allah. And this is clearly revealed in the *Book of Perfection.*

This is the case of a person who has been freed by the hand of another, and who has entrusted himself, or herself, to that other, for he will receive what he takes as a payment. How is it, then, for the person who has helped another to come out of his self (*nafs*) into the seeing of his Lord?

The fifth kind of seekers, of the various arts of knowledge, are those who pursue them without any other purpose, and without seeking any other meaning, nor having any other direction than the Path of Allah; for they have immersed themselves in His service, and they have lost themselves in His words, and in the love of its People, and their bondsmanship to it, until they are satisfied with what they see of it. Those are they who have the Secret, and if they find someone who carries the Qualities of the Folk, they will ask him for more, and if it is not too difficult for them to obey the Truth by being on a nobler rank than those who are negligent, they will remain at that rank. The knowers say about this, "If you see someone who is truthful with the words of the Folk, ask him to make a *du`a* (request) on your behalf, for they are those whose asking is heard by Allah."

The wonder is that this group of people is the most difficult of groups in standing up, and in approaching Allah, because they are satisfied with what they have reached in loving the love of the People of the Path, and in their proximity to their outside manifestations of the love, which they see in them. I have seen many of those who have left the Path after entering it, and reaching to what they could in it, and those who remain in its midst still unaware of its meaning, not knowing the Path nor what is required of them from it. And if you say to one of them, "Stop, for what you wish for is in front of you, and before you," maybe he would answer, "My love for them, and my affiliation to them is enough." How strange! For through their worship of what is not the Truth they have veiled themselves from Allah. So, if you wish to move one of them from the place where he is, you would find him to be deeply rooted like a mountain, and he would not come closer, with you, to Allah, not even by the length of an atom.

The Shaykh of our Shuyuh, al-`Arabi ad-Darqawi, may Allah be pleased with him, said, "The People of this Path have taken from it a stick on which they lean, and the glorification (*'at-tasbih - Allahu Akbar),* but if you say to them: Come close; this will bring you closer to Allah, they say: No, no!" For, in general, they think that what is needed is only to be connected to the Path, and to be able to recite some poems, and to know, by heart, about some of the miracles relating to the senses; and to remain with the *fuqara*. But this is not enough, and this is not what Allah wants from us of the Path; but to reach its goal. "For surely to your Lord is the final limit of it (*al-muntaha*)," (79:44) which is to the Attribute of the witnessing and eye-witnessing, all of which comes from the Master (*al-murshid*), and it is not for the seeker (*al-murid*) to do anything, save to preserve obedience to Allah, through him.

The sixth kind of seekers (*muiridun*) are those who are *indebted* because they have not fulfilled their obligations to the Truth (*al-Haqq*). These are they whose hearts are broken for not having obeyed the order of Allah, having remained at the outer fringes or limits. However, they are closer to Allah than those who are proud of their work, and who have been compelled by their obedience to prove their *breaking*. The case of the former is better than that of the latter, even though their *breaking* came as a result of disobedience, as the words of *The Wisdom of `Ata'iya* indicate: "A disobedience which has brought disgrace and scorn is better than obedience that has afforded you pride and glory." And Sidi Abu Madyan al-Ghawt, may Allah be pleased with him, said, "The disobedience of he who is rebellious is better than the pride of he who is obedient." And the All-Mighty has said, in some Sacred Traditions (*hadith al-qudsiyah*): "I am with those whose hearts are broken for Me." There is no doubt that there are those who know about their debt to Allah, which is a broken heart, as against those who, because of their obedience which is mingled with the existence of the self, and its contentment with itself, see themselves as having a claim on Allah, and this is a fatal sickness. If he who has a broken heart returns to Allah, he will be closer to Him than others; for He, the All-Mighty, says, "Truly Allah loves those who repent, and He loves those who purify themselves." (2:222)

The seventh kind of seekers are those whose hearts are weak, although they desire to walk in the Path like others, and they open their hearts as they are able to do. So, if they meet others on the Path they are like strangers because they do not have the deep yearning (*himma*) for the walking. But their knowledge is beyond that of their people, and they stand in a position of advantage and of favor (*fadhl*) on the Path, because of their knowledge; for the scholar has a concern, and interest which, of necessity, should be supported. Therefore, the Prophet, may peace and blessings be upon him, gave permission for those, who are drawn to this art, to be able to walk on the Path without any kind of conditions, unlike the case of others, for this would be too difficult for them to achieve. But nevertheless their obedience is necessary, so that they can realize some of the *tasting* of the Folk (*al-qawm*), and so that they can take from the Path as much as they can *buy* of it, with what they can achieve of the deep knowing. However, this is not universally so, but only if circumstances require it, and this permission for them is of significance and importance in the time determined for it (*`azim fi-waqtiha*).

The knowers have encountered many scholars, and they have asked many of them to enter the Path and to walk in its Truths without hindrance, as was the case of our Master Mawlay al-`Arabi ad-Darqawi with some of the scholars of his time, when he said, may Allah be pleased with him, "I regret what has happened to me with the scholars. For when they asked me: What is the price of your Way? I answered them: It is to lose one's rank and position. Then they excused themselves, and went away. When we had separated from each other, I blamed myself for what I had said, for I should not have imposed this condition upon them, because such persons should not be turned away from the Secret, for they are beneficial for the Creation."

The eight group of seekers, and the last one, is of the travelers who need the Unseen, for the doors of this art are not closed in front of the seeker for whom this art is destined; for he is the son of the Path. Meaning that he is the Child of the Path, and that his capacity for this art does not evidently need to be proved, for it is enough for him to be a traveler who needs someone to raise him up to Allah. So that, if he finds the one who holds the power to do so, he will be taken onto the Path merely through meeting with him; and it will be clear that this is a seeker (*murid*) of Allah, and that he is turned towards, and is facing, everything that will come to him of Allah's favors. In his case, it is enough for the Shaykh to give him the Essence of the Reality of a thing, and to place him in his Insight so that, at that point, he becomes of those who are *rich* in Allah. Sidi Abu l-`Abbas al-Mursi, may Allah be pleased with him, said about such a murid, "Between me and my murid there is but a glance, and I will enrich him."

We have had encounters with some seekers who were asking for the knowledge of Allah; so we tested them in their asking, and we found them honest, so we gave them what they needed, without hindrance; and the blessings are for Allah, Praised and Mighty is He.

Finally, we say that each of the eight kinds of travelers needs its freedom and its surrender. Meaning, its standing in the station (*maqam*) of surrender. This is the quality of the seekers who are sincere in their desire to be treated with the medicine which will bring about their healing, specially because they do not want to refuse anything which is destined for them, and in so doing, to be free from wanting any other thing than this art, in whose proximity they need to be. And know, that it is necessary to establish the veracity of the state (*hal*) and the yearning (*himma*) of each of the eight above-mentioned categories, before the Secret can be unveiled to them, so that no doubt, which could render their state untruthful, is found in them. But he, who has a clear eye, can see the qualities of the *muridin* manifesting on their backs; and he will act accordingly.

Then we come to the zakat of breaking the fast (*fitr*). For the Folk of Allah *fitr* means the returning to one's original and pure nature, and this return is with Allah, because they see the Reality of the Creation, and what is behind the Creation. For them, the *fasting* is their emergence from the universe, and their annihilation in His Name, the Hidden (*al-batin*). For when this happens their *return* is in the seeing of His Name the Revealed (*az-zahir*) in all beings; and this is the day of the feast (*al-`id*) when they see the Hidden as the Essence (*`ayn*) of the Revealed, and the Revealed as the Essence of the Hidden. It is said:

"The day of meeting is my true wedding feast,
And my happiness, my joy, my intimacy and delight."

And another said:

"Your feast is, for me, a promise,
And my saving from it is the proximity in You."

All of which comes from the realization of the Truth of His words, All-Mighty is He, "He is the First and the Last, and the Revealed and the Hidden." This is the true nature of revelation. What feast could be greater than that, when the First calls to him, and says, "Lift up your intention to eternity, for I am the Last (the Hereafter)." And the Hidden also calls to him, "Open your eyes to the universe, for I am the Revealed." So when he has been overwhelmed by this knowledge, of which, before, he knew nothing, and of which he could not have imagined, nor had he any part in what happened to him of what has been mentioned, then it is an obligation upon him to give *zakat*. Meaning to give to his brothers or sisters some of what he has been granted. And it is an obligation upon him to open up to them some of this new knowledge, so that they will be strengthened on their Path, for the Folk say, "Speak! If you know."

Finally, zakat is a duty upon everyone, even upon he who has the smallest portion of Divine Knowledge, for if he has tasted of it with his brothers, it is important for him to speak of it; but not to speak of this Divine Drink, nor to give it to strangers. For the Muslim, who in that time has been freed, this is not a difficult thing, in comparison with others who are not yet free. Meaning, for he who has surrendered to the Path. So, if he hears these truths from the murid who has reached, he will be strengthened in his intention, and he will be annihilated by the Path, and his heart will feel peace. The words, which come from the seeker (*murid*) at that time, and in that state (*hal*) are thankfulness for the blessings, according to His words, All-Mighty is He, "And proclaim the bounties of your Lord." (93:10)

The thanking for the blessings that have come upon one is the greatest zakat; and they come only from the food of the Folk (*al-qawm*), those who have tasted it and lived it; and not from those who have heard it from the Folk, and who have copied them. Often we have heard the Shuyuh saying to their followers: "Bring us the raw meat and not the dried meat." What is meant by that is not that the words of those who have gone before have no meaning, but it means that there is no zakat except upon a person's own words, and what he has realized himself. The words of those of the past are their words of the past, but what is needed is not merely to learn their expressions, but to live one's life with their manners. This means that when the murid falls upon Allah, and finds Him, that he then goes forth with knowledge which, for the Folk, is known as *the day of the feast*, as it is said of them, "You will then find them speaking about unseen Secrets before their brothers, and often in front of their Shaykh, for everyone needs their words, because through them, they speak about their pure and deep knowledge, and in so doing, they free a Muslim to annihilate himself, in a day." Meaning, that he can free his brother from further searching, merely by his announcing to him what happened to himself on that blessed day. For the Folk have understanding which no others but they can realize. Our Shaykh Sidi al-Buzaydi, may Allah be pleased with him, loved most to speak with his murid in the moment when he would come with the knowledge of the proximity of Allah; and he would say to him, "Speak! For your words are the words, and all other words are non-existent."

Finally, we say that zakat is a duty on all knowers, in whatever state or rank they have reached. Then, all things return to their *nature* and no one comes out of his rank. "Whoever has knowledge lives out his Order and sits under it." For that reason it has been said, "The beginning of the Path is madness, its middle is art and its end is stillness." It may come about that the knower claims ignorance with those who are ignorant, so that he is not known to them; and if he is asked about a matter, he does not answer, because he knows his Destiny, and he stops with his limits. "And he believes that he has a known station." (37:64)

Prayers and peace upon our lord Muhammad and his Family and his Companions, and many greetings of the deep surrender; and peace be upon them until the Day of the Religion (*yawm id-din*).

الله

[1] `Abd al-Qadir al-Jilani was know by this *kunya* because he liked to end the lines of his poems with the word *`ayn*.

As-Sawm
The Fast

To fast, linguistically means: the complete withholding from everything except the Beloved, which is Allah. And there are conditions for it which involve obligations, prohibitions, and the performance of good deeds, the meanings for which the owner of the `ayn,[1] Sidi `Abd al-Qadr al-Jilani, may Allah be pleased with him, said:

"Fasting is restraint from seeing anything but Allah;
And my breaking of fast also goes back to You."

Others have said:

"My self (nafs), through my fasting from everything but Allah
Has become One and pure, by the Bounty of His Generosity for me."

Then, the knower's absence from everything that is not Allah is in a special Presence (*hadra*), which is that of the Essence, and which the Folk refer to as the Presence of Omnipotence (*jabarut*). However, in the Presence of the Names, the Attributes and Actions, it is not obligatory for he who fasts to witness the Essence, because Allah is high above the board (*lawh*) on which the Names and Attributes are inscribed. Therefore if the person in his fasting, does not reach to the Essence of this Presence, his action is nevertheless pleasing, because he is performing a duty which is good. But most of the time it is difficult for the owner of this station to unite the witnessing of these two Presences (the Essence and the Names and Attributes) because of the complexity and arduousness of bringing together the opposites of the Qualities which manifest in them (the Names and Attributes). For this produces in a murid a turmoil and a churning about like that of the waves on the sea which is a hindrance to fasting, except in the Presence of the Unity which is pure of any doubts or opposition. For in the station of the

Unity, if a person wanted to see anything else but it, he would not be able to do so, because the Reality of this Presence would not permit this. And if anything else came to his heart, he would leave this station, and his fast would end. About this, Ibn al-Farid, may Allah be pleased with him, said:

"If a longing, even unknowingly, comes to me to see anything but You, I will be discharged from the Unity."

This is the case for the owner of this advanced Presence of the Remembrance. But, as for the owners of other Presences, they may be veiled by their vision of the Names and Attributes, and therefore it is not obligatory for them to witness the Essence of this station; but if it is possible for them to do so, this is pleasing.

When the Folk of Allah decided that fasting from everything that is not Allah is a duty, the souls were agitated to know of the right time for it. And they were told that this is when the new moon is sighted. So that Allah said, "He of you who has seen the month, must fast." This is the station of the *seeing*; but the *hearing* about a thing is not like the seeing of it. So that whoever sees the month must fast, and refrain from everything that is contrary to it. And know that this *seeing* does not take place in this material world, but it is in the highest heaven. So that whoever does not lift up his head outside cannot see the kingdoms of the heavens and the earth.

Mostly, the yearning (*himma*) of the murid does not come to him from his senses, but he himself is the reason for the change which comes to his heart through a longing to see his Lord, and which is in contradiction to the indications of his senses. Therefore the murid is required to leave everything related to his five senses, which are those of: eating, drinking, vomiting, making love, and of anything reaching his stomach. What is meant here, by the *stomach,* is the place of *Divine manifestation* referred to as *suwayda al-qalb*, and which is the mid-point of the body, also known as Insight and Discernment (*basira*), which can easily, and rapidly change. Therefore, the murid must protect his stomach as far as he is able to do so. And therefore you will find that most of the *muridin*, as they enter to Allah in the Remembrance (*ad-dikr*), close their eyes, so as to be able to be absent, and to control their senses. These are the most important practices for the Path, because the yearning of the murid can only be strengthened when he abandons all sense of things which have mastery in the material world; and this means his senses. The Mawlana ad-Darqawi, may Allah be pleased with him, said, "The senses are the dwelling-place of meanings, and every meaning that comes through the senses leads to annihilation (*fana'*)." This is the reverse of fasting, except if the senses become the Essence of the meanings, in which case there is no contradiction between them. It has been said that this is a most valuable state, which cannot be reached by the mind, although in the beginning, the mind is a necessary factor for *reaching*, as has been said, "In the beginning there is a need for the mind, but in the middle and the end stages it is necessary for it to be erased, in order to reach this station, which exists behind minds."

And know that when a woman is in the state of menstruation, her *nafs* becomes detached and unseated through the blood, and therefore she should stop fasting, for this period makes a veil for the *nafs,* and is therefore a hindrance for her fasting. And we ask Allah to protect us in all impediments; and He is the only One Who is able to do whatever He wishes.

And know that it is disliked of the murid that anything from his senses should interfere with his Insight (*basira*), for the fear that this should become stamped upon his heart so that he would then be cut off from his Lord. For this reason, the *Owner of the Wisdom* (*al-Hikam*), Ibn `Ata'illah al-Iskandari, may Allah be pleased with him, said, "How can the heart be illumined when the images of creatures are reflected in its mirror?" Because even the smallest of things has an effect on the heart. Therefore the murid should very seriously be concerned about his heart, even to standing as a guard at its door; and to do as one of them said, "I stood at the door of my heart for forty years, and I pushed away from it everything that came to me, which was not for Allah." This is how the murid should be.

Know that there are things which are reprehensible for the murid to accept, but which are forgiven of him if they are forced upon him; while there are other things which are disliked of him to do, if he does them purposely; and which are forbidden for him when he continues to do them. Therefore, if certain feelings come to a person who has abandoned his senses to travel towards meanings, and if he rejects these feelings, then he is safe from temptation; but if he even casts a glance at them, this is reprehensible for him; and it becomes prohibited if he lingers with them.

As has been said, the senses are opposed to meanings, so that the murid needs to leave everything related to them, and if he gives in to even a few doubtful feelings, or if he is halted by such insignificant things as flies, or the dust on his path, these will cut him off from Allah. And we have heard about one of the Masters who told a murid to abandon his senses completely. So he threw away everything that he had, not leaving himself with anything except a needle with which to mend his outer garment. But still the murid did not receive any revelation. The Master then told him that it was the needle which he had kept, that was veiling him from his Lord. So, he threw it away, and as soon as he had done that, he began to be in the witnessing.

This is an example of what results from the annihilation from the senses; and at the same time, and on the other hand, there is the need to relinquish meanings; for whoever keeps even the most minute of things as a picture in the mirror of his heart, even if it is only a hair of his body, this can become magnified to such an extent that it becomes a veil between him and his Lord. O Allah! unite us to You and keep us apart from anything which is not You. Amin.

And know, that the veils are so numerous that we cannot speak about them in any detail, but if you want to leave them, little by little, this will come about for you in repeated stages; yet also, only one intention from his heart is needed for him in order to gather together the whole world and what it contains; and to rise above it. And that is the easy Way to Allah, as He, Mighty and Supreme is He, has said, "Say Allah!, and leave the world and what it contains, if you long for completion," because all reasoning which plagues the murid is contrary to his fasting.

But concerning the outside things, they cannot manifest in such a manner as to hinder fasting, for if the senses try to gain the mastery they will not find the means to do so, because in the station of transcendence (*tanzih*), or reaching (*wusul*), as Ibn al-Farid said, it is :

"Purity and yet no water, and gentleness and yet no love,
Light and no fire, and soul and no body."

Moreover, there would be no breaking of the fast unless his *nafs* returns him to his senses. But if he returns with his Lord, this is what is desired, and is referred to as *the separation.* In this case he should not continue fasting, for he is returning to the world, in Allah and with Him. So we leave him where he is (in breaking his fast), and in a state which would appear to be in contradiction to his obligation, but which in the Truth is not so. However, when fasting is a duty which we must not leave, let us go towards it wherever we find it; for we are under the Eyes of Allah in any place where we have knowledge of Him.

Usually the murid flees from his senses for fear that through enjoying the pleasure of their touch and taste, he will be veiled from his Lord. However, when the senses come to be the Essence of meanings, or we can say the *revealed manifestation*, then the murid does not emerge through this. But it is as the case of the *mountain* of Musa (Moses), may peace and blessings be upon him, by which we mean the existence of the complete peace and intimacy (*'uns*) for Musa's presence, which he would know about through his senses, when he asked to see Allah in His Transcendence (*tanzih*) before He showed Himself to him in the picture of His Immanence (*tashbih*), according to His words: "Look at the mountain - if it remains in its place, then you will see Me." (7:143) Then when Allah was manifested to Musa's senses, or let us say, when He revealed Himself to Musa in His World of Immanence, it replaced the World of Transcendence: "For wheresoever you turn, there is the face of Allah." (2:112)

And it is said, "If you cross through the revealed (*zahir*) you will find the hidden (*batin*) in it, and you will then realize the Hidden because it is the Revealed. For there is no inner in what is inner, and no outer in what is outer; and this is the meaning of His words, "He is the First and the Last, the Hidden and the Revealed." (57:3)

Then, when the murid finds his *self* in these meanings, this is his annihilation (*fana'*) in the Name of Allah, the Hidden, and if he finds that this is the Essence of the Revealed, he must return immediately to what he has witnessed. And if he does not return to it immediately, still only knowing and worshipping Allah in His Omnipotence and being ignorant of Him, and not worshipping Him in His Immanence (*tashbih*), we say, "He acknowledged meanings but was ignorant of sensory forms; and in doing this he is unconsciously giving a *place* to Allah."

But the reward for the murid, who abandons the revealed world in which he sees an existence for himself, is that he finds that he cannot, in that world, be described as either existent or non-existent, because he is now veiled from Allah by that which has no existence with Him; as Ibn `Ata'illah, may Allah be pleased with him, said, "What shows you the existence of the Omnipotent is that He veils you from Himself by what has no existence with Him." Then, after realizing this, the murid returns to his true existence in Allah. Therefore, you see that at the completion of their Path, most knowers acknowledge the place for the Creation, just as they found, at the beginning of their Path, the necessity for seclusion (*halwa*) from it; for now their existence has become a *halwa* in which there is nothing except the One; and that is the Essence. And this also means that now the murid is asked to return to the senses, as soon as he reaches to know Allah, just as before, in order to do this he was required to abandon them. About this the Master Ibn `Arabi said, "The Essence cannot be reached without revealed manifestations, although the human being does his utmost, even to tearing himself apart, in his endeavor to do so."

Know, my beloved, that the judgment on he who returns to the Creation with his *nafs* alone, before he is drowned in seeing the Truth (*al-Haqq*), means that he breaks his promise and his fast, after claiming that he will not return to the Creation unless he does so in Allah alone. Therefore, in the law of the Folk he must ask forgiveness (*tawba*) for the contradictions and denials that have taken hold of him, and which have led him to break his promise. How can he do this? He must withdraw himself again totally from everything, and abandon his feelings and his *nafs*, and immerse himself completely in meanings, not returning to creatures except when he is certain that they are, in the Truth, non-existent. And when he is sure that all these things have left his heart, so that they do not enter his mind as an idea, or thought to make him reject what he has built up by his strength and his yearning (*himma*), he should fulfill what I have said; so that he returns to his true existence, and gives proof of it, without the need for any exact interpretation. But if he returns with his *nafs* and starts to interpret what was required of him, and he then finds that it is not as he claims, which can happen, he then has to return to where he was before, without making any interpretation, nor giving any explanations for what he has learnt. Because the knowledge of the Folk is founded on certainty, and not on the need for either approximate explanations, nor for any detailed, nor summary interpretation. As has been said before, it is, generally speaking, very difficult for the murid, in the Presence of the Names and the Attributes, to leave everything which is not Allah; and this should not be so. But, his difficulty lies in the multiplicity of the manifestations of the Names and the Attributes, which hinder him from witnessing the Essence in this world, if he is not firmly rooted in Allah. However, if he lifts himself up, and Allah grants him strength, then when the revelations come down upon him, and he travels through them, and comes to realize the Essence, he should fulfill his message, which is to manifest it in this world.

Above all, the murid has to restrain himself from seeing anything else but Allah, and to remain in this *state* continually. And if he finds this state of restraint pleasing he should not forsake it, nor should he try to use his efforts for anything, except Allah. By so doing he will be able to change in himself what is lower for what is higher; and the Truth, All-Mighty is He, has warned those who are not able to be patient with one kind of food (meaning the Oneness of the Essence) of the danger of the excitement, and the craving, for any other food. Allah, Praised and Exalted is He, has said, "Would you exchange what is better for what is worse? Go you down to Egypt." (2:61) What is meant by *Egypt*, according to what we say, is the center of the *self* in which every desire, either known, or concealed, can be found. About this Allah, the All-Knowing, the All-Wise, has said, "From what the earth provides of green herbs, cucumbers, garlic, lentils and onions." (2:61) For all the appetites of the self can be found together in ignominy and debasement. Therefore, because of their selves (*nufus*), humiliation came to them; for abasement only comes from the existence of the *self*. And the wrath of Allah fell upon them. But, on the other hand, power and esteem (*`izz*) come from the existence of intimacy and familiarity (*'ins*). Therefore, it was said, "If you want power and honor that does not diminish, do not esteem things which die and fade away."

In every case the murid should return to Allah and ask for forgiveness for everything that he has done; and he should begin, without delay, to mend everything that he has broken, and which breaks the fast, and which severs his promise with Allah, in His Presence. Then he will not to be degraded in His Eyes. However, any sins which the murid may have committed before entering into the Presence of Allah do not damage him, because in that case he was far away from Him; and this is the opposite for he who is sitting on the *rug of proximity*, and who needs always to be wary of the state of expansion (*bast*), because of the hazards that lie in it.

Know then, that if the murid feels grief or distress for any misdeeds which break his fast, he should return and make the intention to be for Allah alone. Then he returns with his heart, and with the help of his beloveds, who have clean and pure hearts, asking them to return him to his former station (*maqam*); and he should provide for them generously, for they are the Ambassadors of Allah between Him and His Creation. This he can do by feeding sixty poor brothers (*fuqara*) who know about his situation. And there should be one of them whose asking (*du`a*) is accepted by Allah, and before whom they swear, by Allah, that he is free of his former sinful state, so that he raises him up to Allah and heals him of his misdeeds. For everyone who is for Allah, Allah is for him. Then, understand! And Allah is the One Who helps.

الله

1 "The owner of the `ayn" was the soubriquet (kunya) given to Sidi `Abd al-Qadir al-Jilani, may Allah be pleased with him, because many of his poems ended the lines with a word beginning with the letter `ayn.

بسم الله الرحمن الرحيم

Al-Hajj
The Pilgrimage

The linguistic meaning, in Arabic, of the Pilgrimage is *the complete intention* which also has the meaning of the journey to Mecca and to al-Madina which, for the Folk of Allah, is the absolute intention for, and attentiveness to this station. For the Pilgrimage has a station above which there is no other, and because of that there is no way in which to speak about its hidden meaning and its Reality. And there are no words that can help us to express exactly what it is. And even there are no letters which could make up words which would be able to convey the truth of its meaning. For this reason there are very few of the Folk, normally, and even very few of those who have reached to it, who are able to speak about it, because of their lack of ability to do so. Yet the Pilgrimage is for whoever is able to make his way to it, and therefore it is a duty, for every Muslim, to perform it once in his lifetime.

And know that the Pilgrimage is not complete if its hidden pillars are neglected. The first of these pillars is what is forbidden (*al-ihram*). This means that as soon as the owner of this station puts on the clothes of *ihram*, then everything that was permitted for him before this moment is now forbidden, in addition to what is normally forbidden; and this is because of the magnitude (*ta`azim*) and the holiness of Allah in this station.

The second pillar is the *sa`i,* which is the rite of hastening between the signs of Safa and Marwa. This means the turning about of the knower, from side to side, between the severity (*al-jalal*) of Allah and His beauty (*al-jamal*), until the *jalal* becomes, for him, the Essence of the *jamal,* as a result of the destruction of his self (*nafs*), his desires and his will.

The third pillar is the *standing on `Arafah*, which is the station of the travelers, according to the words of he who is more than my father, the Prophet Muhammad, may peace and blessings be upon him, "The Pilgrimage is `Arafah." Most of the knowers have tried to explain this station but because they were, in some way, incomplete, they were not able to find the right words with which to speak about the truth of its meaning; and we are even less able to do so, than they were. For whenever the owner of this station tries to explain it, the more difficult it becomes. However, a few suitable words have been found to inform about it, but they cannot tell us about its station (*maqam*), which is known to the Folk as *tams*, which can be translated as *blindness*. It means something such as the full-stop, which is very small and very intense, so that there is no space inside it for anything else. Other words, giving something of the same meaning, are also used. But most of the knowers are veiled from *the hidden face* of this station, so that whenever they have tried to clarify it, the more its complexity increases. And when it is spoken about, he who is veiled from it will not believe what he who has reached to it says about it, for he only sees that it is one of the amazing things; but the knower of this station where he himself is standing is satisfied with having reached to it, without needing to explain anything about it. And how then will it be when he is told that in this reaching there is yet more to reach? For there is something which, until you reach to, you may deny, because when a person is still at the beginning, he will not believe in whatever he himself has not yet realized. For that, Sidi Ibn al-Farid, may Allah be pleased with him, said:

"If anyone, other than I, is satisfied with what he has reached,
I am he who is not satisfied with what he has reached."

Also the owner of the *`ayn*, `Abd al-Qadr al-Jilani, may Allah be pleased with him, said in a poem:

"There are things which it is not possible to unveil,
And by which I was fettered with the chains of the Law."

But some have rejected what I am saying, and they have told me that `Abd al-Qadir al-Jilani, may Allah protect his Secret, did not omit anything, but that he revealed everything, and that there was nothing further to explain than what he has said. And I said to him, "Yes, but he has left out something which is very difficult to unveil, and he has designated me to reveal some of this difficult *drink,* and extraordinary Secret which only a few are able to see and absorb, and even fewer to know. But when I made him understand it, both in a direct and an indirect manner, by explaining it to him in the closest meaning that I was given, he said to me, "By Allah! this is a strange matter!" And he was one of the People of Witnessing. Therefore, I now begin by saying:

Look, my beloved, at how valuable for its People, and how precious is this state! So when they arrive at it they begin to walk to Him, from Him. Firstly they walk to Allah, then they walk in Allah. My Master Abu Madyan al-Ghawth, may Allah be pleased with him, said in a Wisdom, "Those who journey travel to Him, but the knowers travel in Him." This is something which is transmitted to a person, and which is therefore removed from all logical reasoning, because of which it is not an obligation for this station to be realized in the perfect way, except by the person who has been given the capability for it. As we have already said: the meaning of this pillar is the Essence, and everything else follows after it.

The fourth pillar is the circumambulation (*tawaf*) of the Holy House, after the standing on `Arafah. This requires the returning to the manifestation of the Essence which has the right to the name of Divinity, because of what it contains of meanings and abstract relationships, and because it is the plunging into the understanding of the ways in which the Creator and creatures manifest; all of which make up the complete performing of the circumambulation.

And know, that in the Pilgrimage there are three kinds of actions. The first kind being those related to the pillars, which are its roots, and which, if not performed, make the Pilgrimage null and void, for there are no other actions which can replace these. The second kind concerns the duties for which a substitution can be made by blood-shedding. The third kind of actions are those to which no blame is attached if they are not carried out.

What is meant by the word *blood*, in this case, is the sacrificing, which means the killing of the nafs, if its death is realized; but in fact, any duty which is imposed in order to destroy the nafs, even if it has only been partly completed, is nevertheless acceptable; and this is not the case for the first and second pillars, which can only be completed by the acts which are obligatory for them. Or we can say that these pillars can only be perfectly fulfilled by themselves; because they concern the Essence. And when the depth of this station of the Essence is realized in accordance with its inner meaning and its Reality, I ask of you, O murid, to bring your heart, and to concentrate your mind in order to have the right understanding, so that when you ask for this station, you will, through your walking in it to Allah, receive Insight which is better than entering it without having any knowledge of it.

If you come to the place of comfort (*ragigh*), it is forbidden in the Law of Islam to cross it without first putting on the *ihram* - the ritual white seamless garment. And know that for every knower there is a *miqat,* a covenant or promise, which means a special time and a special place, each of which has its own conditions which should be satisfied. So that the *miqat of time* is when the murid is established in the certainty of the Oneness of Allah, by bearing witness that nothing exists in this world except Allah. Then if he wants the *standing*, this means that by clothing himself in the *ihram* he asks for the whole station (*maqam*), and the preparing of himself to walk in this station of the Essence, and for the drowning in its depths, and the gazing upon its Secrets. But before that time he is not permitted to put on the *ihram*, and the Pilgrimage is not required of him, for it cannot be entered into before its time, which comes in a well-known month.

The *miqat of place* begins at the borders of the world, or you can say: from the *sidrat al-muntaha*, or you can say: at *the ultimate limit*. And every *miqat* has its own conditions, as has been mentioned, for it is the expression (*kunya*) used to refer to the state of the murid and his excitement in his release, when he emerges from bondage. This is the *miqat* from all directions, whether from above or below, or from the right or the left, or from the absolute of *how,* or from the absolute of likenesses, for it is the release from the limitations of space and time, so that the murid is totally absorbed by this release into the complete freedom of Allah. However, before he has emerged from his state of bondage and its accompanying burdens, he cannot carry the demands of this station, which can be likened to the complete freedom in Allah from everything; for what he is seeking now is the Essence of the Hidden. Then, how can he walk to it if he is chained to the Creation, even though he may know Allah in the existence of manifestations. But he is obliged to emerge from this knowing, abandoning it, so as to reach to a deeper meaning than anything that he has known before. As we have said, "There are some knowers who do not have the words with which to express this knowledge, so we have tried to direct their attention to it, but it proved to be impossible for them to grasp it.

I then remembered Allah's words, All-Mighty is He, in a saying of His Angels, "Not one of us but has an appointed station." (37:164). But if the right time has come for he who seeks to walk in this station, it being the *time* of his Promise with Allah, this will give him dignity and majesty, because this is a station of annihilation which can be compared to the World of Lahut, the Secret of which cannot be reached by any human being.

Therefore, I would like to inform you, before you walk in this station, of the observances and rules for it. The state of comfort or pleasure (*rabigh*) is the place of purification, and the good manners necessary for it, which means the divesting of everything to be pure, leaving both the material world (*ad-dunya*) and the Hereafter (*al-aḫira*) to be with Allah, which is a duty under the Law, and in the murid's promise to it, by which he is bound to this station. Meaning that in this station he is cleansed from his existence so that it can in no way mingle with the existence of the Beloved. This is at the very limits of all human cultures; and it is the order for the first pillar, which concerns the rules and restraints necessary for the fulfilling of the laws of the Pilgrimage. And by this is meant the annihilation of all aspects of highness or lowness, of time or space, which is indicated by the taking off of all seamed clothing, this rite being a sign for the leaving of all material restrictions, so as to be wrapped around by a seamless garment symbolizing the enfolding into the Unity.

For, if the owner of this station does not relinquish all limitations of time and space, and lingering manifestations of the universe, all of which are related to the outer meaning of this station, he will not reach his goal. But as for its inner meaning, there is neither time nor space, because there is only Allah, for whom there is no time nor space, since He is now, as He always was. And when the might of this Creation is manifested to his eyes, he will then begin to purify his conception of the Truth (*al-Haqq*) from any ideas related to time and space, and from directions, and from the established pillars; for from pre-existence the

Truth has been free of all Attributes. And if we would accord them any existence, what then are these pillars in front of the Omnipotence of Allah, except like a mustard seed, and even smaller and more fragile than that, according to what they say?

But the Might of the Truth does not permit of making any comparisons, as some in the Divine Presence have said:

"And is there any wandering that leads to any but Me ?
And is there any emptiness for I fill all space.

For I am the hidden of the Essence, according to it,
And I am the revealed through the Attributes

In multiplicity and in singularity.
And there is no direction without My being the Lord of it.

And does anything other than I have appearance,
For I am the gatherer of all?

My Essence is the Essence of the Creation,
And it is as you see.

My omnipotence has no limits,
And it is the measure of a mustard seed."

If the murid leaves this world behind him, and starts walking without soul or body, and becomes for his Lord, in his Lord, then the hidden truths call to him, by the Divine tongue, speaking of the Presence (*hadhra*) of the Unity, saying, "Have you found existence for anything except My Name? And if you find that there is existence for anything except Myself, then bring proof of what the purpose is of the Attributes by which I have established for you that I am the First and the Last, the Revealed and the Hidden, the Hearer and the Seer. For I am with you, hearing and seeing."

The knower then says, "We see them looking at You, but they do not see." The lofty presence then answers him, from its sublime light: "For the eye does not see its Eye." And whenever the call is repeated, and he is permitted to draw near, he then says: "Here I am. Here I am in front of You." And he renews his answer: "Here I am, O Lord, at Your service," whenever he hears the call.

And if, O beloved, you reach to the Presence of the Unity, which is known as *Makka*, and which the special People refer to as the Essence which is worthy of Divinity, and if you become it, you must change your manners, because each station (*maqam*) and state necessitates its own manners. For the manners of Divinity and Lordship are not like those of the Names of Allah; and it is likewise for the other presences.

It is difficult for the murid to enter this presence because of how it manifests and of the effect which its Attributes and its wonders have upon him. In addition, what makes this station difficult for the human being is that he must abandon both his existence and everything that he has which, in the Truth, is non-existent. This is arduous for most people whose existence is built up of these contradictory states (existent yet non-existent), for now it is required of the slave that his existence passes away, yet he is not, at the same time, described as being existent. But it is necessary for him to know the truth of every Quality. The owner of the Wisdoms said: "The universes are immutable through His immutability yet they vanish in the Unity of the Essence." For in this station the universe is lost, in relation to the Eternal Essence, in the image of the Attributes, and it is but a metaphor (*mital*) which has no effect, except upon those things which are other than Allah, in His Unity.

Therefore nothing can help the person in this station except to surrender; and he can only enter it through this door. But know that the benefits of being obedient in this will shortly be manifested to him. However, if he appears to be separated from the proximity because of its might having overwhelmed him so that he loses all sense of himself, then what use is it for him to ask for proximity, since he is, in fact, already in it? This would mean that he would abandon the manners which have helped him to leave behind everything, even to his own name. About this, it is said: "Allah does not call the person who can see Him, and he who does not call Him, cannot see Him."

So that the good conduct and manners required by this presence is in the concern for seeing Allah, and for surrendering to Him everything that is due to Him; which means the surrender to everything that manifests from His Actions; and that is His Universe. The sign for this surrender is *the kissing of the Black Stone*, which is therefore known as *the Right of Allah*.

And know that if the knower reaches this station, he will understand how the heavens and the earths are folded into the right-hand-side of Allah, which thus veils him from seeing all material things, because these do not manifest from His right-hand-side. But when all things, through His majesty, are revealed and unraveled, then the eyes of the knower see the Essence before they see the things. Then if he praises a thing he is praising the right-hand of Allah, since this is all that he sees, for before he praises a thing he has witnessed the Essence of Allah in it.

And it is also from the required good manners to circumambulate the House seven times; which means the reflecting on the seven Attributes of power, will, knowledge, life, hearing, speech and sight, and the possibility of putting them in their true order, in relation to each other. This is the station of *elaboration and of details*, the knowledge of which accepts neither summation nor abstraction, for that was the case of the murid before; and therefore now it is his duty not to cut short his circumambulations, but to *taste* fully the meanings of the Attributes, and to realize, in himself, the unifying bond between them; and to kiss the Stone, which is revealed to him through the Attributes, saying, "We praise Allah, the Greatest of Creators." The Truth, Praised and Exalted is He, shows Himself, in this form, to His Saints (*awliya*) with His Names and Attributes, after which the revelation of His Attributes becomes so intense that it comes to be the complete Essence which is manifesting in each Attribute separately; and this is *the state of particularization and diffusion.*

And know that those who know are part of the manifestations of the universe, for sometimes Allah manifests in them, and at other times He manifests upon them. Then, if He exalts him and He reveals himself to him, he returns to be like water; and if He reveals Himself through him, then he may say whatever he wishes, because he is giving expression to the Essence of the Truth, with the tongue of the Truth, and not with his own tongue. And it is said:

"This is the station of negation which I have reached,
So say what you wish, either in detail or in summation."

For the pilgrim, on entering the Ka`ba, finds the six directions all facing towards Allah. How is it then for the knower when he is folded up into the Essence of his Creator? And from the truth of His words, Ibn al-Farid said:

"All directions face towards Me.
After my worship, my Pilgrimage, and my `Umra."

Then all that I reveal in this station of the forms of worship is only manifesting separation, for this is a station of separation, although all that is revealed about this station on the tongues of the knowers comes from the radiance of the presence of the Unity. But it is not permitted to speak about the Unity and the Treasury, which are revealed in the standing (*wuquf*) on `Arafah, and in the coming out (*huruj*) from this station. But anyone who desires to continue in the proximity of this station, must stand in the House, in the station of Ibrahim, may peace be upon him, for Allah, Mighty and Supreme is He, says, "And whoever enters it has become a believer." (3:97) For the murid who wishes to remain in the station of the standing-place of the Unity or the Treasury is not safe because of the fear which accompanies this station, and therefore he should go to the Ka`ba, the Holy House, and he should circumambulate it, and pray seven times, because in this place it is possible to worship and to *see*. Whoever enters this place (the station of Ibrahim) is safe, which is not the case with the standing on `Arafah, because there he is unable to do anything, and he should not linger there, because there the devil also is strong. `Arafah is the Ocean, and if anyone remains too long there, hallucinations and illusions will come to him, because he is between his nafs and the devil. This case is well-known to the special People, because they are always aware of the wiles and temptations of the devil, who has enticed many of them from this station; so we ask Allah to protect us from the devil wherever he is.

The Shaykh `Abd al-Qadir al-Jilani, may Allah be pleased with him, said, "The devil called to me in this station, saying: O My slave! I have freed you from prohibitions. When I turned around I felt a constraint inside my heart, saying that Allah does not command abomination, and I answered him as my inner voice told me to do. He said: O `Abd al-Qadir, I have taken many people before from this station."

One of the important excuses offered for the knowers in this station of falling into the devil's trap, and being taken by him, just as their parents Adam and Eve were taken from the Garden, is that they are not aware that he sits in this station. Yet even if the knower were to be forewarned about the devil in this station he may still be deceived by him, unless he looks deeply into his heart which is firmly grounded in the Truth. If he looks deeply and rejects the devil's temptations, then this is what is required of him.

And it is said that when the knower finishes his circumambulation, and has absorbed the *reality of conjunction* (meaning, the gathering together of the Attributes through tasting and realization), he should then reach to the Stone, which is the symbol for the knowledge of the seven Attributes (power, will, knowledge, life, hearing, speech and sight), and from there he must move swiftly between Safa and Marwa, between the majesty (*al-jalal*) and the beauty (*al-jamal*) until the rank of completion (*kamal*). You can, therefore, see the knowers moving between these two stations as the child moves from side to side in its cradle. Their turning about comes from the Hand of the Caring, which keeps them in both these states; and in that they do not lose anything of what they have received through the circumambulation, and of their resting in the Presence of the Unity; until they become a part of it. For now neither the manifestation of the *jalal* nor of the *jamal* can affect their inner *being* because they only touch their outer bodies. This is the case of the Folk of Allah, whereas for others everything is a trial for them, and their entire being enters the Fire. And: "We test you with evil and with good." (21:35)

But for the true knowers, the majesty and severity (*al-jalal*) becomes a source of beauty (*al-jamal*) and therefore they are able to be pleased with either state. Our Shaykh Sidi Muhammad al-Buzaydi, may Allah be pleased with him, used to say, if he was touched by the pain of the *jalal*, that it was from the beauty of the *jamal*, and you would see him then happier and more full of wisdom than when he was in a state of *jamal*. One of the marvelous things was the day when they went to visit him, feeling pity for him because he was in deep pain having lost the use of one of his hands and one of his legs. He, may Allah be pleased with him, began to talk to them about something which had come to him when he entered the Path, for he said, "Once I was sleeping on one of the holy nights, and when I awoke I touched the hand that I could not move with the one I could move, and it felt to me as though it was something that was attached to me, and that did not belong to me; and I felt as though it was dead, and I thought that it was something strange to me. I called to the people of the house to light the lamp, and said: The living One (*al-Hayy*) is with us, and I have caught hold of Him, because the lifeless hand had started moving. When the people brought the lamp I found that my hand had caught hold of the other hand, and there was no other living thing, and nothing else on my body. And I said: Praise be to Allah. This is an example of how illusion takes hold of the murid before he knows Allah."

Then look, my brother and my sister, at the state of the special People, and of how they are able to drink from the *jalal* because they are neither with the *jalal* nor with the *jamal*, but they are with Allah in all their states. They see the contracting (*qabdh*) and the outspreading (*bast*) as they see night and day. "And We bring you night as a covering, and day for going about your livelihood." (78:10) These are two states which are necessary for the human being to know, for the withholding (*qabdh*) is the Attribute for the spirits, and the expansion (*bast*) is the Attribute for the souls. "And Allah grasps and outspreads." (2:245) Then, if the knower is with Allah, he is with the Grasper and the Withholder but he is not with what is withheld; and he is with the Expander and not with what is expanded, for he knows that Allah is the doer of actions, and also He is the receiver of actions. When he understands this, and truly knows it, he becomes one of those for whom nothing is able to overwhelm them.

So, O murid, be with Allah in everything, then you will see that He is with you, and that He is following you; and you are like the prince, for your Fire is also your blessing, and it is the hands of mercy, grace and compassion which are moving you about; and then nothing can harm you, and you do not yearn for anything. Then let it be the station which calls to you, and do not you be the caller; for it has been created for you, but you were not created for it. And walk straight to Allah, and devote yourself, above everything else, in saying: "*La ilaha 'illa'llah*" and "*Allahu Akbar*" and in the crowning or exaltation (*tahlil*); until you find the balance between both states. Then move to Marwa, and stand at Safa. Meaning, cast yourself into the rite of throwing at Marwa, for it is the symbol for the severity (*al-jalal*), and Safa is the symbol of beauty (*al-jamal*). But you, O knower, be described by perfection, or completion (*al-kamal*), which accepts both the meaning of Marwa and of Safa. For he who knows Allah only in the beauty and denies Him in the severity, loses the right to completion (the station of *kamal*), and illusions will turn him away from the Path, and he will not find satisfaction in Allah, nor will Allah be well-pleased with him.

For this Sidi Muhammad al-Harraq al-Maghribi said, in one of his wisdoms: "The honest knower retains his good manners (*`adab*) with Allah in all His appearances, and does not ignore Him in any of His aspects; for he is not present only with Allah in some of His faces whilst ignoring Him in others. He gives their Names to all His faces, and he is not influenced by them."

My brother and my sister, do not only worship the revelations whilst ignoring the withholding of revelations, so that the words of Sidi al-Maghribi have no application for you. Therefore, it is your duty to stand up and to walk, in completion, through every station, so that your nafs, through the anxiety of being confronted in the walking with something unpleasant to it, is not halted by this, and at the same time, moves on to another station without having completed the one before. But be like the people of the Cave about whom Allah (the Exalted) says, "And We moved them now to the right, now to the left," (18:18) because they did not allow their nafs to be reassured by some things, and deterred by others. Until the Hand of the eternal Mercy moves you to the Essence of the Severity (*al-jalal*) and the Essence of the Beauty (*al-jamal*), and you are like a dead person in the hands of those washing his body. You can then call for whatever you want, because the Examiner has marked you down as worthy of trust. And if anyone does not accept this, then that most probably shows that he is a liar.

Then, after the *sa`i* (the moving between Safa and Marwa seven times), and the circumambulation, he abandons everything. But before that he is not permitted to say "I," as has been said, for the Examiner will mark anyone down as a liar who calls making any claim to what he does not possess; except if he has reached to this state of purity from the knowledge of his nafs, and the complete acceptance, at the same time, of the *jalal* and the *jamal*, the contracting and the withholding (*qabdh*) and the expanding (*bast*), poverty and riches, death and life; for this is the proper balance for the *nafs* of the *murid.* Then if he lays claim to anything, he must give proof of it, and if he relies on one thing and ignores another, then he does not have the right to claim what is not his. Allah, Praised and Exalted is He, says about this: "If yours is the Home of the Hereafter with Allah, especially above all people, then wish for death, if you are truthful." (2:94)

One of them said, "A man is not complete until his heart is *ripe* in four things: in what is prohibited (*mana`*), in the giving (*`ata'*), in honor (*`izz*), and in humility (*dul*)."

It is said about Ibrahim, the son of Adam, may Allah be pleased with him, that he said, "I was seldom contented in Islam, except once when I was in a boat, and there was a man telling funny stories, to make the people laugh. This was at the time of the war with the Turks, and this huge man in the boat came towards me, and seized me by my beard, and thrust his head onto my throat, like this, and the people in the boat were all laughing at what he was doing to me, and I felt that there was no-one in the boat smaller than I, nor more despised. Then I became happy about that. And another time I was sitting and a man came and urinated on me."

These stories, and those similar to them, are a manifestation of their states, which are necessary, for if the human being reaches this state he can count himself as being in an elevated and pure rank, because he fears Allah. "And it was said to those who revere their Lord: what did your Lord send down to you? They said: Good." (16:30)

Know, that it is necessary for he who holds the station of the circumambulation to be in a state of purity and of concealment. We have spoken about the purity, but as for the concealment, this is the safeguarding and the restraining of the *self* with the truths, and the preserving of the Divine Secrets. This is a duty upon the person in this station, because it is a distinguished one which is able to bring together the difference existing between the *jalal* and the *jamal*, through the realization of the meaning of the rite of the *sa`i,* which is the running between the *jalal* and the *jamal,* and the circumambulation back through the Attributes to the Unity of Allah; all of which demands the observance of Orders and the safeguarding of a condition of secrecy. He who is in the Presence of the Unity is required, as far as he is able, to preserve the Secrets of this Presence (*hadra*), because he witnesses He Who is the Causer of all things, as well as what He causes, and the influences and effects of His Attributes. For this reason it is said:

"Be wary, and preserve the veil,
For these are the beautiful bounds of Allah.

Then close them, for only in the preserving of the Secret
Resides reverence and solemnity.

And pride in Allah and His Glorification is the source of strength
Amongst the Friends of Allah.

Be satisfied with the Blessing from Allah, from wherever it comes,
And keep it as a treasure from those who deny His Attributes."

In this station it may be more difficult for the person, who is absent from everything about which we have just spoken, to preserve the Secret, for he is so overwhelmed that if he reveals it, he is forgiven for this, because, in his intoxication, he has lost his mind, and in that case of mindlessness he is beyond the state of being commanded.

Know my murid, that he who enters the state of restraint, or prohibition, should remain in it until he reaches the House (the Unity) where he leaves behind him obedience to what is ephemeral and transient, and he becomes content with his new existence. So that when it is the time for him to move on to another station he nevertheless remains waiting to know whether he should re-enter the state of prohibition, or not. Then, tell him here that he should again and again pass through that state of restraint, until he reaches his goal, and he is folded up into it, as he was into the stations before; because in the Truth whenever he enters a new station there are conditions for it, just as there were for the stations before. For what he must understand is that he has to proceed until he reaches to, and realizes the meaning of each station, and he is annihilated in what has been decreed for that station. This means that he must follow what is the complete message coming from each presence (*hadra*) of the Attributes.

Then, after the *tawaf* and the *sa`i* the murid must be prepared to continue walking to a state of worthiness, or it can be said, to a state beyond which there is nothing, and for which the order is the abandoning of everything that he has known, and every realization that he has so far received. Now O murid, you must leave everything that can be described as either *inner* or *outer*, absent or present, because the station to which you are now traveling does not accept any of these manifestations (*zuhur*), nor the witnessing of any Names or Attributes, nor the possibility of attachment to any created thing. And if you do not reach to what we have just mentioned you will not smell the fragrance of the World of Divinity. It is difficult for most knowers to enter this station, because of the extent of its emptiness (*jard*). For this presence may require him to relinquish any vestige of his shadow existence (*shabah*), and his soul, his nafs and his mind, and the Names and Attributes, and all fragrances of manifestations. And you are required now to unite, and to fold up all appearances into the Inner (*butun*), and this Inner into the Outer (*zuhur*); which means the uniting of all in the All, and the folding in of all your appearances into non-manifestations, and your existence into witnessing; and then, if you realize this, to ascend the mountain, which is described as the standing (*wuquf*) on the mountain, other than which there is nothing.

Now your existence is complete because of your absence in the Truth, from the Creation; and in this station there is no tearing asunder nor mending, for it is referred to as *the station of oblivion, or blindness*. The 'Imam `Abd al-Karim al-Jili, may Allah be pleased with him, has spoken about this station saying: "Blindness is a means of speaking about the Truth of the Truths, which is not preceded either by the Reality (*al-Haqiqa*), nor by the Vice-Regency (*al-Halifa*), because it is of the purest Uniqueness to which neither the Reality, nor the Vice-Regency can add anything; and it cannot be brought to an end, because the Names and the Attributes are non-existent in proximity to it." This is the meaning of his words, may peace and blessings be upon him, "Oblivion, or blindness, is that above which there is no air, and beneath which there is no air." For no meaning can be given to this station, and therefore it is referred to as the *standing* or the *bewilderment*, or the *Divinity*, or the *obliteration* (*tams*), or the *Great Fear* (*rabbut*). There is no name for this station, but these words are used by the Sufis for it can neither be reached nor realized except through itself. The knower, therefore, is in the state of obedience so long as he is walking towards this station, until he descends from `Arafah, when this descent is referred to as the coming down, and this is because of the love for the attraction of being absent in the Absent (*al-ghayb*) and of being concealed in the

Concealer, and of being united in the Unity, and of being diminished in the Diminution and Curtailment (*taqsir*). O All-Mighty God, how precious is this station! So that we can see that even the special People are confused as to how to speak about it, and how cautious they are when describing it; as if they were blind and deaf out of the astonishment of not knowing where they are.

Know that the *standing* comes after all that is visible (*zuhur*) has vanished, and after the turning inwards of what is outspread: "When the sun is folded up, and when the stars fall losing their brilliance." (71:1) This station of obliteration (*tams*) is not of any kind, not male nor female, so that he, may peace and blessings be upon him, said, about it, "Above it there is no air and beyond it there is no air." Therefore it is very deep, and its rewards come only after much enduring effort. It is for this reason, therefore, that it is important to descend from it without any lingering, or as soon as one has reached to a *standing* in it.

It has been said that this is a station of fear which should not be dwelt upon, so that the knower must relinquish it, without delay, lest he be harmed by the Fire, which overspreads it. After which the murid, for fear of being enveloped by it, should go to a place which is far removed from it, and therefore he should hasten to the *Muzdalifa*, or proximity, in order that in descending from the station of *standing* the knower becomes known and recognized by existence, in which both He Whom he worships, and He who is the worshipper, are made fast to him; for the Lord is the Truth and the slave is the Truth, and he has become a true worshipper of He Who is worshiped, because His Secret resides in His slave, after which he has a known station, and a recognized Secret.

For that, the knower in this station is taken by the existence in which both the seer and what is seen is confirmed for him, so that the influence of this will manifest in his prostration (*sujud*), and the tongue of his state calls out: "Allah! From the Truth of existence, You are the worshipper, and You are He Who is worshiped. You are the Seer and what is seen. You are the Eye. You are the Beauty, and You are the Where. You are I, and no I is there but You. There is no other Essence with You, so kill me through Your soul, O Soul of the souls," as it is said:

"O Soul, the soul of the soul, the great 'aya.
O last consolation, the free heart.

O eternal hope, or final destiny,
How beautiful are Your words to me, and how bitter."

Know then, that when true existence merely touches the person in this station so that he enters into the witnessing, then he has to be aware of the onslaught of the Devil (*ash-shaytan*) because this station is surrounded by deceptions and a multitude of enviers. For in this station the Devil, with all his deceptions and damnation stands in the Path of the knowers the moment they become separated from Allah. Therefore, it is important, when returning from this station, to hasten on until the safety of Makka is reached; and that is the Presence of the Unity, in which the knower is secure.

And what the Truth (*al-Haqq*), All-Mighty and Powerful is He, has told us about the Devil, suffices us, and of how he greets the traveler on the Straight Presence (*al-hadra al-mustaqim*), for he said: "Then I will assault them from in front of them, and from behind them. From their right hand and from their left, and in their belief, and in their hearing." But Allah protects the Muslims from this evil, for the Devil has no power over those whom He has taken by His hand: his authority is only over those who take him as their guardian." (16:100)

But it is because of the wiles of the Devil that the knower is asked to hasten from this place of dangers, so that when he finds tranquillity again he should stop and pray the morning prayer, and in so doing purify the reason for which he is traveling and wandering; and by this I mean his soul, to which after having lost it, he needs to be reunited; so that he can worship in his new-found existence.

And after that, O knower, hasten onwards, and be careful of your *self* so that the Devil cannot seize you unawares from in front of you, nor from behind you; and do not trust him, but stone him before he reaches you, for if you stone him he will return fearing you, instead of you fearing him. But do not fear him, but fear Allah, for He it is Who protects you from the Devil. For Allah, Praised and Exalted is He, has said: "So do not fear him, but fear Me, if you are believers." (3:175) At the same time beware. But the state of the knower does not become steady, nor does his fear leave him until he reaches the House, which is the symbol of the Unity, the station of Ibrahim, where all those who enter it are protected, for there is no safety before entering this stronghold, and the presence of *la ilaha illa'llah* is reached. This is what is meant by the *hadiṯ al-qudsi* in which Allah, Praised and Exalted is He, spoke through His Prophet Muhammad, saying: “La ilaha illa 'llah is My stronghold, and whoever enters My stronghold is safe from My punishment.” And this is the presence which is worthy of the worshipper and He Who is worshiped, and the seer and what is seen, which is unlike the presence which we mentioned earlier, which is that of total annihilation.

For this reason we have said that the knower must not linger in that station, and not even on the Path to it, but he must abandon it totally, because the Devil lies in wait in front of the knowers on this Path, receiving each one of them with a special exclusiveness with which he deceives them, thus confusing knowledge with ignorance. And do not think that the Devil is only on this Path. Here we are referring to the Devil of the mind and the senses, for each presence has its own Devil. For this reason it is said that the king is the Devil of the World of the Kingdom (*al-malakut*), and the kingdom is the Devil of the World of Dominion (*al-jabarut*); meaning that each of these worlds has a Devil of its own nature. And the knower is approached by the selfsame door from which he entered, so that the Devil takes him from the very place where he is. The Devils are everywhere and in all stations, “For the water is the color of the glass which contains it.” Even when the knower is in the Presence of Allah, not having anything, and not seeing anything but Him, the Devil calls to him with the Tongue of Divinity, as has happened to some of them; so that they have said, “The Devil called to me in the Presence of Proximity (*qu'ub*) and Witnessing, saying: O My slave, I free you from all prohibitions! And if Allah had not joined my heart to His, the Devil would have taken me from the place in which I was not aware of him, because I was witnessing only Allah.”

Most of the knowers have been seized in this state, but what excuses them is that they do not realize that the state has a Devil, until they are shown him. So that the knower is taken from where he is because of being unaware of him; but if he is forewarned, and alerted, the Devil would not be able to take him. I have met some of them in this state, in the midst of the *valley of Fire*, and I warned them of the wiles of the Devil, and of his deceptions, and I told them to be on the alert and watchful for him. Some of them listened to my advice, and were forewarned of his tricks, and they said, “No-one is safe from the deceptions of Allah, except the People who are *lost*." Others of them did not believe my words, and answered me, "You are veiled from Allah, for where is the Devil in this presence; we can see nothing but Allah here?" And their estimation of me became low in their eyes. "So some were saved and some were drowned." And when I met some of them, whom I had warned, I asked them, "How did my station manifest to you, and how did you find my advice?" They answered me, "We were not aware of what you told us, and we ask the Truth (*al-Haqq*), Exalted is He, to be merciful to us, so that we may be taken back, for we are being sorely oppressed."

Therefore, O traveler on the Path, be aware, for I am a faithful adviser for you, and I warn you against the whisperings of the Devils, and I am telling you about the states of your Path, and what you may meet upon it.

Then, if you have success in the presence of Actions, and you are annihilated from your own individual acts in the Actions of Allah, He will speak to you in the Secret, with beneficial words, being drowned by Him in the witnessing of Actions. But there exists a deadly poison for you if you are not aware of the deceptions of the Devil, as he says to you, "All that you see are performing the Actions of Allah, but they are veiled because they are annihilated in the actions." You answer him, "Yes!" Then he says to you, "How do you know, for I do not see that you are absent from your actions, for you look upon your actions as coming from yourself?" And you say, "This is forbidden (*haram*) and this is permitted (*halal*) so then where is your knowledge of His words, Exalted is He: "And Allah has created you and you do not know." (37:96)

Then if the Divine Caring were not there, you would be taken like the wretched ones are taken. If you are in the Presence of Attributes, annihilated from your own attributes in Allah's Attributes, the Devil says to you, "Say O Allah! Who is beyond everything, for there is no seer, nor hearer, nor speaker, nor capable one, nor knower, nor alive, nor seeker to the Truth, except Allah." You then say to him, "Yes," and he says to you, "The knowers are annihilated from their attributes and Allah has taken charge of their concern. If goodness comes from them they do not ask for a reward for it, and if evil comes from them, the blood-money (*diya*) is upon the killer, for he is dead and not alive."

If the knower is in the Presence of the Essence, annihilated from his own essence in the Essence of his Creator, the Devil comes to him, to the shore of the presence, and calls to him, saying, "There is no existence but Allah's existence." Then the knower turns towards these noble words, which are the most precious to him, and when he meets with the Devil he says, "The Truth (*al-Haqq*) manifests in all things - a Mighty Manifestation - and it is the ultimate Truth of existence." But he who cannot be pleased with the manifestations, in which Allah is the Manifester, has missed many wonderful and praiseworthy things. For what is the benefit of knowing that you know Him in some manifestations, but you do not know Him in this manifestation? But he who is permitted to see Him in both what is prohibited and what is permitted, says to Him, "All beauty is the Beauty of Allah." But if you are still fearful of punishment, what then is the benefit of removing the veil? Do you not know that the reason for suffering is the existence of the veil?

Then if he listens to his advice the Devil takes him just as he took his parents before him; and may Allah protect us from this evil. But he who is taken by the Hand of Allah does not turn to the Devil, because Allah has made him understand from the beginning about him, and he sees that every word which he hears, coming from Allah, is like the beautiful cloth (*kiswa*) which shrouds the Ka`ba; and he sees also that, in this way, Allah obscures His words. But this does not deter him, and he does he follow the words of the Devil.

It is for this reason, and with this meaning, that the owner of this station is required to stone the Devil with three stones, for it is said by the People of the Path, that the Devil has three ways by which he misleads, and that when the knower reaches any one of them he must stone him, and not be beguiled by his deceiving suggestions, for if he does not throw stones at him, he will incline towards his words, and the Devil will take hold of him with nothing but evil consequences; and he will not allow him to escape from his clutches. Then the Light of the Truth will be changed into falsehood and a false Reality, and the soul will give place to the nafs, and the king will be replaced by the Devil. And the armies of darkness, repression, and disappointment will conquer him: "Surely we are of Allah and to Him we return." (2:156)

This is a very difficult station which only few can reach. Whoever tries to walk in it must be steadfast in his *self*, and in what he has realized in understanding and knowledge; and to keep the prayer, and not to lose any of the pillars of the Religion, all of which goes back to being well grounded in the wisdoms of the Law (*ash-shari`a*). Whoever cannot follow this, nor is able to be in this state, should stay away. We are therefore required to stone the Devil wherever he manifests and stands in our Path; and to be always vigilant for him, and aware of what his Reality demands of us. Therefore, you, O murid, are ordered to stone him and not to turn away from him, nor to turn on your heels before him. And know, that with the throwing of the very first stone, strength comes to the knower, because this is a sign, and a proof of his willingness, and his standing firm at the door of his heart, and of his intention to cleanse it for the Truth (*al-Haqq*), and to rid it of falsehood (*batil*). After that, in facing up to the Devil, things become easier, for now he knows about his tricks, when he begins to play and to tempt, and he also knows how to discharge him from his Path. For this reason it is said: "He who in the beginning is illumined, will in the end be illumined."

So if you, O murid, in such difficult places, find safety and protection, you will have reached to what is required of you, because in this way, you have become one who knows that the Devil is one of the manifestations of the Creation; and that each manifestation, according to its Reality, demands the answer of he who walks on the Path of Allah. For the Devil is only fulfilling his appointed role, just as you are ordered to fulfill the role for which you have been created.

We have been speaking about the station of *the standing on `Arafah*, and that it is one of complete drowning, and that the owner of this station neither sees nor hears anything, nor does he have any cares, and that his treasure is sealed, for he is in an Ocean without shores. Does he, then, in this Ocean take heed of prohibitions (*haram*)? Your answer is: "He is absent and is not able even to see what is permitted of him (*halal*) so how, then, could he see what is not permitted?"

Then, when he is in this Ocean it is not permitted for him *to hunt on the land*. Meaning, that he is required to keep the separation between his *self* and his senses, the metaphor for this separation being that the pilgrim is not permitted, while he is wearing the garments of the Pilgrimage, to hunt on land. Allah, Exalted is He, has said, "Permitted to you is water-game and its use for food, for the benefit of yourselves and those who travel; and forbidden for you is hunting on land so long as you are in the Sacred Precincts." (5:99) This means that so long as you are drowned in the great Ocean and you have left your senses, then everything connected with the senses has no meaning for you; but when you emerge from the Ocean of drowning, to the *self*, and you see *land*, then the rules of the Law (*ash-shari`a*) should be followed, because you have now returned to be aware of your senses, as the special People say, then the permitted (*halal*) and the forbidden (*haram*) return to their usual domain. For in the Ocean there are no pictures and no vessels, but when the knower comes out of the Ocean and he is received by the land, he finds that there are dense objects and distinctions written on the faces of manifestations, which indicate to him that this is permitted and this is forbidden. But the state in which there are no pictures, no names, no manifestations and no wisdom, is like the obscurity of a dark night, one layer above another. Who is it then who allows what is permitted, and upon whom were all things, which are not permitted, made forbidden? He says: "Whose is the kingdom this day? Allah's the One, the Omnipotent." (40:16) When the knower's heart is not open to leave this station in the perfect way; meaning to leave it not only in his soul, but also in the deeper place of the Secret inside his heart, then he emerges from it uncompleted, for in this case he has not abandoned the Ocean in all his states and conditions; yet in the Truth everything is always under the protection of this Ocean, when he understands how to emerge perfectly from it. So what can the knower do with this Ocean, which is now a part of himself? It is said:

"The Ocean is an ocean as it has been since Eternity,
And happenings are its waves and rivers."

Therefore, if he hunts in the sea, he cannot harm anything by this, because ultimately everything is in, or from, the Ocean. In the eyes of the knower this Ocean includes all things, and the Devil is one of the creatures (*'afrad*) of the Creation; then how can the knower throw stones at him?

I answered, "The Devil is part of what Allah has created of the land-game, and were the Ocean to absorb him completely we would then be required to stone him, not only on the Mountain of `Arafah, but also in every place away from it, because he would then exist between the state of annihilation and the state of the Presence of the Unity. And if we were to find the Devil in the Ocean, during the state of drowning, we would eat him, and eating him would be permitted for us, according to Allah's words: Permitted to you is the game of the sea." (5:96)

For this reason you can see that most *majadib*, who are drowned in the Ocean of the Oneness, do not find any meaning, nor sense, for the Devil; nor are they subjected to any of his tricks. And if they were to find him they would swallow him up, as if he were a piece of food. Yet this would not bring them any closer to destroying him, because whenever the *majadib* happened to find him, he would disappear to another hunting-ground; for the Devil only hunts the murid who is on land. Meaning, when he is likely to be overmastered by his senses, and to begin to taste the desires of his nafs. But if the Devil finds the knower freed from the imprisonment of his human nature, how then can he reach him in order to tempt him, because he whom he is trying to entice is not able to hear him? And this is the case of the special people of drowning.

But the Masters of the art of blending, or mixing (*mazj*), those who are well-grounded and established between, on the one hand, intoxication and, on the other hand, sobriety, follow a different law, so that they can distinguish between what is beneficial and what is harmful, and they are always in a balanced state of being able to see, and be aware of, all things. But although their eyes are in the Glorification and Exaltation of their Lord, they still fear the harmful things of the Creation, such as scorpions, owls, fierce dogs, and the suggestions of the raven; all of which are metaphors for the nafs, the Devil, the dunya, and human inclinations, which are found on land (*barr*), and which exist with the human being who is rooted in his senses; which is the case of all those who are drowned in this lower material world.

However, the knower is, nevertheless, required to accept, recognize and realize, the meanings coming from his senses, as being a part of the totality of all created things. Therefore, he should have respect for them, but he should not be caught by them, because both the nafs, the Devil, and the material world, and everything to which they incline, are in opposition to the Oneness of the Unity, which is the goal of the knowers, and the intention of the Unity; and he only truly fears whatever prevents him from meeting with his Lord. He fears both the *dunya* and the inclinations of his desires (*hawa*) when he comes to realize their harmfulness. But when he is absent in witnessing the Truth (*al-Haqq*) and enjoying His protection, nothing can harm him; for in that case he takes whatever he needs from everything, yet at the same time, nothing can take away anything, of which he has true knowledge, from him. Everything yearns for him, but he does not yearn for anything. And this is the state which no other state can deny. But the Devil will enter him if he finds in him the slightest inclination in his favor - an opening through which he can enter - so that it is from that door that he has to be stoned. For the human being, because of his nature, is never free nor safe from the invasion of the Devil who, like the nafs, is very persistent in his demands and his enticements.

Therefore, in this station, the *stoning* is a holy Law, which the pilgrim is obliged to honor and fulfill; for whenever the knower returns to his nafs and acts in accordance with its desires, such as drinking, eating and clothing himself, he starts recognizing what pleases and contents him in the way of deceptions and of appraisal and approval, so that he must be wary of every one of these manifestations, in face of what his Truth demands of him. And when he is veiled by words or thoughts, and he does not know what Allah wants of him, then let him refer to the ancient words of the Straight Path, which have been laid down, and ordered for him to follow: "Verily, this is My Way, leading straight: so follow it." (6:153)

For in the Holy Qur'an there are righteous norms for reference, so leave aside, and do not follow any word that does not carry the might of the Qur'an, because Allah, the Exalted, the Supreme, has said, "Nothing have We omitted from the Book." (6:38)

Now, let us return to what we were speaking about earlier, regarding what is forbidden on the Pilgrimage. For example, it is forbidden to hunt even in retaliation, for meanness does not exist in this presence (*hadra*). So how can he hunt when he sees everything to be the Presence of Allah? It was said that Majnun Layla found a dog which he took into his house, and fed, and respected, and occupied himself in caring about. But the people, mocking at him, said, "What are you doing with this dog?" He said to them, "How can I not respect this dog when I found it in Layla's quarter of the town?" For this it is said:

"I pass by the houses, the houses of Layla,
And I kiss these walls and those walls.

But it is not the love for the houses that fills my heart,
But it is the love for the One who lives in the houses."

Say: "Behold all that is in the heavens and the earth." (10:101)

I have found that, in this station, most knowers observe good manners towards the Creation as if they are with the Truth Himself. Our Master `Abd al-Qadir al-Jilani, may Allah be pleased with him, said about this:

"In the Truth there is nothing but Allah,
So smell His fragrance, for He is the fragrance in the Creation."

Therefore, you see that the people who enjoy this presence (*hadra*) never hurt anything, and even if they are but few, they are enough; for the wisdom of the pilgrim is such that he neither harms nor kills anything, not even a louse, for he finds that he and all the Creation of Allah are in this noble presence, and therefore he is polite with everything. And I myself remained in this state for more than five years, witnessing the lights of this presence surrounding the Creation which was overflowing with its Secrets. You would see me absorbed by its creatures, in deep politeness, even if I was attacked by them, for I reached to great peace, and a state of deep expansion, until Allah moved me to another station, and I became occupied with Him, not knowing if I was, after that, impolite with the Creation, or not.

In every case, the owner of this station cannot harm anything of Allah's Creation, except as we have mentioned, that he fears, through this, the existence of any separation of a harmful nature, in which case he must repel it before it oppresses him. And the most dangerous source of separation is the nafs, so that he must put an end to its evil, and in no case trust it. Allah, Praised and Exalted is He, says, "If it offered every ransom none will be accepted from it." (6:70) For if the murid does not forbid his nafs it will get the mastery over him, and once it does this, it is difficult to repel it. Therefore, he should fear his nafs from the very beginning.

As has already been said, the owner of this station is beyond the confines of the Universe, both in space and time; and if he is not completely free from his surroundings, and from the most seemingly insignificant thing of the *dunya*, as was the case of the murid with his Shaykh and the needle (mentioned by us in our Chapter on Fasting, *as-sawm*), he will not reach to the complete freedom.

Therefore let us now speak about what he is supposed to do. We have mentioned that if the murid remains in this state and becomes immersed in the hidden Absence, his vision of the universe having been cut off from all influences of material existence, yet he does not say, "I have understood the meaning of this," it means that he has returned to his senses, which, in this case, he is not permitted to do, so long as he is in this station which is one of total effacement, without any trace of the senses. Then it should be clear to him that he cannot penetrate deeper into this state, for it is only possible to do that when he no longer has any perception of time or space, as the words of Ibn `Arabi, the great Master, explain, "He who is not grounded in this knowledge of ours, dies insisting upon the big sins." By this, he, may Allah be pleased with him, means that he who is not deepened by the Ocean, until he becomes unaware of its waves, because he is absent from all his senses, and it is impossible for him to see anything which it is not necessary for him now to see, has still not completed his drowning in the Ocean; for it should be known that the owner of this station of drowning cannot return to any of his customary habits. The proof of this is his continual traveling ever more deeply into the Center of the Unity. This being his goal, he must abandon all his usual ways, because he is now in a state in which it is impossible for him to see himself, because he has surrendered all control over himself, as if he were unaware of himself, yet Allah and those who are deeply rooted in knowledge know of his state. In this case he cannot do anything to make himself appear pleasing, and he does not cease to abandon things that exhaust him. For now everything to him is praiseworthy, as it is for the special Folk (*qawm*) when they destroy their *nafs,* throwing off all restraints, shamefulness and indignity, which the *nafs* hates because of the humility which it feels in front of this; thus making it flee far away. About this Ibn Farid has said:

"I have thrown off all my restraints and my excuses,
Wearing the gown of depravity,

Happy with what my manners have torn off.
For it is my duty to You to throw off all restraints.

And it is through You that I come closer to my people,
For my depravity is also my sunna.

Those who mock at my shamefulness are not of my People,
For they have distanced themselves from me,

And are pleased, thinking You have pushed me away,
And abandoned me because of my behavior.

My family in the religion of the love, are His Family,
Who are content with my shamelessness, finding my dishonor delightful."

The knowers, may Allah be pleased with them, have experienced what is an unimaginable indifference for their skins, because of their immersion in their *tasting* of the Secret of the Unity, which is hidden in the manifestation of the ramifications of distinctions and separation. For they know that they cannot dissolve anything, nor alter it, nor discard it, because they are also held and encompassed by the vision of all things in a Wholeness and Unity; all of which make up the Divine Presence. At the beginning, when they enter this presence it is known that the pilgrims should forego intercourse with their women, so that you see them separated from their wives, not fulfilling their duties towards them, and exhibiting complete firmness in this, for they are in a state of exhalation, far removed from any desires. And you can see their wives, also desiring to follow this art, although in the beginning they may be angered by this, accusing their husbands of failing to be men. But all this comes from the state of complete bliss, in which the knower now finds himself; a state of witnessing the delight of being rescued and saved.

But do not think that the knower has abandoned all that his humanity demands of him in this life, because this is not so. Only when he enters this station, and he begins to flee in the witnessing of it, is it forbidden for him. But when he has been established in the station, and has gained knowledge of it, and is moving out of it into the station of the subsistence (*baqa'*), then it is not forbidden for him again to be in the complete love with his wife; and she with her husband. Then he can busy himself with his human needs, so that what was forbidden for him a while before, is now permitted; and he participates in human matters as is the usual case of the human being. For he has returned to the world of bodies, so that because he is a member of the human race what is permitted to them is also permitted to him, even though he is removed, with his soul, from the normal human senses, and is absent in the Unity. And after this sometimes he returns to the humanity because this is necessary for him, and it is permitted.

It is also permitted for the knower, when he is in the highest of Heights, which is the Throne, to be sometimes shaded from it, and yet he has not left it, but he remains under its protection, which is the case that we have now been speaking about. At those times it is necessary for him to trust, and to know with certainty, that when returning to the Creation nothing can harm him from human states, even though those who do not know him may imagine that his *himma* is no longer upheld and protected by the Throne. But because he has been annihilated from all illusions, it is possible for him to be embraced by the Throne at some times, yet not at all times. In the times of his being in the embrace of the height of the Throne (meaning the state of returning to its Center) it is possible for him to deal with the Creation, and at the same time, to love his wife. So do not understand from this, that his *himma* is reduced to coming only from the Creation, as is the case for the people generally; no, for he is always aware of the sun of the Truth, which is behind the clouds. He who is shaded from the zenith of the light of the sun is not deterred by this, for he is then neither completely absent, nor completely present. And nobody can understand this case, except he who has *tasted* it, for he is then always aware of the Unity in the midst of opposition; and this is something that is accepted by the special People, who say:

"If I wanted to see nothing but Allah always, I could not.
And if I insist, I find it is a mirage in the air.

If I look for them I do not find them
For they are only a mirage which does not truly exist."

When everything has been said about the well-known facts of the Pilgrimage (*al-hajj 'ashur ma`alumat*) (the *standing* which the knower should observe at least once in his lifetime), what is meant by this is the absorption into the Unity, as we have mentioned. And now we will speak about the presence (*hadra*) which is required by the Essence, and which he can enter into at any time.

The Lesser Pilgrimage al-`Umra

The `Umra means the state of mind necessary for being in this holy presence because it is like a fortress in which the owner of this state does not have to fear either difficulty or severity. For that reason it is referred to as the House, the Stronghold of Allah, which brings security from suffering, as we have said, because the `Umra does not include the pillar of the standing on `Arafah. But the performer of the `Umra is required to circumambulate the Ka`ba and to complete the *sa`i*, which is the hurrying seven times between Safa and Marwa, and to witness as much as possible of the House, which is the presence of He Who is worshiped, and of the worshipper. But the knower should be knowledgeable in every aspect of this presence, by realizing all that it manifests and reveals, so that he will accept, and face, everything that appears to him from all the faces of this presence. It is said about this:

"And my Pilgrimage to it is like the standing,
For to be at its door is like all standings up,

For at its door all standings are nullified,
All the lands of Allah appearing therein,

But I do not see them, for to my eyes there is only Makka,
For in the haram all places are brought together and joined.

And I see that every place has it dwelling in the hijra."

If the knower understands the meaning of the rites of the Lesser Pilgrimage, he will be protected, in the same manner as he likewise preserves it, so that he will never want to leave it, and in this he will reach to an elevated station, and his attention will be absorbed by his realization and understanding of the meanings of the many diverse revelations and lights coming from the Attributes of Allah, so that the Creation will be illuminated to him through the Light of He who *is*; and the earth will shine with the Attributes, for the *Book of the Manners of the Knower* is written down in this presence.

The state of the knower, when he passes through the standing on `Arafah, has already been spoken about, and of what he should accomplish in the Pilgrimage, in both the presence of the circumambulation, and in that of the *sa`i,* all of which are metaphors and signs for those who possess the art of the knowledge of Allah. So let them fulfill it in the *`Umra* just as they do in the Greater Pilgrimage.

Then know that this station is a mighty and important one, for to realize it, he must make use of all the existing kinds of manners required by it. One of these is the regarding of it with humility and modesty, for these are the qualities needed in this presence.

Therefore, when you find yourself in Makka come to respect this place when you are near the House, and be even more a slave, because this presence knows of you as a slave, therefore it requires of you politeness. If you are not in the right state of surrender and willingness with this station, you will not find ease in it, for it will not take you to itself, because this presence only calls to those who are perfectly polite. But when you are polite, and when this presence seizes you, it will be content to give itself to you, and you, on your part, will receive from it the very best of behavior and manners.

For this reason it is said that it is necessary to stand in this presence in simplicity, and to be able to expand and grow in it, for in it there is a scale which measures everything that comes from you, so that it is for you to be noble, because many revelations are contained in this presence, and many possibilities for growth and expansion. It wants you to accept, and respect, each revelation as fully as you can, even though they have no limit. Therefore we have said that in this station the knower, so far as he is able, should have the complete politeness with every manifestation, as also it is the duty of the owner of this station to strive always, even when he is in those states of serenity and delight.

And if your intention is for the presence of Muhammad (*al-hadra al-muhammadiyya*) this does not mean, in the Truth, any emerging from where you are in the station of the presence of the `Umra, because the presence of Muhammad is one of the manifestations of the Presence of the Unity. However, there can be no real peace for the knower until he enters into the presence of Muhammad, which is realized through visiting the most excellent of leaders, may the peace and blessings of Allah be upon him, and his Family.

Visiting the Beloved Prophet
may Allah bless and grant him peace

Know my beloved, that when the knower reaches to whatever he has reached, and has not entered this presence of Muhammad to travel in it according to his politeness, until its lights shine upon him, one may be concerned for him, because he has reached, without going through this station. Therefore, it is necessary for him to return to it. For which it is said: "The Reality of the end is the return to the beginning." And it has been said about that: "How can anyone who loves, not love the Prophet, nor give his attention to him, for he is the Door to Allah, and entering to Allah can only be through His Door."

If, in his Path, the murid manifests the presence of Muhammad in witnessing the presence of the Unity, he must go through the owner of this presence, may peace be upon him. Because if it were not for the light of Mustafa, which protects him, he would not be able to move even one step forward, for if he tried to do so he would be burnt up. Therefore, it is a duty for every knower to return to this presence, and to be humble at its threshold, for it is the perfection of completion, and the completion of perfection, and any other perfection without it is useless. Then, he who does not establish himself in this presence is lacking, and imperfect; or it can be said that he has been turned upside down. But if he is not subverted in this way, nor veiled, then he returns back and is veiled. For know that, in this station, the Truth of the Prophet is revealed to the knowers. Meaning, his Truth which is answerable to Allah, of the Oneness of Existence, about which the owner of the *burda* (Muhmmad's outer garment) Al-Busayri, may Allah be pleased with him, said, "How can sleeping people in the *dunya* dream that they can get his truth without effort?" Because the Truth of Mustafa is the Truth of the Unity of Existence, so that when it is revealed the veil of its face is lifted, showing the light of the beauty of existence. For every Prophet is from your army; and your light is everything, yet the light of everything is part of your light. Then the knower is certain of the Muhammadan Truth, and he then begins to give expression to such sayings as: "If the Prophet of Allah were veiled from me for one moment, I would not consider myself to be a Muslim." Others said: "If he vanished from me for one hour I would die immediately."

And I say: Those to whom the Truth of Muhammad, may peace be upon him, is revealed, have uttered many similar sayings, some of which can be seen in the following verses:

"She told me that I am the Pole (qutb) of beauty,
The Essence of perfection, which is the goal.

The Secret of life, the light of the Attributes.
The fortress of safety, and the house of peace.

My intention is my earth, my wine my intoxication,
The source of the Essence in this world.

The unifier of the Unity, the cave of yearning,
For every knower cares for him.

The Secret of the Truth; the meaning of the Path,
The strong bond that does not sever.

A branch of the Divinity of the Light of Lahut.
His is the station of the Mercy of Allah.

The treasury of meanings, the Secret of time,
The soul of the special of the special; and I said: Yes."

Then know, that he to whom the Reality (Haqiqa) has been revealed, has to observe the most complete politeness, which is known to the special People.

Therefore, go to the grave of the Prophet in politeness, which means to put every effort into being in the correct manner, for which this station has been created. For some *muridun*, the *fana* comes in this *presence* so that he starts speaking with the tongue of the owner of this presence, may peace be upon him, as has been the case of most of the knowers, who have witnessed him in this place. For the deeper that the knower penetrates into this presence, the closer he comes to Allah, until neither the caller, nor his calling, can be refused. Know then, that the owner of this station should not cease asking, for if he reaches to it, he should continue his invocation of the *good* as long as he is able to do so.

And, in this way, the visit of the knower to Mustafa, the chosen one, is a revelation of the Truth, whose station the special People refer to as subsistence of subsistence (*al-baqa li-'l-baqa*), so that he who carries the Attributes of this station is more complete than others, because he is firmly grounded between a state of sobriety and of intoxication.

The knower should emerge from the three presences, so that his vision is from the Muhammadan presence, and the Presence of the Unity. Then his hidden is in the Presence of the Unity, just as his Revealed presence should be in the Law (ash-shari`a), and his soul in the Path (at-tariqa), and his Secret in the Reality (al-Haqiqa). Meaning that he should, in this way, unite the three presences. For if he is confirmed in the Muhammadan Truth he is then removed from considering anything else, because in it the universes are dissolved in the Oneness, as regards both its hidden and its revealed manifestations. So when you have affirmed, and have deeply realized, the name of the owner of this presence you will find a mighty sign, in our words: "Muhammad the Messenger of Allah" (muhammadun rasulu llah). For Muhammad is the Kingdom (al-mulk), and Messenger is the Dominion (al-malakut), and Allah is the World of Omnipotence (al-lahut). And this is contained in his name; so how then is the case of he who carries this name? Or you could say: "How is his Truth?" And he who knows the Truth of Muhammad, is not satisfied with anything else: "For whoever follows the Messenger obeys Allah."

He who knows the Reality of the Messenger of Allah must speak out, but he who does not know it should remain silent. Muhammad the Messenger of Allah: "Joins the two seas between them a barrier which they do not cross." These are two opposites that do not meet. Meaning, that what is a happening (hudut) and is transient and ephemeral cannot meet with the eternal (qadim). But Muhammad, may peace be upon him, is the barrier (barzakh) between the two boundaries, the land of the two seas, having two sides and faces.

As for his Revealed face, he is a spot in the soil, and as for his Hidden face, he is a Vice-Regent of the Lord of all the worlds. So it is said: "Muhammad rasul Allah." And by that, you can reach the whole meaning and its order. If you take away the word *Messenger*, the meaning is changed, so that what is ephemeral (*muhammad*) meets with what is eternal (*qadim*) which is Allah; then what is ephemeral and transient disappears, and only the eternal remains, because you say: "Muhammad Allah." So the pillar of this meaning becomes the source upon which you lean, and which does not need any link; and this is the meaning of Allah's revelation.

But it is not possible to be in the deep politeness of these presences except through the word: "Muhammad rasul Allah," and through the standing in the presence of each name, in the manner that our duty towards it requires of us. For the name of Muhammad demands that the knower should worship Allah, and the name of the Messenger demands that we come to proximity with Him, and to fear Him; and the Name of Allah demands of us to be seeing Him, and to look upon His Face.

And all praise is to Allah, the Lord of all the worlds!

الله